D0225871

THE FOREVER FUEL

Also of Interest

Energy from Biological Processes: Technical and Policy Options, Office of Technology Assessment

* *Renewable Natural Resources: A Management Handbook for the Eighties*, edited by Dennis L. Little, Robert E. Dils, and John Gray

* *Energy Futures, Human Values, and Lifestyles: From SRI International, A New Look at the Energy Crisis*, Richard C. Carlson, Willis W. Harman, and Peter Schwartz

Energy Transitions: Long-Term Perspectives, edited by Lewis J. Perelman, August W. Giebelhaus, and Michael D. Yokell

* *Climate Change and Society: Consequences of Increasing Atmospheric Carbon Dioxide*, William W. Kellogg, and Robert Schware

* Available in hardcover and paperback

About the Book and Author

THE FOREVER FUEL
The Story of Hydrogen
Peter Hoffmann

In a world increasingly plagued by pollution, where limited availability of fossil fuels creates international tensions, and where global disaster from proliferating technology lurks on the horizon, the search for alternative synthetic fuels is no longer an idle scientist's dream—it is necessity.

Hydrogen—with its vast and ready availability from water, its nearly universal utility, and its inherently benign characteristics—is one of several attractive synthetic fuels being considered for a "post–fossil-fuel" world, and it may well be the miracle fuel of the future. It is of special interest because, technically at least, it is so easily produced and because it produces simple water vapor in the combustion process rather than loading an already burdened environment with more hydrocarbons, carbon dioxide and monoxide, sulfur, particulate matter, and even more exotic pollutants.

Journalist Peter Hoffmann describes worldwide scientific work toward a future hydrogen economy, looking at the auspicious prospects of this potential fuel, at its applicability to powering everything from automobiles to airplanes, and at the principles and technologies involved in making hydrogen a viable energy alternative. He examines how—and how soon—nature's simplest element may become available as an energy carrier, as well as the economic conditions that will accompany its introduction and the social impact of "clean" hydrogen energy. The picture he paints of the fuel future is a welcome alternative to the now-common prognostications of impending doom.

Peter Hoffmann is deputy bureau chief of McGraw-Hill World News in Bonn, Germany. His interest in hydrogen began in 1972.

THE
FOREVER FUEL
The Story of Hydrogen

Peter Hoffmann

Westview Press / Boulder, Colorado

Copyright © 1981 by Westview Press, Inc.

Published in 1981 in the United States of America by
  Westview Press, Inc.
  5500 Central Avenue
  Boulder, Colorado 80301
  Frederick A. Praeger, Publisher

Second printing, 1982

Library of Congress Cataloging in Publication Data
Hoffmann, Peter, 1935–
  The forever fuel.
  Bibliography: p.
  Includes index.
  1. Hydrogen as fuel. I. Title.
TP359.H8H63   665.8'1   80-20965
ISBN 0-89158-581-8

Printed and bound in the United States of America

Contents

List of Illustrations ix

Acknowledgments xi

Abbreviations xiii

1. Introduction 1

2. The Basic Element: The Discovery of Hydrogen 9

3. Early Visions: The History of the Hydrogen
    Movement 19

4. Hydrogen from Natural Gas, Electrolysis,
    Thermochemistry: Present and Future Production 51

5. Solar and Nuclear Power: Hydrogen's
    Primary Energy Sources 81

6. Water Vapor From the Tailpipe: Hydrogen
    as Automotive Fuel 105

7. Clean Contrails Over Lake Erie: Hydrogen
    as Aircraft Fuel 139

8. The Invisible Flame: Hydrogen as Utility Gas 167

9. Fertilizer, Steel, and Protein-Producing
    Microbes: Nonenergy Uses of Hydrogen 193

10. The Hindenburg Syndrome: Is Hydrogen Safe? 209

11. Scenarios for the Future 219

Notes 241

For Further Reading 249

Index 257

Illustrations

2.1 Antoine Laurent Lavoisier 11
2.2 Henry Cavendish 14
2.3 Lavoisier's apparatus to split water 16
3.1 Rudolf A. Erren 26
3.2 A German self-propelled rail car 28
3.3 An Australian commission investigating
    Rudolf A. Erren's hydrogen-burning bus 29
3.4 Cesare Marchetti 35
3.5 Derek Gregory's hydrogen-powered cuckoo clock 41
3.6 The "H₂indenburg Society" credo 42
3.7 William J. D. Escher....................................43
4.1 The Mark 13, a thermochemical, water-splitting
    apparatus at the EURATOM Research Center 73
5.1 An artist's conception of a 100-megawatt
    "Solar Chimney" 86
5.2 The 100-kilowatt "Solar Chimney" demonstration
    plant in Spain 87
5.3 A cross section of the experimental 15-megawatt
    high-temperature reactor in Jülich, West Germany 90
6.1 The first U.S. car to run on hydrogen 106
6.2 A staff member of the Jet Propulsion Laboratory
    demonstrated that the exhaust of a hydrogen-
    powered car consists of almost pure water 110
6.3 Roger Billings's hydrogen-fueled minibus 113
6.4 Roger Billings with one of his
    hydrogen-fueled engines 114
6.5 Daimler-Benz's first hydrogen-powered minibus 121
6.6 The hydride storage tank in Daimler-Benz's
    first hydrogen-powered minibus 122

6.7 Two recent Daimler-Benz developments: a sedan that runs on hydrogen and gasoline and a hydrogen-powered city bus that uses hydrides as storage elements 124

6.8 One of the first methanol-fueled VW "Rabbits" 137

7.1 A B-57 airplane with a hydrogen system 140

7.2 Hydrogen system for a B-57 airplane 141

7.3 The 1956 Lockheed design of a hydrogen-fueled, supersonic, reconnaissance plane, the CL-400 142

7.4 Daniel Brewer of the Lockheed Corporation 146

7.5 Early Lockheed designs of liquid-hydrogen–fueled transports with a capacity of 400 passengers over 5,500 nautical miles 148

7.6 A NASA rendering showing the locations of the liquid-hydrogen tanks inside the fuselage 149

7.7 Lockheed's version of a Mach 2.7, 234-passenger, advanced supersonic transport, fueled by liquid hydrogen 153

7.8 British Aircraft Corporation's "notional concept" of a liquid-hydrogen–fueled, Mach 3 to 3.5, 500-passenger airliner for the 21st century 156

7.9 A liquid-hydrogen–fueled, Mach 6, 200-passenger airliner 156

7.10 A rendering of a Lockheed L-1011 Tri-Star converted to liquid-hydrogen operations under the "LEAP" concept 164

8.1 Roger Billings's "Hydrogen Homestead," a residence fueled entirely by hydrogen .172

8.2 A hydrogen-based house-heating and -cooling concept 181

9.1 Peter M. Bell and David Ho-kwang Mao with their experimental high-pressure cell setup with which they produced solid, crystalline hydrogen in early 1979 200

Acknowledgments

Many people helped with this book, starting with Cesare Marchetti, who initiated me into hydrogen lore in the early seventies when I was working for McGraw-Hill World News in Milan, Italy. Others who generously provided information and who later assisted this nonscientist in spotting the more glaring errors include Bill Escher, Heiko Barnert, Karl-Friedrich Knoche, Dan Brewer, Bill Witcofski, and Rudolf Erren. Thanks are also due to Fabrizio Serena di Lapigio, formerly of Alitalia Airlines, Bob Ingersoll, Irmgard Wilksen, and Roy Koch.

Special gratitude for their forbearance with years of hydrogen-induced dementia is due to my wife, Sarah, who read and helped edit the manuscript, and my children, Peter, Jr., Rembert, and Benjamin.

P.H.

Abbreviations

ADT	Adenosintriphosphate
ARPA	Advanced Research Projects Agency
AST	Advanced supersonic transport
ATP	Adenosine triphosphate
AVR	Arbeitsgemeinschaft Versuchsreaktor
bhp	Brake horsepower
Btu	British thermal unit
BWR	Boiling water reactor
atm	Atmosphere
cc	Cubic centimeter
CO_2	Carbon dioxide
CWH	Chemische Werke Hüis
DOC	Direct operating cost
DoE	Department of Energy
DFVLR	Deutsche Forschungs und Versuchsanstalt für Luft und Raumfahrt (German Aerospace Research and Experimental Institute)
ENI	Ente Nazionale Idrocarburi
ENR	*Engineering News Record*
EPA	Environmental Protection Agency
EPNdB	Effective perceived noise level in terms of decibels
ERDA	Energy Research and Development Administration
EURATOM	European Atomic Energy Community
GA	General Atomic
GM	General Motors
GNP	Gross national product
HEST	Hydrogen Energy Systems Technology
HgO	Mercury Oxide
HIT	Hydrogen induction technique
hp	Horsepower
HTR	High-temperature reactor

HST	Hypersonic transport
HYCSOS	Hydrogen Conversion and Storage System
IEA	International Energy Agency
IGT	Institute of Gas Technology
IIASA	International Institute for Applied Systems Analysis
JPL	Jet Propulsion Laboratory
kg	Kilogram
kv	Kilovolt
kwh	Kilowatt hour
lb	Pound
LEAP	Liquid-hydrogen Experimental Airline
LH$_2$	Liquid hydrogen
LNG	Liquid natural gas
MIT	Massachusetts Institute of Technology
mpg	Miles per gallon
mph	Miles per hour
Mw	Megawatt
Mwe	Megawatt (electric)
Mwth	Megawatt (thermal)
NACA	National Advisory Committee for Aeronautics
NASA	National Aeronautics and Space Administration
NATO	North Atlantic Treaty Organization
NOX	Nitrogen oxides emissions
OPEC	Organization of Petroleum Exporting Countries
OTEC	Ocean Thermal Energy Conversion
oz	Ounce
ppm	Parts per million
psf	Pounds per square foot
psi	Pounds per square inch
PWR	Pressurized water reactor
Q	Quadrillion Btus
SNG	Substitute natural gas
SPE	Solid-polymer electrolyte
SPTL	Superconductive power transmission line
SRI	Stanford Research Institute
SST	Supersonic transport
TI	Texas Instruments
TiO$_2$	Titanium dioxide
TVP	Textured vegetable protein
UCLA	University of California at Los Angeles
USGS	United States Geological Survey
VW	Volkswagen

A Hydrogen Song

(to the tune of Cole Porter's
"I get a kick out of you")

I get no kick from methane,
Pure ethanol does not thrill me at all,
Only a fool thinks syn-fuel,
My yen is for pure hydrogen.

—Anonymous

1

Introduction

There are two prime sources of energy to be harnessed and ex-
pended to do work. One is the capital energy-saving and storage
account; the other is the energy-income account. The fossil fuels
took multimillions of years of complex reduction and conservation,
progressing from vegetational impoundment of sun radiation by
photosynthesis to deep-well storage of the energy concentrated
below the earth's surface. There is a vast overabundance of income
energy at more places around the world, at more times to produce
billionsfold the energy now employed by man, if he only knew how
to store it when it is available, for use when it was not available.
There are gargantuan energy-income sources available which do
not stay the processes of nature's own conservation of energy
within the earth crust "against a rainy day". These are in water,
tidal, wind, and desert-impinging sun radiation power. The ex-
ploiters of the fossil fuels, coal and oil, say it costs less to produce
and burn the savings account. This is analogous to saying it takes
less effort to rob a bank than to do the work which the money
deposited in the bank represents. The question is cost to whom? To
our great-great-grandchildren who will have no fossil fuels to turn
the machines? I find that the ignorant acceptance by world society's
presently deputized leaders of the momentarily expedient and the
lack of constructive, long-distance thinking—let alone comprehen-
sive thinking—would render dubious the case for humanity's earth-
ian future could we not recognize plausible overriding trends.

—R. Buckminster Fuller[1]

The big powers are seriously trying to find alternatives to oil by
seeking to draw energy from the sun or water. We hope to God

1

they will not succeed quickly because our position in that case will be painful.

—Sheikh Ahmad Zaki Yamani, Saudi Arabian oil minister[2]

WASHINGTON, April 22 (UPI)—*A shift to solar energy could create 2.9 million jobs and cut spending for conventional fuels by $11.8 billion by 1990, according to a study released yesterday by Sen. Edward Kennedy, D-Mass.*[3]

Hydrogen as fuel? It's still Buck Rogers stuff.[4]

These quotes sum up what this book is all about—hydrogen as fuel. Hydrogen: a normally invisible, tasteless, colorless gas that happens to be the most abundant element in the universe; a basic building block and fuel of stars and galaxies; a very reactive material essential in innumerable chemical and biological processes; a very energetic and yet nonpolluting fuel.

Even before Buckminster Fuller's observations, many people had been calling for the use of nature's current energy account—solar power in its various manifestations—instead of robbing the world's energy savings account—coal, oil, and gas. As Fuller points out, the problem has been to a large extent not only how to collect but how to store this essentially free energy. Tapping solar energy for purposes other than basic solar heating so far has meant producing electricity. But electricity has a basic flaw: Essentially it has to be consumed the instant it is produced. Electricity is difficult to store in large quantities (leaving aside for the moment concepts such as pumped storage, compressed-air caverns, flywheels, battery farms, or supraconducting magnets, all of which are clumsy, expensive, unproven, or all three). Another aspect frequently overlooked is that electricity supplies only a fairly small share of an industrialized country's total energy needs—typically between 15 and 25 percent. By far the largest share of the total energy demand requires *chemical* energy—gasoline, diesel fuel, heavy oil, kerosene, natural gas, coal—to propel airplanes, cars, and ships, and to run plants and heat homes, offices, and schools.

When burned in any internal-combustion engine—V-8, diesel, Wankel, jet—hydrogen produces virtually nothing but harmless water vapor as exhaust. There are no carbon monoxides or dioxides, no unburned hydrocarbons, no stench, no smoke, nor any of the other carbon-bearing, earth-befouling discharges we suffer today.

"Hydrogen, H_2, atomic weight 1.00797 . . . is the lightest known substance," reports the *Encyclopedia of Chemistry*.

> The spectroscope shows that it is present in the sun, many stars, and nebulae. Our galaxy . . . plus the stars of the Milky Way is presently considered to have been formed 12 to 15 billion years ago from a rotating mass of hydrogen gas which condensed into stars under gravitational forces. This condensation produced high temperatures, giving rise to the fusion reaction converting hydrogen into helium, as presently occurring in the sun, with the evolution of tremendous amounts of radiant thermal energy plus the formation of the heavier elements. Hydrogen gas has long since escaped from the earth's lower atmosphere but is still present in the atmosphere of several of the planets. In a combined state, hydrogen comprises 11.19% of water and is an essential constituent of all acids, hydrocarbons, and vegetable and animal matter. It is present in most organic compounds.[5]

Today, hydrogen is used in many industries as a chemical raw material (especially in the production of fertilizer), but also in making dyes, drugs, and plastics. It is used in the treatment of oils and fats, as a fuel for welding, to make gasoline from coal, and to produce methanol. In supercold, "cryogenic" liquid form and combined with liquid oxygen it is a powerful fuel for space rocketry.

Hydrogen is produced commercially in almost a dozen processes. Most of them involve the extraction of the "hydro" part from hydrocarbons. The most widely used process is "steam reforming," in which natural gas is made to react with steam. Water electrolysis, in which water is broken down into hydrogen and oxygen by running an electrical current through it, is used where electricity is cheap and where high purity is required (see Chapters 4 and 9).

Hydrogen gas can be stored in a variety of ways. As a cryogenic fuel it promises to lead to better, faster, more economical, and obviously environmentally "clean" airplane designs. Metallic hydrogen, a rare laboratory curiosity today, holds promise as an ultraenergetic fuel and for large advances in electrical ultraconducting technology.

Since the early and mid-seventies a growing number of environment-minded scientists, energy planners, and industrial executives have begun to think of hydrogen not only as a chemical feedstock but also as an almost ideal chemical fuel and energy storage medium. As a fuel it doesn't pollute. As an energy storage medium it would answer Fuller's call for some method "to store it [energy] when it *is* available for use when it is *not* available."

To be sure, hydrogen is *not* an energy *source*; that is, it is not primary energy like natural gas or crude oil that exists freely in nature. It is an energy carrier, a secondary form of energy that has to be manufactured, just like electricity. Hydrogen can be manufactured from many primary sources, an advantage in itself since it reduces the chances of a cartel similar to the Organization of Petroleum Exporting Countries (OPEC) dictating global energy prices. Today hydrogen is made mostly from polluting fossil fuels but tomorrow it will be made from clean water and clean solar energy, probably also "cleaner" second-generation nuclear energy. As it can be made from both nonrenewable and renewable sources, it can be phased into the overall energy structure by whatever method is most convenient and least wrenching in a given locale—coal gasification in the western United States, solar-based electrolysis in a Saudi desert with water from the Persian Gulf.

Put in its simplest terms, the broad outlines of a future "hydrogen economy" run something like this:

• Solar energy as well as cleaner, safer nuclear power plants (discussed in Chapter 5) would produce electricity to be used to split water into hydrogen as fuel, with oxygen as a valuable by-product. Alternatively, solar or nuclear power plants would produce high-temperature heat to crack water molecules thermochemically in processes now under development. Other, more exotic methods are also being investigated.

• Hydrogen would be used as an energy storage medium—as gas under pressure, in hydrogen-absorbing alloys called "hydrides," or as cryogenic liquid. Hydrogen would fulfill the indispensable storage function to smooth out daily and seasonal fluctuations of solar power—Fuller's "gargantuan energy-income sources."

• Hydrogen would be burned in conventional internal-combustion engines—jet engines, turbines, Otto motors, Wankels, diesels—but also in fuel cells, producing mostly harmless water vapor as exhaust emission. Water vapor returns immediately to nature's cycle as fog, clouds, rain, snow, and groundwater to rivers, lakes, and oceans, and water can be split again for more fuel. As a gas, hydrogen can transport energy via long-distance pipelines much more cheaply than electricity, driving fuel cells at the consumer end to make electricity plus water.

• As a chemical fuel, hydrogen can be used in a much wider range of energy applications than can electricity. In addition, hydrogen does double duty as a chemical raw material. Unlike other chemical fuels, it does not pollute.

Currently, the overriding goal of the international hydrogen research community is to find *economical* ways of splitting large volumes of water molecules; this is the prerequisite to using the element as a fuel. Many hydrogen advocates believe the global "hydrogen economy" will begin to take shape near the end of the present century, with hydrogen ultimately serving as the universal energy carrier by the middle of the twenty-first century, fueling almost all machinery as it now does for biological processes. Others think hydrogen will not completely supplant but rather complement electricity; each will be used in areas where it serves best. In addition to large-volume, industrial-scale "hard technology" production methods, the "forever fuel" can be made by "soft technology" routes that should appeal to "Ecotopia" adherents and environmentalists who distrust big government and big industry.

What about nuclear power? Since hydrogen is a secondary fuel, any primary energy, including nuclear, can in principle be used to fire machinery that breaks down water molecules. During the past decade, in fact, the hydrogen community counted on atomic energy as the mainstay of cheap power to split the water molecule. The concept has an almost mystical elegance—a near-cosmic energy dance combining the elementary force that heats the sun and the stars to produce a chemical fuel that happens to be the most abundant element in the universe and that also represents the elementary chemical building block of all matter.

But while a nuclear fire burning far away in the cosmos is one thing, building a nuclear reactor or breeder in the neighborhood is another— or so it has seemed to the increasingly powerful antinuclear forces throughout the world. Since the mid-seventies, the nuclear energy industry has felt the opposition's growing impact as new plant orders dropped toward ground zero.

And then there was Harrisburg. To the antinuclear forces and to many others as well, the Three Mile Island incident in early 1979 in effect spelled the end of nuclear power. It almost felt as if the lights were beginning to dim already. But the new round of oil price increases a few months later muted much of the opposition to nuclear power in many countries.

To the hydrogen community, the message of Three Mile Island was never that clear-cut. As scientists and technicians, many hydrogen advocates believe that the power of the atom will be needed for at least a few decades as an interim solution until solar is well on its way. This does not mean that they do not appreciate or share the fears about *current-generation* reactor types. They are fully aware of the dangers of a meltdown, of nuclear contamination, of the spill of nuclear material during transport, or of its theft to make home-made nukes, and of the problem of storing wastes safely over thousands of years.

What is the answer then?

First, some pro-hydrogen planners believe that Three Mile Island provided an impetus toward the stepped-up development of safer, more efficient second-generation nuclear power plants, the so-called high-temperature reactors (HTRs). As will be mentioned in Chapter 5, HTRs are more efficient, but more important, they have a fail-safe mechanism and are inherently meltdown-proof—if the reactor cooling system fails, they shut themselves down. And since these reactors operate at higher temperatures than current types, they can do double duty: In addition to producing electricity, they can also serve as a more efficient and safer heat source for various hydrogen production techniques requiring high temperatures that are unavailable from current light-water reactors.

Second, hydrogen people believe that Three Mile Island also provided an impetus for removing nuclear power plants from population centers, decoupling them from humanity by moving them far away to deserts, inside distant mountains, or to remote islands thousands of miles from large metropolitan areas. This, in turn, would favor introduction of hydrogen as an energy carrier; energy transport from remote power plant sites thousands of miles away can be handled efficiently only by hydrogen as an energy carrier. Energy losses in electric cables are just too great over extremely long distances.

The view of some hydrogen experts thus is that while Three Mile Island may indeed have been a setback for current nuclear technology, it may yet turn out to be a stimulus for new, inherently safer, and more efficient nuclear power plants that will be more acceptable to the public. These new reactors in turn may accelerate the introduction of hydrogen as fuel.

One other factor that favors a massive switch to hydrogen should be mentioned—the so-called greenhouse effect, the atmospheric heat buildup due to the massive accumulation of carbon dioxide (CO_2) in the atmosphere. CO_2, which is produced by burning fossil fuels as well as by natural causes, acts like a greenhouse in the atmosphere: It lets solar radiation through to the earth's surface from space, but it prevents the reradiation of energy from the earth into space. CO_2 traps heat, and the more CO_2 there is in the atmosphere, the more heat is trapped. CO_2 is taken in by plants as part of their metabolic process. But in part because of decreases in the world's forestation and consequent decrease in global CO_2 absorption and apparently also because of increasing burning of fossil fuels (as well as other causes), the atmosphere's CO_2 content has been going up steadily over the decades.

The fear is that as more heat is trapped, the global temperature-and-climate balance may be upset. There has been speculation that the polar icecaps might melt, raising the level of the oceans and inundating whole stretches of coastline, including some of the world's biggest cities.

So far the evidence is inconclusive whether global CO_2 buildup will, in fact, be dangerous to our children and grandchildren. Still, fear has been expressed that the atmosphere's CO_2 content may double by the years 2030–2050, causing an average global temperature increase of 1.5 to 2.0 degrees centigrade. In regions such as the polar caps the increase could be as much as 10 degrees.

A British Broadcasting Corporation (BBC) documentary about hydrogen, "The Invisible Flame," quoted a meteorologist stationed in Hawaii, home of one of the world's most important CO_2 monitoring posts, as saying, "we don't know at this point whether it [CO_2] will build up so that it can do damage. The oil crisis may have slowed it a little." But he added, "A lot of people believe we could get into trouble, irreversible trouble, in about ten years' time."[6]

Hydrogen contains no carbon at all, and burning it produces no carbon dioxide. Burned as a fuel, it would reduce at least the man-made share of CO_2 deposited in the atmosphere. Switching to hydrogen from fossil fuels soon may save our children's lives.

Time will undoubtedly tell.

2

The Basic Element: The Discovery of Hydrogen

Water is everything. So taught Thales of Miletos, a settlement on the western coast of Asia Minor, today the Turkish town of Miletus. Thales, who lived from about 624 to around 545 B.C. was a pre-Socratic Greek philosopher, reputedly the founder of the Milesian school of philosophy. Although he apparently wrote nothing, he was regarded as one of the Seven Wise Men of Greece in his time. He was the first Western philosopher of record, and he is said to have introduced astronomy to ancient Greece.

Prior to Thales, the design and substance of the universe was explained mostly in mythological terms. For Thales, water was the basis and beginning, the original stuff, primordial material, the essence of everything else in the world. Thales's ideas, said to be traceable to Babylonian beliefs, become

> easily understandable in that the observation of water turning into rigid ice and its transformation into an air-like state led to the thought that all things were derived from matter of middle characteristics.[1]

Other early philosophers added air (Anaximenos of Miletos), fire (Heracleitos of Ephesus), and earth (Empedocles of Agrigentum) to the list of elements.

In a way, Thales was not so far off the mark. He taught that water is the basic element, but we know that it consists of two elements, hydrogen and oxygen (H_2O). Nevertheless, the preponderant part of water is hydrogen—*Wasserstoff* in German, the stuff of water—and hydrogen is the most abundant material in the universe. As Steven Weinberg related in *The First Three Minutes*, 70 to 80 percent of the observable universe consists of hydrogen and the rest mostly of helium, a ratio believed to be essentially unchanged since the beginning of the cosmos 10 to 20 billion years ago.

9

Discovery of Oxygen

Hydrogen had been unknowingly produced somewhere around the end of the fifteenth century, but its discovery was a process that took about two hundred years. The discovery involved the contributions of many scientists and was closely intertwined with the identification and chemical isolation of oxygen. It was not until the seventeenth century that the notion that air is one of the basic elements came to be doubted. A Dutch physician and naturalist, Herman Boerhaave (1668–1738), was the first to suspect that there is some life stuff in the air that is the key to breathing and combustion: "The chemists will find out what it actually is, how it functions, and what it does; it is still in the dark. Happy he, who will discover it," he wrote in 1732.[2]

In England the brilliant scientist Robert Boyle (1627–1691) also maintained "that some life-giving substance," probably related to those needed for maintaining a flame, is part of the air. The English physician and naturalist John Mayow (1645–1679) claimed that "nitro-aerial corpuscles" are responsible for combustion (nitro-aerial because they occur also during combustion of saltpeter).

The discovery that both oxygen and hydrogen are gases was long delayed by the phlogiston theory, a first, erroneous attempt to explain what combustion is. Promulgated by a German physician and scientist, Georg Ernst Stahl (1660–1734), and first published in 1697, the theory held that a substance called phlogiston disappears from any material during combustion. This phlogiston was supposed to impart burnability to matter, but it was also believed to be impossible to reduce it to a pure state. According to modern chemistry, to burn a material is to add a substance, oxygen, to it; Stahl held the reverse to be true: that combustion was the release of phlogiston from the burning material. Similarly, he interpreted the reverse chemical reaction, reduction, in which oxygen is removed, as the addition of phlogiston. Even the increase in weight during oxidation, a fairly clear indication that something is added rather than removed, was explained in an altogether artificial fashion: Stahl claimed that phlogiston was so light that it was repelled by the earth. When phlogiston was removed from a compound, the material gained weight because it had lost a component that had lightened it—a balloon effect, of sorts. Stahl was regarded as more of an abstract thinker than a pragmatist, "sharply logical but erring, a brooding human, little interested in human society and inclined to melancholy."[3] In his prime he was "basically difficult," reports one biographer. "He did not hesitate to exclude facts if they violated his ideas: unity of thought was his ultimate goal above all factuality," said another.[4]

Figure 2.1. Antoine Laurent Lavoisier (1743-1794), France's most famous chemist of the 18th century. He was the first to produce water from hydrogen and oxygen, and he named both hydrogen and oxygen. In the wake of the French Revolution, he was executed by guillotine.

Stahl's phlogiston theory gained wide adherence throughout Europe and the rest of the civilized world. Compared to the stormy development of chemistry during the nineteenth and twentieth centuries, the science made only slow progress during the eighteenth century—largely because Stahl's notions held sway.

Meanwhile, scientists like the British preacher Joseph Priestley (1733–1864) and the Swedish-German apothecary Carl Wilhelm Scheele (1742–1786) had discovered oxygen but without naming it as such. Scheele isolated and labeled the burnable component of the atmosphere "fire air." He was the first to produce pure oxygen sometime between 1771 and 1772 (the exact date is not certain), ahead of Priestley and Antoine Laurent Lavoisier. It was his bad fortune that his publisher put off publication of his major work, *Chemical Treatise on Air and Fire*, until 1777, while his chief competitors, Priestley and Lavoisier, published their discoveries in 1774. In that year Priestley discovered oxygen—he called it "dephlogisticated air"—when he heated mercury oxide without the presence of air. The resultant gas produced sparks and a bright flame in a glowing piece of wood kindling. Priestley inhaled the gas, and he "felt so light and well that he regarded it as curative and recommended it as a means of improving the quality of air in a room and as beneficial for lung diseases." Priestley made himself unpopular in England by his sympathies for the French Revolution, aggravated by his less-than-good-natured character. Having lost most of his friends, in 1794 he emigrated to the United States, where he ended his days near the springs of the Susquehanna River, as he put it himself, a "broken philosopher."[5]

Priestley's and Scheele's experiments came to the attention of France's foremost chemist of the day, Lavoisier (1743–1794). Lavoisier had been studying gases for years, and he had noted that burning phosphorus and sulfur absorb part of the surrounding air and gain weight. During a visit to Paris in October 1774 Priestley told Lavoisier about his mercury oxide experiments. Just about this time Lavoisier had received a letter from Scheele about his discovery of this gas that makes flames burn "lively and that animals can breathe." Lavoisier repeated Priestley's experiments. In 1772, he had been among the first to make precise weight measurements to quantify how much "air" disappeared during combustion of phosphorus and sulfur. In an elaborate 12-day experiment, he had heated mercury and air in an airtight retort, producing that same gas so conducive to combustion and breathing. Lavoisier labeled this gas "oxygen." He concluded one of his papers by saying, "we shall call the change of phosphorus into an acid and in general the combination of any burnable body with oxygen as oxidation."

Lavoisier was not content to refute Stahl's phlogiston theory with scientific evidence but resorted to what today would be called "show biz" to put Stahl down. In 1789 Lavoisier staged a play in Paris to destroy the phlogiston theory completely. Wrote a German visitor:

> I saw the famous M. Lavoisier hold an almost formal auto-da-fé in the Arsenal in which his wife appeared as a high priestess, Stahl as advocatus diaboli to defend phlogiston, and in which poor phlogiston was burned in the end following the accusations by oxygen. Do not consider this a joking invention of mine; everything is true to the letter.[6]

Discovery of Hydrogen

The discovery of hydrogen as an element also proceeded by fits and starts. The early Chinese reportedly were the first to doubt that water was an indivisible element. In the Middle Ages, Theophrastus Paracelsus (1493–1541), the famous physician, was apparently the first to produce hydrogen when he dissolved iron in spirit of vitriol: "Air arises and breaks forth like a wind," he is reputed to have said of his discovery, but he failed to note that hydrogen is burnable. Turquet de Mayerne (1573-1655) noted hydrogen's burnability after he mixed sulfuric acid with iron, a phenomenon rediscovered by the French chemist and apothecary Nicolas Lemery (1645-1715), who described the burning of the gas as *"fulmination violente et éclatente."* Still, there was no thought that this gas was an element but rather a sort of burnable sulfur.

The final isolation and identification of hydrogen happened more or less concurrently with the unraveling of the secrets of oxygen in the second half of the eighteenth century, largely because the same scientists were investigating both air and water. Boyle, for instance, was researching artificial gases—"factitious air," as he called them—producing hydrogen from diluted sulfuric acid and iron. Boyle did not regard these gases as significantly different from common air; he saw them as a type of air with different characteristics, a view shared by many chemists of those days.[7]

Henry Cavendish (1731-1810), a rich English nobleman, who was "extremely strange" in his personal characteristics, was the first to discover and describe some of hydrogen's qualities. The problem was that he did not name the element hydrogen; caught up in the prevailing belief in phlogiston, he thought he had discovered phlogiston in a pure state, a belief he clung to until his death. Taking off from investigations of "factitious air" by other scientists, Cavendish proved that there were different types, "fixed air" (carbon dioxide) as well as "inflammable air" (hydrogen). Describing these findings in the first paper of his scientific career, which he presented to the Royal Society of London in 1766, Cavendish gave precise readings of specific weight and specific density for both gases. He proved that hydrogen was the same material, even though it was derived from different metals and different acids, and that it was exceedingly light—about 14 times as light as air.

Hydrogen buoyancy was quickly put to aeronautical use: "Since then, our colleague has put this knowledge to practical advantage in making navigation in the air safe and easy," said a eulogizing contemporary the year after Cavendish's death.[8] He was referring to Jacques Alexandre César Charles (1746-1823), a French physicist who confirmed Benjamin Franklin's electrical experiments and who became interested in aeronautics. Charles was the first to use hydrogen's buoyancy in a balloon known as a "Charlière"; in 1783 he flew a balloon to an altitude of almost 3.2 kilometers (2 miles).

In fact, one can say that without Cavendish's discovery and Charles' ap-

Figure 2.2. Henry Cavendish (1731–1810), the British nobleman who was the first to discover and describe some of hydrogen's properties. (© Deutsches Museum, Munich)

plication of it, the Montgolfiers' achievement would scarcely have been feasible, so dangerous and cumbersome for the aeronaut was the fire necessary for keeping ordinary air expanded in the montgolfières . . .

said the orator. (Montgolfières were the first hot air balloons.)

Cavendish also demonstrated that inflammable air (hydrogen) mixed with air and ignited by an electric spark produced water, usually together with a remnant of air. In other experiments, he ignited hydrogen with pure oxygen, which, when the ratio was right, yielded water only, thus definitely establishing the makeup of that first "element." A lifelong bachelor, Cavendish was taciturn, shy, and lacking in social graces. Perhaps because of these traits, he did not publish many of his findings for a long time. His experiments, begun in the late 1770s, involving electric sparks and hydrogen and oxygen, for example, were not published until the mid-1780s in his famous treatise *Experiments on Air*.

Lavoisier, meanwhile, had been trying for some time to find out the nature of "inflammable air," which he also had obtained by the solution of metals in acid. On combustion of this gas he expected to obtain an acid again but this was not the result. In 1783, Lavoisier heard of Cavendish's work through an intermediary, Charles Blagden, secretary of the Royal Society. Lavoisier immediately repeated the experiment but failed to impress fellow scientists with its significance in his first attempt. In other efforts, he took the reverse route—splitting water molecules in a heated copper tube. Iron files in the tube turned black and brittle from the escaping oxygen, and inflammable air, as gas that could have come only from the water, emerged from the tube. In a landmark experiment, he combined hydrogen and oxygen, producing 45 grams (about 1.6 ounces) of water that are still preserved in the French Academy of Science. His classic, definitive experiments proving that hydrogen and oxygen constitute the basic elements of water were made before a large body of scientists in February 1785. In collaboration with other experimenters he published his major work, *The Method of Chemical Nomenclature*, which is the basis of chemistry even today, and in which he labeled the "life-sustaining air" oxygen and the "inflammable air" hydrogen.

Lavoisier had been a member of the Ferme-Générale, a financial corporation that leased from the French government the right to collect certain taxes. The system was open to abuse and some of its members were widely hated by the public. Lavoisier, who was also one of the commissioners in charge of gunpowder production for the government, got caught up as a victim of the French Revolution. In 1794, all members of the Ferme-Générale were convicted on trumped-up charges and Lavoisier had "to sneeze in the bag"—a cynical colloquialism of the day for execution by guillotine. Mourned a German necrology the next year:

During the last half of 1794, chemistry lost one of its most splendid favorites in M. Lavoisier. He was guillotined following the sentence of the revolutionary tribunal under the terrible despotism of Robespierre. . . . we weep a commiserating tear as admirers of a science at the urn of a man by whom this science was elevated so much. . . . we see him as the originator of a new teaching that created fame for him, [that was] epochal for chemistry, fruitful for practical usage—honorable for our age and inviting for every thinker.[9]

Figure 2.3. Lavoisier's apparatus to split water, employing a heated copper tube. (© Deutsches Museum, Munich)

Lavoisier's work thus represented the culmination and repository of hundreds of years of investigation that began by noting changes in the properties of materials when burned, included doubts about the nature of air, produced the phlogiston detour as a brilliantly ingenious, if false, explanation of the nature of combustion, and resulted in Cavendish's discovery and description of "inflammable air." Lavoisier's achievement was to pull all these strands together with his own discoveries into the final recognition of hydrogen's unique role as a basic element in nature.

Early Visions:
The History of the
Hydrogen Movement

Early Visionaries: The Reverend Cecil,
Jules Verne, and *The Iron Pirate*

On November 27, 1820, the dons of Cambridge University in England assembled to hear a proposal of the new machine age—suggested by a clergyman, no less. As recorded in the transactions of the Cambridge Philosophical Society, the Reverend William Cecil, M.A., Fellow of Magdalen College and of the society, that day read a lengthy treatise "On the Application of Hydrogen Gas to Produce Moving Power in Machinery." His invention described an engine operated by the "Pressure of the Atmosphere upon a Vacuum Caused by Explosions of Hydrogen Gas and Atmospheric Air." Cecil first dwelt on the disadvantages of water-driven engines—they could be used only "where water is abundant"—and steam engines, which at that time were slow in getting under way. According to the clergyman, their utility was "much diminished by the tedious and laborious preparation which is necessary to bring it into action. A small steam engine not exceeding the power of one man, cannot be brought into action in less than half an hour: and a four-horse steam engine cannot be used under two hours preparation."

A hydrogen-powered engine would solve these problems, Mr. Cecil averred: "The engine in which hydrogen gas is employed to produce moving force was intended to unite two principal advantages of water and steam so as to be capable of acting in any place without the delay and labour of preparation." Rather prophetically, he added, "It may be inferior, in some respects, to many engines at present employed; yet it will not be wholly useless, if, together with its own defects, it should be found to possess advantages also peculiar to itself."

According to Cecil's explanations, the general principle was that hydrogen, when mixed with air and ignited, will produce a large partial vacuum. The air rushing back into the vacuum after the explosion can be harnessed as a moving force

> nearly in the same manner as in the common steam engine: the difference consists chiefly in the manner of forming the vacuum. . . . If two and a half measures by bulk of atmospheric air be mixed with one measure of hydrogen, and a flame be applied, the mixed gas will expand into a space rather greater than three times its original bulk.

Mr. Cecil went on to discuss the workings of his engine in considerable detail. The transactions of the Cambridge Philosophical Society did not record whether Cecil actually ever built such an engine, but in any event, Cecil's proposal represented the first known instance of an early technologist attempting to put the special qualities of hydrogen to work.

Cecil's proposal was made only 20 years after another fundamental discovery, electrolysis—the breaking down of water into hydrogen and oxygen by passing an electrical current through it. The discovery was made at the turn of the century, six years after Lavoisier's execution, by two English scientists, William Nicholson and Sir Anthony Carlisle, just a few weeks after the Italian physicist Alessandro Volta built his first electric cell.

In the next 150 years or so, hydrogen's peculiar properties and energy characteristics were discussed with increasing frequency, not only by scientists but also by writers of early science fiction. Probably the most famous example, well-known in the hydrogen community, is Jules Verne's uncannily prescient description in one of his last books of how hydrogen would become the world's chief fuel. *The Mysterious Island* was written in 1874, just about 100 years before worldwide research into hydrogen began in earnest.

In this remarkable passage, Verne describes the discussions of five Americans, Northerners marooned on a mysterious island 7,000 miles from their starting point of Richmond, Virginia, during the Civil War after a storm-tossed escape by balloon from a Confederate camp. The five were "learned, clear-headed and practical" engineer Cyrus Harding; his servant Neb; "indomitable, intrepid" reporter Gideon Spillett; a sailor named Pencroft; and young Herbert Brown, an orphan and Pencroft's protégé. The five were discussing the future of the Union, and Spillett raised the specter of what would happen to commerce and industry once coal ran out:

"Without coal there would be no machinery, and without machinery there would be no railways, no steamers, no manufactories, nothing of that which is indispensable to modern civilization!"

"But what will they find?" asked Pencroft. "Can you guess, captain?"

"Nearly, my friend."

"And what will they burn instead of coal?"

"Water," replied Harding.

"Water!" cried Pencroft, "water as fuel for steamers and engines! Water to heat water!"

"Yes, but water decomposed into its primitive elements," replied Cyrus Harding, "and decomposed doubtless, by electricity, which will then have become a powerful and manageable force, for all great discoveries, by some inexplicable laws, appear to agree and become complete at the same time. Yes, my friends, I believe that water will one day be employed as fuel, that hydrogen and oxygen which constitute it, used singly or together, will furnish an inexhaustible source of heat and light, of an intensity of which coal is not capable. Some day the coalrooms of steamers and the tenders of locomotives will, instead of coal, be stored with these two condensed gases, which will burn in the furnaces with enormous calorific power. There is, therefore, nothing to fear. As long as the earth is inhabited it will supply the wants of its inhabitants, and there will be no want of either light or heat as long as the productions of the vegetable, mineral or animal kingdoms do not fail us. I believe, then, that when the deposits of coal are exhausted we shall heat and warm ourselves with water. Water will be the coal of the future."

"I should like to see that," observed the sailor.

"You were born too soon, Pencroft," returned Neb, who only took part in the discussion with these words.

Of course, Verne did not explain what the primary energy source would be to make the electricity needed to decompose water, but in the overall context of nineteenth century scientific knowledge, Verne's foresight is nothing but remarkable.

Hydrogen also figured in a juvenile adventure novel published, apparently, shortly after the turn of the century in England. A British scientist interested in hydrogen, W. Hastings Campbell, referred to the book briefly when introducing a hydrogen paper read in March 1933 at Britain's Institute of Fuel. Campbell told his distinguished audience that *The Iron Pirate* by Max Pemberton had made a great impression on him when he was a boy. Pemberton's potboiler described the adventures of a gang of international crooks, who owned a battleship that attained terrific speeds due to the use of hydrogen engines—"another instance of the very annoying persistence with which art always seemed to anticipate discoveries," said the account of that meeting in the *Journal of the Institute of Fuel.*

Hydrogen Pioneers: From Haldane to Erren

The 1920s and 1930s witnessed a flowering of interest, especially in Germany and England, in hydrogen as fuel, a historical phenomenon that has been largely forgotten. On the conceptual level, one of the most important advocates was the brilliant Scottish gadfly scientist J.B.S. (for John Burdon Sanderson) Haldane, a physiologist turned geneticist, long-time editorial board director of the communist *Daily Worker,* and ultimately an emigré to India and guru in the sixties to India's growing science establishment. In 1923, when he was only in his late twenties, Haldane gave a famous lecture at Cambridge University in which he said that hydrogen—derived from wind power via electrolysis, liquefied, and stored—would be the fuel of the future. In a paper read to a university society known as the Heretics, Haldane said,

> liquid hydrogen is weight for weight the most efficient known method of storing energy, as it gives about three times as much heat per pound as petrol. On the other hand, it is very light, and bulk for bulk has only one-third the efficiency of petrol. This will not, however, detract from its use in aeroplanes where weight is more important than bulk.

This view was repeated in more technical detail 15 years later by the American helicopter pioneer, Igor Sikorski.

In the same paper, Haldane prophesied that 400 years from now Britain's energy needs will be solved by

> rows of metallic windmills working electric motors which in their turn supply current at a very high voltage to great electric mains. At suitable distances, there will be great power stations where during windy weather the surplus power will be used for the electrolytic decomposition of water into oxygen and hydrogen. These gases will be liquefied and stored in vast vacuum jacketed reservoirs probably sunk into the ground. . . . In times of calm the gases will be recombined in explosion motors working dynamos which produce electrical energy once more, or more probably in oxidation cells.

(The latter was a reference to the fuel cell. The first fuel cell was constructed in 1829 by the Englishman William Grove, producing water from oxygen and hydrogen, but no electricity. Development of modern fuel cells that also produce electricity did not start until the 1950s.)

Haldane went on:

> These huge reservoirs of liquefied gases will enable wind energy to be
> stored so that it can be expended for industry, transportation, heating, and
> lighting, as desired. The initial costs will be very considerable but the run-
> ning expenses less than those of our present system. Among its more ob-
> vious advantages will be the fact that energy will be as cheap in one part of
> the country as another, so that industry will be greatly decentralized; and
> that no smoke or ash will be produced.

On the practical level, men like Franz Lawaczeck, Rudolf Erren, Kurt
Weil, J. E. Noeggerath, and Hermann Honnef in Germany were actively
pursuing various aspects of hydrogen research and were advocating the
use of hydrogen as a fuel. Some of them admitted to being influenced by
Jules Verne in their quest. A 1937 article in the Italian journal *Rivista
Aeronautica*, which introduced Erren's work to Italian aviation circles,
mentioned in passing the experimental efforts of an Italian engineer, A.
Beldimano, to adapt liquid hydrogen for use in aircraft engines. In Britain, H. R. Ricardo, one of the pioneers in the development of the internal
combustion engine, and Professor A. F. Burstall of Cambridge University were among the first to investigate the burn characteristics of
hydrogen. Men like Campbell, joined by Erren, who spent most of the
1930s in that country, and R. O. King, then a captain with the British Air
Ministry Laboratory, worked on, or were interested in, using hydrogen
as a fuel.

In the United States, Igor Sikorski mentioned hydrogen's potential as
aviation fuel in a 1938 lecture before the American Institution of Electrical Engineers in Schenectady, New York. After predicting the development of a new type of aircraft engine that would permit planes to fly at
speeds of 500 and 600 miles (800 and 965 kilometers) per hour and
altitudes of 30,000 to 50,000 feet (9,000 to 15,000 meters), he said that introduction of liquid hydrogen would bring about a profound transformation of aeronautics:

> If a method of safe and economical production and handling of liquid
> hydrogen were developed for use as a fuel, this would result in a great
> change, particularly with respect to long-range aircraft. This would make
> possible the circumnavigation of the earth along the equator in a non-stop
> flight without refueling. It would also enable an increase in the perfor-
> mance of nearly every type of aircraft.

One of the early twentieth-century founding fathers of the hydrogen
era in Europe was Franz Lawaczeck, a German turbine designer by

trade who, inspired by Jules Verne, became interested in hydrogen as early as 1907. Lawaczeck was somewhat of a loner who was far ahead of his time. By 1919 he was sketching concepts for hydrogen-powered cars, trains, and engines. Another part of his inspiration came from contact with a cousin, J. E. Noeggerath, an American of German birth who worked in Schenectady, New York, and later in Berlin. Lawaczeck and Noeggerath collaborated in developing an efficient pressurized electrolyzer.

Lawaczeck was also acquainted with Hermann Oberth, the German inventor and rocketeer of the late twenties whose work led to the German V-2 rockets of World War II and ultimately, via his student Wernher von Braun, to the U.S. Apollo Program and space shuttle. According to his son, Franz Jr., an engineer now living in Sweden, Lawaczeck at least indirectly contributed to Oberth's belief that a chemical space rocket needs to have three stages and that the combination of liquid hydrogen and oxygen is the best possible fuel. In the thirties Lawaczeck was apparently the first to suggest that energy could be transported via hydrogen-carrying pipelines, similarly to natural gas. Despite Lawaczeck's position in the technical avant garde, his economic and political opinions seem to have made life difficult for him, especially during the early years of Nazi Germany.

Another German engineer, Hermann Honnef, dreamed up huge steel wind-power towers up to 750 feet (230 meters) in height, with either three or five wind generators 480 feet (150 meters) in diameter, to produce up to 100 megawatts (Mw) each, stored in the form of hydrogen. Honnef's mid-thirties concepts, the precursors of wind-power designs developed in the late sixties and seventies for New England offshore regions by William Heronemus (see Chapter 5 for more on Heronemus) never went beyond the 50-meter (164-foot) prototype tower stage. Albert Speer, the engineer of Adolf Hitler's war machine, recalled that Honnef's towers didn't live up to expectations, according to a February 10, 1977, report on alternative energy in the German magazine *Der Stern*.

One of the earliest and most fascinating efforts involving hydrogen was its use not only as a buoyancy medium, but also as a booster fuel for the huge German dirigibles, the Zeppelins, that provided leisurely and elegant transatlantic air travel in the 1920s and 1930s. Normally, these big skyships carried large amounts of liquid fuel, usually a benzol-gasoline mixture, to drive 12- or 16-cylinder engines, typically propelling the Zeppelins at altitudes of only 2,400 feet (730 meters) and speeds of not quite 75 miles (120 kilometers) per hour, provided there was no headwind.

Fuel economy was one problem the Zeppelins encountered; another was how to cut down the ship's buoyancy as its weight decreased as fuel was consumed. According to a 1929 report by the Zeppelin Company in Friedrichshafen, on Lake Constance, the rule of thumb was that the Zeppelin captain had to blow off about one cubic meter of hydrogen for every kilogram of fuel burned up during nonstop cruises, which typically lasted from three to five days. Better fuel economy could be achieved by certain engine modifications such as increasing the compression ratios, but what about the buoyancy problem?

The solution was as simple as it was ingenious: Why not burn the blow-off hydrogen as extra fuel together with the main fuel supply? And if this was done, could the hydrogen be burned at higher compression ratios? Zeppelin's engineers found that it could. The addition of anywhere between 5 percent and 30 percent hydrogen to the main fuel at compression ratios as high as from 10:1 to 6:1 produced substantially higher power output—as much as 325 brake horsepower (bhp) compared to a normal output of 269 bhp. It also achieved substantial energy savings. The testbed findings were confirmed by an 82-hour, 10,000-kilometer (6,000-mile) cruise over the Mediterranean Sea in 1928, which showed a fuel reduction of about 14 percent.

Experimenting along the same lines but using diesel rather than gasoline engines, the Royal Airship Works in Great Britain found that "it was possible to replace almost the whole of the fuel oil by hydrogen without loss of power." On a typical England-to-Egypt trip the airship would have saved almost five tons of fuel oil, according to these experiments. But it seems that neither the British nor the Germans ever actually applied these findings to any significant extent to their routine dirigible operations.

Rudolf Erren

The best known of the early hydrogen advocates of 40 and 50 years ago was Rudolf A. Erren, a brilliant visionary German engineer who had trucks, buses, submarines, and internal combustion engines of all kinds running on hydrogen as well as other fuels, both conventional and unconventional. Erren engines were powering vehicles in sizable numbers both in Germany and England. Contrary to a prevalent impression in the international hydrogen community today, Erren, a vigorous octogenarian who looks at least 20 years younger, is alive and well in Hannover, where he is still working as a consulting engineer.

A flinty engineer from Upper Silesia (now part of Poland) with a rather pronounced disdain for academics and theoreticians, Erren began investigating combustion processes as early as 1926, forming his first company, the Erren Motoren GmbH Spezialversuchsanstalt, in a grimy industrial section of northern Berlin in 1928. Two years earlier he had

Figure 3.1. Rudolf A. Erren, one of the earliest
hydrogen pioneers, who converted trucks and
buses to hydrogen fuel in the 1930s in England
and Germany. The picture was taken in 1979 in
Germany.

begun his investigations of hydrogen and its properties, an interest that
went back to his childhood. When I visited him in Hannover in 1976, he
told me that he also had read the Pemberton book in his childhood. He
recalled it "described a pirate group that had kidnapped a German professor who had developed a hydrogen engine which made the pirates'
ship much faster than other ships." Like many teenagers, Erren ex-
perimented with hydrogen while attending high school in Katowice; his
interest in hydrogen carried over as a hobby through his university years
in Berlin and Goettingen and also in England: "During summer vacations
when other students went on vacation, I worked in engine workshops to
learn something because I wanted to get to know these things in practice.
Theory alone doesn't work."

He won his first patents in 1928 for a hydrogen engine as well as for a
multi-fuel engine and other energy-related projects. Erren presented his

data at the 1930 World Power Conference in Berlin and, he says, the terms "Erren Engine, Erren Process, Erren System" were then officially recognized to differentiate his combustion process from any other.

That same year he went to England at the invitation of several British firms, founding the Erren Engineering Co., Ltd., in London. There he continued his work of developing advanced combustion processes that permitted the use of hydrogen alone or as a "clean-up" additive to normal fuels. "Errenizing" any type of internal combustion process was relatively well known in the thirties, at least among automotive engineers. Essentially it meant injecting slightly pressurized hydrogen into air or oxygen inside the combustion chamber, rather than "sucking" the air-fuel mixture via a carburetor into the engine, a method that commonly resulted in violent backfire. Erren's patented system involved the addition of special fuel injection and control mechanisms but left the other engine components intact. With hydrogen used as a booster, the "Erren" system eliminated backfire and achieved much better combustion of hydrocarbons with higher output and lower specific fuel consumption.

Kurt Weil, a German-born engineer who was Erren's technical director in the thirties and is now professor emeritus at Stevens Institute of Technology, Hoboken, New Jersey, says this idea of not permitting hydrogen to come into contact with the oxygen of the air prior to the combustion chamber was representative of Erren's "genius." Weil, who has been in the forefront of promoting hydrogen in the 1970s and has obtained contracts from a number of U.S. government agencies, including the army's Advanced Research Projects Agency (ARPA), explained: "when the valves were closed we injected hydrogen which had a supercharging effect as well . . . about 15 percent more power." This engineering approach was not revived until the early seventies.

In the mid-thirties, Erren and Weil proposed to the Nazi government, which was by then vitally concerned with economic self-sufficiency and lessened dependence on imported liquid fuels, the conversion of most internal combustion engines to the Erren multi-fuel system. In addition to using carbon-based fuels produced from Germany's plentiful coal by the Fischer-Tropsch and Bergius systems,[1] it would also be possible to use hydrogen produced via off-peak power from Germany's closely knit grid of electric power stations, which normally ran at only about 50 percent of capacity. As a beneficial side effect, the congested highways and railroads would be freed of much of the need to transport fuel.

By 1938, when Weil left for the United States, about one hundred trucks were already running between Berlin and the industrial Ruhr area in the west, a distance of some 350 miles (560 kilometers), switching from

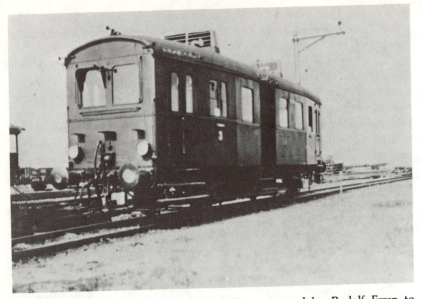

Figure 3.2. A German self-propelled rail car converted by Rudolf Erren to hydrogen operations.

one fuel to another along the way "with the truck fully loaded, on a steep incline with a switch in the cockpit." All kinds of different truck makes had been converted—MAN, Deutz, Daimler-Benz, and Büssing. Weil recalls that the engine adaptation was not that difficult, but it was easier for some types of engines than for others: "For a six-in-line it was much easier than for a V-type engine." As to conversion costs, "I'd say under today's conditions the cost would have been a few hundred dollars per engine." Erren himself believes that the total number of cars and trucks converted to his multi-fuel system was more than 1,000; one British report put the total at between 3,000 and 4,000.

The German railway system test-operated a hydrogen-powered self-propelled rail car in suburban operations out of Dresden. The train was powered by a 75-horsepower six-cylinder N.A.G. gasoline engine, a make that has disappeared today. It was "much worn" and running harshly, according to a 1932 report by a Reichsbahn maintenance depot, but run on gasoline and primed with hydrogen, the engine developed up to 83 brake horsepower, an increase of 9.7 percent. Powered by pure hydrogen, the engine produced a maximum of 77 brake horsepower.

In England, meanwhile, errenization was catching on as well. Erren converted busses with Beardmore diesel engines and Carter-Paterson delivery vans to hydrogen usage for better fuel consumption and less

Figure 3.3. An Australian commission investigating Rudolf Erren's hydrogen-burning bus poses in front of the vehicle after a successful demonstration in 1936. A handwritten note on the back of the original reads,

"Very successful demonstration of the Erren Hydrogen Motorbus, at which the Agents General for the various Australian States and their Technical Advisors were present.—This photo was taken at the Roehampton Club at the conclusion of the Trials on December 16th 1936. (sgnd) James C. Brand, Eng. Captain RAN ret.

"Remarks: The engine was operated on liquid and /or gaseous fuels, no leaded fuels, clean exhaust, compression ratio 12:1 (Beardmore Diesel converted to the Erren-System). Supervision on all bench and road tests: Prof. Dr. S.J. Davies, King's College, London University." Erren (arrow).

pollution, which then, as Weil said in a paper, was "not yet considered more than a nuisance." Erren himself turned into an energy hero to an extent today's hydrogen advocates wouldn't even dream about. British publications, both technical and popular, carried a sizable number of stories about the man and his work. He was sought out by delegations from various governments asking his counsel on energy matters. In July 1935 he was invited to France and Spain for a series of lectures on hydrogen as a fuel and related topics.

Erren tells of an incident involving an Australian commission that spent two or three weeks in his shops checking his claims and his engines. Finally, the commission wanted to conduct an open road speed test with a bus and the site chosen was a climbing road outside of London.

The police there were always on the lookout because the gentlemen from a nearby club drove faster than the thirty miles per hour speed limit. Well, we wanted an official confirmation [of our claims]. The police were pretty well hidden, but we saw them anyway, switched to hydrogen and instead of driving at thirty miles we did fifty or fifty-two miles up the hill. The police stopped us, told us that they had timed us with a stop watch and we had exceeded the speed limit, which we had to admit. We paid our fine but thanked them profusely, which in turn astonished them until we explained that we now had official proof of our claims.

In 1935, Erren made the popular British press with news that warmed the hearts of Jules Verne fans and promised actual achievement. "Secret Fuel to Smash Air Record" headlined the *Sunday Despatch* of March 24, 1935, subheading the one-column story "Non-Stop Round the World with Liquid Hydrogen." The story reported that engines were being perfected "in secret" in London that "will enable aeroplanes to smash the distance record; make long flights in the stratosphere; and fly non-stop around the world without refuelling." The effort was being organized by a Captain Richard Humble, "a business man who has made several outstanding flights in Africa, and Mr. Rudolf Erren, a brilliant German engineer who was an airman during the war." The paper said the effort will be all-British since both plane and pilots will be British. The story gave few details saying only that the secret was to use liquid hydrogen "in conjunction with another fuel" and that for the first attempt probably a "standard monoplane" would be adapted.

The paper went on:

> Mr. Erren, who fought under Baron von Richthofen and General Göring in the Great War, has already achieved distinction in this country with his hydrogen engines.
> Last year, a British company was formed to exploit his plan for ships to distill sea water and to split it under pressure into oxygen and hydrogen for use in an engine which was really a combination of the steam and internal combustion engine.

The project never went beyond the conceptual stage, and nothing came of the "non-stop round the world" flight. Erren says the prototype plane, a Rolls-Royce–powered De Havilland, was "ready to go," but the idea fell by the wayside because of disputes within the company having to do with whether the attempt would be made from Britain or from Germany.

Erren made news in the financial world of London as well in 1938 when he sold patent rights to the National Gas and Oil Engine Company, a subsidiary of the United Kingdom Gas Corporation. According to the *Sunday Express* of December 4, 1938, National Gas ordinary shares jumped on the stock exchange from a little over 9 shillings to 12 shillings when the transaction became known.

Other Erren inventions, the oxy-hydrogen submarine and the trackless torpedo, which operated on the same principle, literally made waves in Britain in 1942. The trackless torpedo, fueled by oxygen and hydrogen, was beguilingly simple in concept. Erren started from the realization that torpedoes leave "tracks"—a trail of exhaust gas bubbles. Because hydrogen and oxygen recombine into water vapor condensing back into the sea water, no bubbles are formed that would drift to the surface for a giveaway trail.

The oxygen-hydrogen–burning submarine eliminated almost entirely the need for big batteries and electric motors for underwater running. Instead, during diesel-powered surface runs the sub's engine also drove an electrolyzer, generating oxygen and hydrogen, both of which were then stored under pressure. When diving and running submerged, the same diesel engine burned the oxygen and hydrogen without any exhaust bubbles. Weight savings from the elimination of batteries and electric motors translated into the ability to carry more fuel and extended the sub's range—one report claims by as much as 15,000 miles (24,000 kilometers). In addition, the hull was strengthened, enabling the submarine to dive deeper and faster. The generated oxygen was a valuable safety addition for crew survival in an emergency, and the pressurized hydrogen could be used to blow out tanks for surfacing if other air supplies were exhausted.

These marine applications were developed by Erren in the 1930s in Britain, where he had applied for naturalization. He demonstrated the oxy-hydrogen submarine propulsion system to the British Admiralty "some years before the war," according to an account in the November 19, 1942, issue of *Shipbuilding and Shipping Record*. The Admiralty said, in effect, "no thanks." However, when the German navy heard about Erren's ideas it began taking an interest as well. The Admiralty, for reasons that are not clear—a sense of gentlemanliness perhaps, professional courtesy of one navy to another—did not raise any objections to the Germans' sending emissaries to Erren in England to study his ideas.

What had seemed before the war more or less a technical-scientific issue surfaced during the war as a British national security problem. In 1942, the Allies captured German submarines, which, according to contemporary press reports, were using just these self-same Erren-type oxy-hydrogen propulsion units with all the advantages cited. Erren, who by this time had been interned as an enemy alien and sent to Canada, says the investigation by British and American marine experts involved only a single such German submarine, but the news hit home "like an atomic bomb." (Ironically, only seven months before his British internment, Erren had been given one of the highest recognitions awarded by the British energy industry—he was made a Fellow of the Institute of Fuel, only the third German to receive this honor. The others were two famous German chemists, Professors Friedrich Bergius and Hans Tropsch, known worldwide as inventor and coinventor, respectively, of two basic chemical industry processes, the Bergius and Fischer-Tropsch processes.)

Erren was repatriated to Germany in 1945. All of his personal and business possessions in England had been confiscated during the war, and in Germany the papers of his company, Deutsche Erren Studien GmbH, located in what is now a part of East Berlin, were lost when the firm's buildings were gutted by Allied bombing. He moved to Hannover, where he helped set up the German Association of Plastics-based Manufacturers, and he has worked since then as an independent consulting engineer in pollution control, industrial combustion processes, and related areas.

None of his engines seem to have survived the collapse of Hitler's Germany, although in England a few may still be around as multi-fuel engines. To prove his ideas once again, Erren converted one engine in Germany in the early fifties to multi-fuel operations. Despite a warm letter of recommendation from a transportation expert to the German Transportation Ministry pointing out the fuel savings and other beneficial aspects, Erren did not even receive an acknowledgment.

Erren's efforts to interest other agencies or companies in his concepts proved equally fruitless. Erren told me he talked to officials and engineers at Volkswagen, Daimler-Benz, and Dornier, a German aerospace firm researching high-pressure, high-temperature electrolysis of water.

> I've been down to see Dornier and have shown my work. The engineers were convinced and wanted to work with me, but nothing happened. I've demonstrated to the Volkswagen people that their approach using methanol[2] is complicated, doesn't work and is nonsense but again, no.

Several researchers at Volkswagen and Daimler-Benz acknowledged that their companies have talked to Erren, but they felt his data are old and are no longer relevant because they have been bypassed by events, especially advances in instrumentation since the thirties that permit a much more precise analysis of emission and combustion data.

Erren isn't buying that argument. The experience of the fifties and sixties have made him rather bitter, especially because in the seventies his name began cropping up as a historical reference whenever hydrogen advocates assembled to talk shop. Erren believes the main reason German companies do not want to work with him is that they are afraid of losing government research money that might dry up once funding agencies realize they are financing what amounts to reinventing the wheel in the area of hydrogen research. It's hard for an outsider to judge who is right. But it does seem a waste not to draw on the experience of a man who has spent most of his productive life not only in theoretical research but in building and successfully operating practical hardware in a field that is just beginning to emerge from the status of a virtual energy subculture. Erren is convinced that the German pattern of corporate research militates against the individual inventor and in fact is consciously designed to shoot down the outsider:

> Unfortunately, the way it is in Germany is that if some engineer comes with an invention to a company and asks for, just to name a number, one thousand Deutschmarks, he won't get it. But the company will spend ten thousand or fifty thousand Deutschmarks to wring your neck.

There is a happy footnote: In early 1978, a research group in Hannover received a $75,000 grant from the research ministry of Lower Saxony (where Hannover is located) to experimentally reestablish the same data that Erren had proved on hundreds of engines in the 1930s. Initially, the Institute of Crude Oil Research converted a small 11-horsepower single-cylinder diesel engine to Erren's multi-fuel system for evaluation, on the assumption that Erren's approach is still worth testing, and other tests followed. It looked as if Erren would once more, belatedly, receive the recognition he deserved. Later that year, Rudolf Erren showed up at an international hydrogen conference in Zurich. When he was introduced at the final session, the applause was loud and a long-fitting tribute for a man who had been ahead of everybody else by four decades.

The War Years and After:
Sporadic Interest in Hydrogen

During World War II, interest in hydrogen as fuel flickered in some corners of the world where fuel supplies were threatened or cut off because of hostilities. In Australia, the industrial use of hydrogen was considered early in the war because of wartime demands for fuel oil and because of the loss of oilfields in Borneo to the Japanese. In Queensland, the state government became attracted to hydrogen after the coordinator for public works, J. F. Kemp, had learned about hydrogen progress in England and Germany on a 1938 visit to Britain. After Kemp returned he ordered some studies of his own. However, it was not until the last year of the war that another Australian engineer, J. S. Just, completed a report dealing with hydrogen production via off-peak electricity in Brisbane, to be used mostly for trucks. The report found that hydrogen fuel costs would be roughly equal to the cost of gasoline per truck-mile. The Queensland government authorized construction of an experimental high-pressure plant with plans for a commercial-size plant later on and several electrolyzer cells were actually set up in an electricity substation in Brisbane, but not much was heard about it afterwards. It appears that the Allied victory in 1945 and the availability once more of cheap oil and gasoline brought progress on hydrogen to a halt. One exception was R. O. King, who after having moved to Canada continued hydrogen research, investigating combustion characteristics with a team of scientists at the University of Toronto in the late 1940s and 1950s.

Hydrogen became of interest again as early as 1950, this time to power fuel cells. Francis T. Bacon, a British scientist, developed the first practical hydrogen-air fuel cell at about that time, a development that was to be of great significance later in the American space program.

In the fifties a German physicist working not too far from Erren was becoming interested in hydrogen as an energy storage medium. Eduard Justi, a distinguished German electrical chemist at the Institute of Technical Physics of the University of Braunschweig, had been working for years on the development of new, more efficient fuel cells. In a 1962 monograph entitled "Cold Combustion—Fuel Cells" Justi and a coworker, August Winsel, discussed the prospects of splitting water into hydrogen and oxygen, storing these gases separately, and recombining them in fuel cells. Justi later amplified his ideas in a book published in 1965 in which he proposed hydrogen production via solar energy along the Mediterranean. The resulting hydrogen gas would be shipped to Germany, for instance, in long-distance pipelines such as a 2,150-kilometer (1,350-mile) line linking Gibraltar and Karlsruhe, a suggestion Justi made in a 1974 lecture in Lausanne. Unlike others, right from the start Justi proposed collecting and piping the by-product oxygen as well to energy or chemical raw material users.

In 1962 John O'M. Bockris, an Australian electrochemist, proposed a plan to supply U.S. cities with solar-derived energy via hydrogen. Bockris, who in 1975 published the first detailed overview of a future solar-hydrogen economy,[3] says the phrase "hydrogen economy" with all its economic and environmental implications was first coined during a discussion at the General Motors Technical Center in Warren, Michigan, in 1970. Bockris, at the time a consultant to General Motors (GM), was discussing with the center staff and others prospects for other fuels to replace gasoline and eliminate its attendant pollution, a subject that was then beginning to loom large in the public consciousness. The group con-

Figure 3.4. Cesare Marchetti, the Italian physicist, who is one of the key advocates of hydrogen in Europe. Since his retirement from the EURATOM Reseach Center in Ispra, Italy, in the mid-seventies, Marchetti has been working at the International Institute for Applied Systems Analysis in Laxenburg, near Vienna, Austria, an international think tank funded by more than a dozen governments, including the United States and the Soviet Union. (Photo courtesy of IIASA)

cluded that "hydrogen would be the fuel for all types of transports," Bockris related in his book. Although GM did some experimental work on hydrogen (see Chapter 6) it did not give it the attention, or at least not the degree of publicity, that Daimler-Benz, the only major automotive manufacturer to do so, gave it six years later. (Renault also did some studies involving hydrogen-powered fuel cells to drive an R-4 model, but they apparently never went past the planning stage.)

An Italian scientist, Cesare Marchetti, delivered a lecture at Cornell University, also in 1970, that outlined the case for hydrogen in lay terms. Marchetti, at the time head of the Materials Division of the European Atomic Energy Community's (EURATOM) Research Center in Ispra, Italy, had been calling both in Europe and the United States for the use of hydrogen since the late 1960s. Hydrogen, produced from water and heat from a nuclear reactor—in those days nuclear energy had not yet acquired the odium it has today—could free humanity from dependence on dwindling fossil fuels: "The potential for hydrogen is very great, and a smell of revolution lingers in the air," he told the Cornell crowd. Marchetti, who has the gift of putting complex relationships into simple terms, stated the hydrogen proposition like this:

> The reason why the studies of industrial utilization of nuclear energy have concentrated on the production of electricity is that a substantial 20 to 25 percent of the energetic input in a developed society is used in the form of electricity and that its production is lumped in large blocks where reactors can show their economies.
>
> But almost nothing has been done to penetrate the remaining three-quarters of the energy input: food, fuel, ore processing and miscellaneous uses where society is geared to using a wide variety of chemicals.
>
> The problem is to find a flexible intermediate, produced in large blocks in which nuclear heat can be stored as chemical energy and distributed through the usual channels. . . .
>
> In my opinion, the best candidate to perform such a task is hydrogen: on one side hydrogen can be obtained from water, a cheap and plentiful raw material. On the other side, hydrogen can be used directly and very efficiently for:
>
> 1. ore reduction, as an alternative to coal,
> 2. home and industrial heat as an alternative to oil,
> 3. in chemical synthesis, in particular [for making] ammonia and methanol,
> 4. producing liquid fuels, such as methanol, for transport; ammonia and hydrogen themselves have potential in the future,
> 5. producing food, particularly proteins, via yeasts such as *Hydrogenomonas.*
>
> Points one to four cover most of the 80 percent of the energy input, excluding electricity.
>
> Point five can solve once and for all the problem of feeding a growing world population.

The same message was spread in lectures, papers, and articles in the United States by a handful of scientists and engineers who had come to the same general conclusion in their respective disciplines. Derek Gregory, a British scientist at the Chicago-based Institute of Gas Technology (IGT), had become interested in hydrogen as a clean substitute for natural gas. Bob Witcofski, a young researcher at the National Aeronautics and Space Administration (NASA), had detailed the genuinely exciting prospects of liquid hydrogen as fuel for types of aircraft, including nonpolluting supersonic and hypersonic airplanes of the future. Lawrence Jones, a particle physicist at the University of Michigan, had become interested in hydrogen as an offshoot of his scientific work as well as because of the rising concern over automotive pollution. Larry Williams, a cryogenic specialist at the Martin-Marietta Corporation, had also recognized the usefulness of supercold liquid hydrogen as a fuel. Bill Escher, a former rocket engineer, had come to recognize hydrogen's potential as a down-to-earth fuel through his involvement with the U.S. space program.

The Institute of Gas Technology early on became one of the leaders in the hydrogen movement. Bockris requested help from the institute's staff in the fall of 1969 on extensive computations to evaluate an overall hydrogen concept—production via nuclear reactors or solar heat, shipping of hydrogen through pipelines, and use in households and industries. The institute team published an initial report in 1971. Gregory, who has become one of the main spokesmen at IGT for hydrogen energy, and two coworkers published an amplified paper a year later in what has become one of the early standard volumes in the field, a collection of papers called *The Electrochemistry of Cleaner Environments* (New York: Plenum Press, 1972), edited by Bockris.

While GM, Ford, and Chrysler largely practiced benign neglect of hydrogen, at least publicly, hydrogen's potential as a nonpolluting car fuel caught the eye and enthusiasm of a number of American academics, engineers, and automotive enthusiasts in the early seventies (see Chapter 6). Beginning roughly with the work of the Perris Smogless Association in California and the University of California at Los Angeles (UCLA) hydrogen-powered car that won the 1972 Urban Vehicle Design Competition, efforts to utilize hydrogen in cars and trucks sprang up, primarily in the United States, Germany, and Japan but also in France and even in the Soviet Union.

The U.S. military, especially the air force and the army, were also seriously looking into hydrogen as a fuel. Starting in 1943, the air force began investigating hydrogen properties in a program at Ohio State University, a development that eventually culminated in the combined use of liquid hydrogen and oxygen as rocket fuel in the U.S. space program. Much less known outside the hydrogen community were efforts in the sixties to use liquid hydrogen as jet fuel. In one secret project, Lockheed began work on a long-distance high-altitude reconnaissance plane, a forerunner of the U-2. In a parallel program, the National Advisory Committee for Aeronautics (NACA)[4] was gathering actual engine flight data in a B-57 twin-jet bomber operating partially on liquid hydrogen. Both efforts, which will be described in Chapter 7, were eventually halted; the reconnaissance plane was never built, and the evaluation program was stopped after it was shown to everybody's satisfaction that jet planes could indeed fly on liquid hydrogen.

Similarly, the navy had been investigating hydrogen as a fuel for a variety of ships, including hydrogen plus oxygen as a fuel for a deep-diving submarine rescue vessel that would be powered by fuel cells. One revolutionary idea tossed around in the mid-fifties was to tap reactors powering nuclear aircraft carriers to make liquid hydrogen fuel for carrier-based airplanes, a concept that in theory would make such a carrier and its planes virtually independent of cumbersome and (in time of war) unreliable fuel supply by tanker.

Another significant military effort of the sixties was the army's so-called Nuclear-Powered Energy Depot, "an early experiment in the hydrogen economy," according to a paper at The Hydrogen Economy Miami Energy (THEME)[5] conference, held in 1974 in Miami Beach. The idea was to develop a portable nuclear reactor, presumably available near the battlefield, that could split water into hydrogen and oxygen, making hydrogen available as a chemical fuel for battle tanks and trucks. An alternate version envisioned ammonia production from air, with ammonia serving as fuel. The concept was the outgrowth of the "recognition that the dominant problem in the combat theater is the transportation of petroleum," said John B. O'Sullivan, an army chemical engineer, adding that a reactor core "held the equivalent of many tons of petroleum." In the 1962–1966 program, the army studied "thousands of hydrogen production cycles [and] did a fairly large amount of experimental work," which resulted in "six feet of reports." The idea was dropped because of efficiency problems and because the researchers "were not getting the power densities that were needed." It was also realized that such a portable nuclear hydrogen plant was, after all, a "very vulnerable item" that "needed a lot of people" and that lost its main advantage, mobility, if it had to be buried or protected in some other way to keep it out of reach of enemy attack. Another reason for discontinuing the project was the belief that the United States had another 100 years worth of petroleum, coupled with the implicit assumption that prices for petroleum would not rise. Commented O'Sullivan wryly: "All concepts should be periodically reviewed because reasons and conditions change."

The 1970s: Hydrogen Research Takes Off

With the arrival of the seventies, interest in hydrogen began to grow by leaps and bounds. Almost all of the initial enthusiasm was a by-product of the growing environmental awareness, especially the concern over automotive pollution and the mounting conviction that alternative nonpolluting transportation systems and energy forms were needed. Hydrogen fit the bill neatly. Hydrogen researchers, as they began combing the literature, found to their surprise that others like Erren, Campbell, King, Ricardo, and Lawaczek had developed many of the same concepts—for reasons that had little to do with pollution—decades earlier. Then, Jules Verne's prophetic words on the subject, plus those other rediscovered pronouncements by the likes of Haldane, gave the idea of hydrogen-as-fuel an almost mystical sense of historical rightness and inevitability, a sort of belief that this element was *meant* to be used to deflect mankind from at least one of many paths towards self-destruction.

Next came the oil shock of 1973, the first of the many instances since then when OPEC flexed its cartel muscles, driving world oil prices sky-high. The shock announced that the short age of cheap, convenient liquid fuel was coming to an end and that it was urgent that substitutes be found. Again, hydrogen seemed to provide an easy, fairly fast answer: Produced via electrolysis "cheaply" from "safe, clean" nuclear reactors, so went the conventional wisdom then, hydrogen could be substituted readily for fossil fuels. Thus, the twin impulses of environmental concern and search for alternative sources of energy combined to speed up the investigation of hydrogen.

The reasons for the renewed widespread interest in hydrogen in the early seventies were, of course, different for different people. But the idea of a "totally benign energy metabolism," as the University of Michigan's Lawrence Jones put it, was a large factor. The cosmic wholesomeness, "a kind of gut appeal to people was the kind of thing that frankly turned a lot of us on," Jones observed.

Jones put it more formally in a 1971 article in *Science* magazine, in which he wrote that the possibility of using liquid hydrogen as an ultimate replacement for fossil fuels occurred to him in casual conversation "related to the logistics and use of large quantities of liquid hydrogen in a cosmic-ray experiment"—the normal scientific habitat for Jones, a particle physicist. "In remarking on the drop in price of liquid hydrogen in recent years, I noted that the cost per liter was about the same as that of gasoline." As he began reading up on hydrogen in the available literature, "I recognized that . . . it had an inherent self-consistency and appeal which warranted broader discussion. The conclusion I have reached is that the use of liquid hydrogen as a fuel not only is feasible technically and economically, but also is desirable and may even be inevitable."

Those early discussions took place in 1969, a time when concern about the environment, especially automotive pollution, was on the rise throughout the United States. Like many scientists and engineers, Jones was profoundly troubled by what looked like technological Armageddon. He organized what he had learned about hydrogen and presented it at an environmental teach-in at the University of Michigan in March 1970. He published it later as a University of Michigan Technical Report and then as the *Science* article quoted above.

Said Jones in another article two years later: "It soon became apparent that a surprising number of widely-separated individuals and groups had very similar thoughts." That phenomenon became evident at the watershed spring 1972 meeting of the American Chemical Society in Boston where Marchetti and De Beni presented their first thermochemical water-splitting process and especially at the seventh Intersociety Energy Conversion Engineering Conference in San Diego that autumn.

Business Week's story was timed to appear for the San Diego meeting, and the effect on the assembled scientists was notable. Marchetti, who attended, wrote later in a personal note,

> The big cats of hydrogen had tears in their eyes seeing their names and work printed in full letters . . . the success was great and the sessions on hydrogen did depopulate the parallel sessions; out of 650 participants about 500 were concentrated in the one on H_2.

Hydrogen researchers' recognition that they were not alone in their interest produced a chain reaction of correspondence and meetings leading to a climax of sorts with the creation of the informal "H_2indenburg Society" on the thirty-fifth anniversary of the *Hindenburg* disaster (May 6, 1972) as a group dedicated "to the safe utilization of hydrogen as a fuel."

The society has no statutes and no by-laws. The only way to recognize a H_2indenburgian is by his stark black-and-white, gothically scripted "H_2indenburg" lapel button, a collector's item by now seen rarely only on people like Derek Gregory, who sported one in Zurich. Gregory's puckish sense of humor led him to design the world's first, and so far only, hydrogen-powered cuckoo clock, a Rube Goldberg-type contraption (see Figure 3.5 for an early sketch). Another early relic held in amused reverence by the H_2indenburgians is the society's credo, drawn up by Ben Bova, former editor of the science fiction magazine *Analog*, and first published in the magazine's September 1973 issue. (See Figure 3.6.)

One of the original chain reactors, Bill Escher, was named secretary of the society. Escher is one of the main hydrogen movers whose name seems to appear on just about every other bit of paper published in the United States on hydrogen as coauthor, consultant, advocate, or in some other capacity. In 1976 he recalled:

> I became very much interested in hydrogen because it was paying my

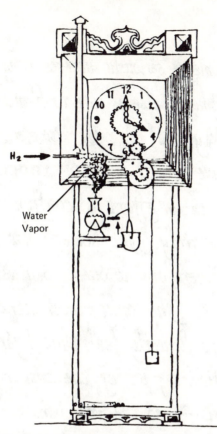

Figure 3.5. Derek Gregory's celebrated design of a hydrogen-powered cuckoo clock.

salary in 1958 when I began work on hydrogen-oxygen rockets at NASA Lewis [Research Center]. My job was to help run tests and lay out thrust chambers that worked on hydrogen and oxygen which was considered a far-out rocket fuel. Today it is a staple fuel. The space industry has already made the conversion.

His "transition to real life," as he calls it, came in the late sixties when he went to Rocketdyne, a maker of rocket equipment in California, where he drew the assignment to sell rocket technology to the outside world.

I made a few trips to the public utilities and other such people with potential hydrogen interests. It was interesting and immediately it churned up

42

Whenever someone seriously suggests using hydrogen this way, someone else is sure to blanch and scream, "My God! the Hindenburg!" So they have formed The H₂indenburg Society in an effort to confront the problem squarely. The society has no real structure, there are no dues, no newsletters, no meetings. The only requirement is that the members honestly feel that hydrogen might be a significant part of the answer to the energy crisis — so the members will face up to the frozen-minded attitudes of the heathen and attempt to get them past the emotional block that has stoppered thinking when it comes to hydrogen as a fuel.

Ben Bova

analog September 1973

Figure 3.6. The "H₂indenburg Society" credo. (Courtesy *Analog* Magazine)

Figure 3.7. William J. D. Escher.

into a big activity, and a year later, in 1970 I left and became an independent consultant

on hydrogen and hydrogen-related alternative energy systems.

In Marchetti's case, the interest in hydrogen also started in a roundabout way back in the late 1950s when he was working for the Italian national oil company, Ente Nazionale Idrocarburi (ENI), trying to find ways to make use of the off-peak power of nuclear reactors. "The idea then was to somehow use electricity to make adenosine triphosphate [ATP] which is the energy carrier of biological systems," he recalled. Marchetti tried to find ways to make synthetic ATP to act as intermediary between an electrical energy source, like a reactor, and a biological system. Eventually Marchetti found "this didn't work because ATP never leaves the individual cell, therefore you cannot put it into a cell." Later, in the sixties, after he had switched to the EURATOM Research Center in Ispra, he recalled that in his high school days he had read that there were certain bacteria able to metabolize hydrogen and oxygen and grow on that, "and so I thought this material would be the right interface between food chain and electricity because you can make hydrogen and oxygen electrolytically." A bibliographic search of the literature under H—for hydrogen—turned up all kinds of chemical processes "that could do almost everything—reduce materials in chemistry, reduce minerals to metals, run engines and things like that." Looking at the problem more generally, "I decided from a systems point of view electrolysis was not very good for a number of reasons. So, going to the root of the problem, that of transferring free energy from a heat source to a chemical system, I decided that the best way was to go to a chemical system via a multistep process." That was about 1969, and the way he tells it with a smile, "I told De Beni to invent such a system, and he did invent one."

In a landmark presentation Marchetti and his coworker Gianfranco De Beni introduced the first workable—theoretically, at least—thermochemical water-splitting cycle at the 1972 meeting of the American Chemical Society in Boston. Gregory acquainted the scientific community and interested lay people with the concept of a hydrogen economy in an article in the January 1973 issue of *Scientific American*. The popular media followed suit. *Business Week* was among the first to lay out the hydrogen picture in a September 22, 1972, article timed to coincide with the opening of a conference in San Diego devoted largely to hydrogen. *Fortune* carried a longer story two months later; it was followed by articles in *Readers' Digest, TIME, Popular Science,* and other magazines.

NASA organized a working symposium on liquid hydrogen-fueled aircraft in May 1973 at its Langley Research Center in Hampton, Virginia. THEME, which was the first major international hydrogen conference, yielded a fat volume of conference proceedings. Two years later, at the next international meeting, the First World Hydrogen Conference, the proceedings had swollen to three volumes. At THEME the groundwork for setting up the International Association for Hydrogen Energy was laid. Officially chartered in the fall of 1974, the association had about 2,000 members by 1979. It began publishing a quarterly (later a bimonthly) in January 1976 with contributions from hydrogen researchers from all corners of the globe. As of early 1980, the *International Journal of Hydrogen Energy* counted some 3,000 subscribers.

At the 1978 Zurich conference four volumes were published. While at previous conferences papers tended to be more general and occasionally somewhat messianic, extolling the virtues of hydrogen, Zurich was all business. "There is much more emphasis on describing problems of individual processes," observed Heiko Barnert, a scientist from West Germany's Nuclear Research Center in Jülich, during the meeting. Typical of the down-to-earth, analytical approach was a Jülich paper entitled "The Anodic Oxydation of Sulfur Dioxide in the Frame of the Sulfuric Acid

Hybrid Cycle." Noted Barnert: "The earlier enthusiasm has cooled off, but many researchers are now doing more basic work and go much more into detail."

Governments and international organizations began taking notice as well. In the United States, where hydrogen research funding passed the million-dollar mark only in the mid-seventies, $24 million was budgeted in fiscal 1978 for hydrogen research—far too little in the opinion of hydrogen advocates, who compare this to the $200 million the Department of Energy (DoE)[6] had allocated that same year for researching means of converting coal into synthetic natural gas, for example. Having decided that coal would be the mainstay of America's energy supply in the next few decades, government energy planners tend to give priority to coal. "There's a lot more emphasis on things that can be commercialized by 1985," acknowledged James H. Swisher, DoE's assistant director for physical storage systems and one of the department's people most intimately involved with hydrogen, in a September 4, 1978, *Business Week* story on hydrogen developments. "We all agree that hydrogen is worth considering but other alternative fuels can be developed more quickly."

West Germany also began funding hydrogen programs on a small scale, earmarking $2 million between 1978 and 1980. Beginning in 1976, the Paris-based International Energy Agency (IEA) began to support hydrogen programs; in 1978, the IEA's hydrogen budget stood at somewhat more than $16 million, spread over several years.

Since 1972 the European Economic Community has spent an estimated 60 to 70 million Units of Account (roughly $72 to $84 million) on hydrogen. The outlays mainly supported Marchetti and his team's early efforts towards finding a viable thermochemical water-splitting cycle at EURATOM, parallel investigations of the interface between thermochemical hydrogen production and the required high-temperature nuclear reactor at Jülich, and computer studies at Aachen Technical University attempting to narrow down the field of thousands of theoretical cycles to a few promising ones. With interest in hydrogen cooling, the European Community budgeted 13.2 million Units of Account (roughly 10.2 million dollars) for the 1975–1979 period. In the next four years, 1979 to 1983, the figure was to be even smaller—only about 8 million Units of Account (about 6.2 million dollars).

What looked initially like a truly gigantic alternative energy program, comparable in scope to the Apollo space program, is Japan's Project Sunshine, a 26-year undertaking begun in 1974 that was supposed to assure Japan of clean and plentiful power by the end of the century. Early reports in the mid-seventies circulating among Western European scientists mentioned total outlays of up to $15 billion over the lifetime of the program. One German scientist reported home that the hydrogen budget alone amounted to $3.6 billion (other main research areas were: solar energy, geothermal energy, coal gasification and liquefaction, and supporting programs). By 1978, it had become clear that these early reports were wildly exaggerated and some Japanese researchers charge that their country's hydrogen program actually lags behind the efforts in other countries. Professor Tokio Ohta of Yokohama University, vice president of the Hydrogen Energy System Society of Japan, said in a 1978 interview that by and large Japan's hydrogen program is on the right track, but he complained that funding is inadequate compared to nuclear R&D, which gets 30 times as much money as the 5.5 billion yen ($25.6 million) earmarked for the entire Project Sunshine in 1978, of which hydrogen received only 720 million yen ($3.3 million). "It's far too small an amount compared to [the programs of] the United States or of European countries," Ohta said. Project Sunshine as a whole should receive at least "one-tenth of the nuclear budget since diversification of energy sources is very important in the next century because of the limitations of natural resources," he suggested. "To get a national consensus on hydrogen as future energy, many more industries or people should be involved."

Japanese planners have conceded, though, that their programs are perhaps among the world's most advanced. Some European and U.S. hydrogen researchers have suspected as much in recent years but facts have been hard to pin down because of the frequent reluctance of Japanese scientists visiting the United States or Europe to discuss their work in detail. One European researcher (who preferred to remain unidentified) told me, "the Japanese are being very reserved [about divulging technical information]. Even where we asked very insistent questions about details, the usual reply was 'well, we can't talk about this so far, I have to query back home, and that's very, very difficult.'" Another scientist said that when he visited Japan in the late 1970s, "we were totally amazed how far along they were." He said one had to at least "consider the possibility that they are ahead" of everybody else in hydrogen research. He complained of "barriers that hamper the exchange of information." For example, this scientist noted that some Japanese technical diagrams of chemical processes involving hydrogen, so-called flowsheets, failed to include key data needed to make them comprehensible and repeatable, a precondition to any scientific claim. Maybe it was only a problem of language, but it just wasn't quite clear, the researcher said.

Perhaps the ultimate, ironic indication of spreading interest in any given field is the arrival of quasi-perpetual motion machines, usually greeted by rampant skepticism in the field. Hydrogen already has a couple. One of them was a U.S. device that, fed with water and air and without any additional energy, would, it was claimed, produce heat. A 1975 patent describes the "invention" as an energy system in which steam is generated by combustion of hydrogen in ozone-enriched air. Skeptical outside engineers who met with the inventor said the heart of the device was a semipermeable barrier of some sort that separated dissolved gases like hydrogen from the water molecule. They concluded that the proposal was in violation of the first law of thermodynamics and was therefore unworkable.

The following year the hilarious Leach-and-Mirkin hydrogen caper surfaced in southern California, with approximately the same claims of getting hydrogen from water free for the asking. It produced, according to the *New York Times*, "a flurry of speculation on Wall Street, a federal investigation of possible stock manipulation and virtually unanimous skepticism from scientists who say the machine cannot do what its inventors say it can." That machine was a steamer trunk–sized stainless-steel box with six dials and a gas jet spurting hydrogen. The inventor, Sam L. Leach of Los Angeles, claimed the machine was able, using an unidentified reacting metal, to continuously break down water molecules into hydrogen and oxygen with no outside energy except for a small electric start-up charge. Leach was being backed in this venture by, among others, Morris J. Mirkin, founder and former head of Budget Rent-A-Car, who started a new company, MJM Hydrotech, to exploit Leach's alleged invention. Another backer was the president of a California group of home-construction firms, the Presley Companies, whose stock almost quadrupled between December 1975 and March 1976, leading to an investigation by the Securities and Exchange Commission of the possibility of stock manipulation and other violations. The whole affair took on show-biz aspects when, according to *Newsweek*, an MJM Hydrotech vice president commented, "it's the greatest thing since sex." Patrick McDonald also gushed, per *Newsweek*'s account, "there will be no reason to strip-mine for coal, no reason to run supertankers full of oil or build nuclear power plants."

Despite the hydrogen community's skepticism, Leach has not given up. After what he called "first generation" technology involving thermochemical and photochemical reactions in a two-stage process—typically a manganese reactant operating at 1400° to 1500° F. (760° to 815° C.), generating infrared radiation that splits the water molecule—Leach in 1977 announced a "second generation" method. This one operates at lower temperatures and employs "laser-like" devices that bombard steam, generating hydrogen and oxygen. Leach has refused invitations to discuss his invention with other hydrogen researchers, and scientists are still generally unbelieving. However, a federally funded clearing house for inventions, the Experimental Center for the Advancement of Invention & Innovation at the University of Oregon, checked Leach's mathematics and found no errors, according to a July 10, 1978, account in the *New York Times*. The Oregon researchers emphasized that they had not tested a working model of Leach's new S.L.X. process, as it is called, that the efficiency of the process is still in question, and that no conclusions about the method were feasible until they had a chance to test the hardware. In 1979 the center refuted Leach's assertions that the center's tests supported his claims; according to a May 21st *Business Week* story the center had never looked at that entire process. As of early 1979, U.S. researchers were "still waiting for results," as one put it.

Broadening the Base: Detail Work Replaces the Brotherhood

During the past decade, a subtle shift in attitude has taken place among the hydrogen workers, while the ranks have swelled. At the end of the 1960s and in the early 1970s, relatively few, highly idealistic people scattered on different continents formed a kind of elite international movement. They worked more or less independently, often as an after-hours labor of love in addition to their normal jobs. Communication among the members of the international hydrogen order was apparently spotty, and the field was pervaded by a sense of the avant-garde and underground—a subculture of energy research. In the mid-seventies the scene began to change as more information about hydrogen began to percolate through the international scientific community, corporations, and energy planners, and more and more researchers took up the cause full-time. Whether the early enthusiasts saw themselves as members of a new energy order is hard to say. Bill Escher says that even in the first heady days of the late sixties there was no such thing as an international "hydrogen mafia. . . . I don't think that at any one point there were identified guys who knew each other. There were guys who were working on the problems, quite separately and quite independently." The Boston and San Diego meetings did provide an opportunity to get together "for identification of the brotherhood, so to speak. We're phasing out of that right now, which is good. We have a lot of new people coming in." A more sober sense of purpose had replaced the euphoria and underground fellowship that earlier seemed to sprout around the edges of the "movement." The early small band of visionaries who charted the broad outlines of a hydrogen economy have been joined by growing numbers of sober, dedicated workers filling in the blanks.

The hydrogen economy is on its way, noted Marchetti in Zurich, "because a lot of people have committed themselves. They are locked in now." The Soviet Union, which sent only observers to the 1976 meeting, weighed in internationally for the first time with papers of its own dealing with "plasma-chemical" hydrogen production and with nuclear plant requirements for hydrogen production. (Romania had also announced two papers but they were not presented.)

The feeling of "brotherhood" Escher was referring to is more subdued now because of the growth of interest of so many people and institutions in the field and its inevitable bureaucratization, but it also could be the result of a gradual disillusionment. In part this disillusionment has to do with too high expectations at the start. U.S. researchers and enthusiasts in particular grabbed onto the idea of a hydrogen economy as almost instant panacea for both energy and environmental problems. When neither the full-bore hydrogen economy nor the beginnings of hydrogen hardware evolved within a few years, the letdown was inevitable, given the American penchant to immediately put new ideas into action. The Europeans were perhaps more realistic or maybe slower on the uptake, depending on one's point of view. As will be discussed in Chapter 11, Marchetti and others argue that any new energy system requires several decades after introduction before it can take over a sizable share of the total energy pie.

Derek Gregory, keynote speaker at the 1976 Miami Beach hydrogen conference, said even then that he was more pessimistic about the chances for quick introduction of hydrogen as a universal fuel than he was two years earlier at the initial THEME conference. NASA's Bob Witcofski agreed, but the delay hasn't affected his enthusiasm:

Some day, I don't know when, the hydrogen economy is going to come. And I would like, years from now, whenever it is, to be able to stand up and say, all right, our hydrogen airplane has improved 20 percent over the first crude model that was demonstrated back in the year 1990 by a [fellow] who worked for NASA—and I would like to be that [fellow].

4

Hydrogen from Natural Gas, Electrolysis, Thermochemistry: Present and Future Production

The April 1972 meeting of the American Chemical Society in Boston promised to be just another of the thousands of scientific congresses held every year. The general public usually doesn't pay much attention to them, but to scientists they are useful and enjoyable, with peer-group gossip in the hallways, cocktail party banter, exchanges of scientific information, and the chance to see in person the people who are ordinarily known only as authors of papers.

For advocates of a future hydrogen economy, the Boston meeting turned out to be a landmark gathering. Cesare Marchetti, the Italian scientist largely responsible for rekindling the interest in hydrogen in Europe, and his collaborator, Gianfranco De Beni, a slight, unassuming chemist, presented their groundbreaking Mark 1 cycle in a paper titled "A Chemical Process to Decompose Water Using Nuclear Heat." While most of the other sessions of the ACS meeting enjoyed more or less normal, ho-hum attendance, "it was standing room only" at the Division of Fuel Chemistry session, Marchetti recalled a few months later in his modest, paper-strewn office at the EURATOM Research Center in Ispra, a campus-like research establishment on the shores of Lago Maggiore, in view of the towering Alps and an hour or so from Milan in Northern Italy.

Economical Production: Key to a Hydrogen Economy

The interest was obvious. Marchetti had been discussing and calling for the introduction of hydrogen as a chemical fuel since the late 1960s. He and other charter members of the international hydrogen movement realized early on that the *economical* production of hydrogen from water, was the key problem that needed solving if hydrogen was to play a major energy role in a future "hydrogen economy." Technically, the problem was solved long ago: Electrolysis, the cleaving of the water molecule by running a current through it, was well known and is used industrially in some places where electricity is cheap. But the economy of water-splitting is the linchpin. There are many technical problems in the storage, handling, and safe use of hydrogen, but almost everybody in the field agrees that once hydrogen can be produced at prices competitive with fossil fuels, half the battle would be won. At that time, Marchetti felt electrolysis was inherently inefficient because of the many steps between the power source and the final product, all of them causing some energy loss: Electricity has to be produced from a primary heat source (a nuclear reactor or a solar power plant); it has to be transformed, transported by cable, and manipulated many times before the electric current can attack the water molecules. Why not, he reasoned, use the heat directly with the help of some chemicals to break down water? Elimination of the various electricity-making steps would constitute a significant saving of energy and thus would help make hydrogen production more economical.

Another relevant point here is that water breaks down directly into hydrogen and oxygen at extremely high temperatures—so high that they are not industrially available in any type of boiler, furnace, or nuclear reactor. However, this dissociation process can be divided into smaller steps with an assist by certain chemicals that can be recycled; in this way, the heat requirements come down to the temperature range at which nuclear reactors—or future solar power plants—operate, an idea Marchetti picked up from concepts developed a few years earlier for the U.S. army.

Splitting water in a heat-assisted, closed-cycle chemical process rather than via electrolysis was first explored in the early sixties when Brookhaven National Laboratory began investigating what it called then "chemonuclear" processes. The idea was to use a large nuclear power plant to produce both hydrogen and ammonia to meet the then skyrocketing demand for fertilizer. This research, however, did not generate a great deal of attention even among scientists.

But in 1966 two scientists at GM, James E. Funk and Robert M. Reinstrom, wrote a fundamental paper that still crops up in the literature as one of the hydrogen economy's basic documents. Funk and Reinstrom were working then for GM's Allison Division in Indianapolis, Indiana; Allison was making tanks for the U.S. Army. At the time the army was investigating the Nuclear-Powered Energy Depot concept mentioned in

Chapter 3—an effort to become independent of long logistical supply lines and to produce tank fuel from locally available raw materials such as air or water at a remote site. Funk and Reinstrom concluded that, at that point at least, there were no known compounds that would permit an efficient two-step water-splitting process. "It appears unlikely," they said, "that a compound exists, or can be synthesized which will yield a two-step chemical process superior to water electrolysis." Pessimistically, they added that although another process might have a higher thermal energy efficiency than water electrolysis, "the possibility appears to be remote."

In the intervening years, that view has been modified considerably in the sense that many researchers have been investigating multi-step processes involving several compounds that indeed are believed to yield better efficiencies than the single-compound, two-step cycles that caused Funk's and Reinstrom's scepticism. Since the 1970s, dozens of laboratories around the world have been investigating, so far largely on paper and by computer, hundreds, perhaps thousands of theoretically possible cycles. Marchetti in his Cornell lecture described the effort to devise the first thermochemical production process, the Mark 1 cycle, almost as if it were the easiest thing in the world—which it certainly isn't. Nevertheless, the search is still going on, and a couple of cycles have been identified and refined to the point of constructing small, bench-scale experimental setups that actually produce small amounts of hydrogen. The two best-known ones, both employing sulfur as the main chemical assist, are cycles set up in 1978 by the Ispra Research Center in Italy and, shortly afterwards, by Westinghouse in the United States. However, most teams still limit their hardware activity to testing materials and verifying parts of such cycles.

What Marchetti was describing was really the first new attempt to at least *theoretically* construct such a cycle on paper:

"I asked a collaborator of mine [De Beni], an ingenious chemist, to see whether it would be possible to devise a process, entirely chemical, to decompose water using as input heat at less than 800° C.," Marchetti related. Such temperatures can be obtained in a high-temperature nuclear reactor, a type that was developed but later abandoned by General Atomic in the United States. It is now under active development in West Germany (see Chapter 5).

After a couple of months or so, he came out with a viable process. We can visualize it as a black box containing as working materials calcium, mercury, and bromine. One puts in water and heat at 500° to 800° C. and takes out oxygen and hydrogen and a certain amount of degraded heat. We call a plant using a process of this kind a Water Splitter. The clever trick consists of breaking the water molecule in two [separate] steps.

This is the principle of the Mark 1 cycle presented in Boston by Marchetti and De Beni. Other cycles developed in the meantime use as many as four or five steps but for a number of highly technical reasons, the rule of thumb is that the fewer the steps, the simpler and more efficient a water-splitting cycle tends to be.

Breaking up the water molecule is always a difficult, energy-intensive business because of the strong binding forces between hydrogen and oxygen atoms. Hydrogen ordinarily does not exist in a free state but almost always as a compound of some sort. Water can be broken up without chemical help by running a current through it—the electrolysis process well known to high school students—or by applying extremely high temperatures directly. However, in the latter case the temperatures needed are so high—direct thermal watersplitting requires temperatures above 2,500° C. (4,500° F.), far above the heat output of current nuclear reactor types, which operate at around 220°–320° C. (428°–608° F.)—that this approach is all but impossible. Attempts to use solar furnaces have been disappointing so far, yielding very little hydrogen and oxygen.

Electrolysis, on the other hand, is a proven process for making hydrogen and oxygen on an industrial scale, but it has been extensively used only in places where electricity is extremely cheap, such as Canada and Sweden with their vast hydropower. Electrolytic hydrogen was considered economically justifiable only as a chemical feedstock and only where high purity is required. In the late sixties and early seventies, many researchers believed that electrolysis was almost hopelessly outdated and inefficient. Today, most hydrogen used in the chemical and petrochemical industry is produced much more cheaply from natural gas. The big attraction of thermochemical processes was that heat from primary sources could be applied directly, while in the electrolytic process the energetic detour via electricity entailed the waste of practically two-thirds of the primary energy, which escaped through the power plant's smokestack. At the time, Marchetti put it succinctly in a review for a Japanese publication: "A complicated machinery is used to transform heat into mechanical energy; then into electrical energy and then into chemical energy. . . . The overall efficiency is 30 percent at best, and capital investment is large."

Since then the pendulum has swung back. It is being increasingly recognized that the laws of thermodynamics that postulate a certain conversion loss of energy in any "heat engine"—an internal combustion motor, a steam turbine—apply to thermochemical cycles as well. Use of more sophisticated materials such as solid plastic electrolytes instead of the classic alkaline water electrolyte, electrolysis of steam at very high temperatures, and use of high-temperature-resistant electrodes are persuading many experts that advanced electrolysis may well be among the more promising methods to produce hydrogen fairly economically from water.

Beyond that, it now appears there may be a meeting of the two schools of thought. The compromise consists of so-called hybrid cycles—water-splitting processes that combine a thermochemical and an electrolytic step. Both the experimental Ispra cycle (dubbed Mark 13) and the Westinghouse cycle, regarded by many as the most promising approaches, are such hybrids.

The Ispra and Westinghouse cycles have another thing in common: They both use sulfur in one form or another as a key chemical in helping to break up the water molecule. Sulfur is also a main ingredient in other processes such as the three-step "pure" thermochemical cycle (now under development by General Atomic), which in addition to sulfur employs iodine. Marchetti explains that sulfur is attractive because its chemistry is relatively simple and well understood. Typically, in the first step a sulfur compound is broken up by heat, followed by a second electrolytic step that liberates the hydrogen and reconstitutes the main basic compounds needed to start the process all over again. One indication of the high hopes held out for sulfur-based thermochemistry is the fact that the International Energy Agency has designated sulfur-based cycles as the subject of one of the three main hydrogen research "tasks" over the next few years—clear recognition that this approach is perhaps the most promising among the thousands of theoretically possible cycles.

In the late sixties, Marchetti's and De Beni's work at Ispra was ahead of most everybody else's by a couple of years, by Marchetti's own reckoning. But as the decade neared its end, research into the ways of splitting the water molecule economically spread across the Atlantic and Pacific. At the Second World Hydrogen Conference in Zurich in August of 1978, around 100 of the 160-odd papers dealt with hydrogen production.[1]

Hydrogen from Fossil Fuels

At the beginning of the 1980s splitting water molecules economically and in large volumes is still a future proposition. The common industrial approach has been to strip hydrogen out of hydrocarbon fuels. Most hydrogen is made from natural gas by catalytic reforming, a method in which steam reacts with natural gas. Most hydrogen has been used in liquid form as a fuel in the U.S. space program—Centaur, Apollo, and now the space shuttle projects. Hydrogen is also required in large amounts for fertilizer production. The biggest plant in the United States, in Donaldson, Louisiana, turns out about 130 million cubic feet (3.7 million cubic meters) a day.

In 1979, total hydrogen production in the chemical industries of West Germany, Britain, Italy, France, and Spain amounted to 1.463 billion cubic meters (51.7 billion cubic feet). In the United States that year merchant hydrogen production was close to 1.2 billion cubic meters (44 billion cubic feet). However, these figures exclude captive production, according to a 1980 report in the industry magazine *Chemical Engineering*, which said much more hydrogen is produced by small on-site units, possibly as much as ten times the recorded merchant hydrogen output.

In the pecking order of ease in making hydrogen from fossil fuels, methane, the main ingredient in natural gas, occupies the top spot because methane has so far been cheap and is easier to handle industrially than a liquid like crude oil or a solid like oil shale or coal. It contains the most hydrogen per carbon atom: four hydrogen atoms for each carbon atom. Next comes petroleum, with a hydrogen-to-carbon-atoms ratio of 1.5–1.6. Oil shale has a ratio of 1.6, but it's solid and therefore more difficult to handle than petroleum. Coal poses the greatest difficulties for hydrogen extraction and has a ratio ranging from 0.72 to 0.92.

However, as most Americans are painfully aware, natural gas is beginning to run short and become expensive. Massive imports from Algeria and elsewhere are unlikely to redress the balance. In Europe, several countries were planning to import huge amounts of natural gas from the Soviet Union and, before 1979 at least, from Iran. In any event, natural gas is on the decline as a viable energy source in the long term. Otherwise there would be no need for research to make natural gas synthetically—Substitute Natural Gas, SNG for short.[2]

Coal, in all of its various forms—brown coal or lignite, subbituminous, bituminous anthracite coal with small amounts of chlorine, sulfur, and metal traces—is the "ugly duckling" of fuels. As Australia's John Bockris observed,

> Its products [ashes and slag] corrode and foul the plant. A plant built for one coal may be fouled by the use of another. The prospect of its reintroduction as a main source of energy clashes with environmental considerations.

Because it is so intractable and because it entails all sorts of conversion losses before it can be used in cars or gas boilers, coal's rejuvenation as a major fossil fuel will require all sorts of stimuli and legislative support. It certainly won't make an automatic comeback merely because of high oil prices, and the process may be slow and painful.

Upgrading coal into easy-handling gases or liquid fuels will be the name of the game in the decades ahead. Hydrogen extraction will also get some attention, but not quickly and not to the same extent as coal technology, much to the chagrin of "pure" hydrogen supporters.

In fiscal 1979, for instance, the Department of Energy's budget for coal gasification and liquefaction totaled $381 million while only $7.4 million was allotted to hydrogen as part of a $32.6 million package for energy storage research. (Research into other hydrogen areas such as production or applications was funded at less than a million dollars, or at decimal point-levels, as one U.S. government source put it.) For 1980 the corresponding amounts were estimated at $376 million, $2.5 million, and $32 million, respectively. In 1981, according to *Business Week*, funding of *all* hydrogen research is to go up to $12 million.

These priorities bothered a lot of people committed to hydrogen: "DoE doesn't know where hydrogen fits in," complained T. Nejat Veziroglu, president of the International Association for Hydrogen Energy and also director of the Clean Energy Research Institute of the University of Miami, Coral Gables, Florida. "They put money into new energy sources but these sources don't have the good properties of petroleum. You can't put solar or wind power directly into a car or plane. You have to create a chemical fuel from these sources." Vast availability of coal is a bane rather than a boon to hydrogen, Veziroglu suggested: The people who want to use up coal before turning to anything as exotic as hydrogen "should remember that coal pollutes, and it won't last forever."

Not all hydrogen advocates buy that argument. Some argue that (1) coal will and must be used as a transition fuel before the advent of the hydrogen millenium, and coal upgrading is a basic precondition for that; (2) existing coal gasification-liquefaction processes are largely uneconomical but can be vastly improved by using the higher temperatures obtainable from the safer, high-temperature nuclear reactors of the future; and (3) the nuclear industry and governments will not risk vast investments and decades of research to produce a high-temperature reactor for hydrogen production, say, 40-50 years in the future; but (4) since coal gasification and liquefaction with the help of a nuclear heat source is much nearer reality, it is the kind of challenge that will be accepted by industry and government. In other words, walk before you run.

Another way of looking at the situation, some say, is to let the coal people pay for the development of these reactors, which hydrogen-makers can't afford to finance so far, but which will be needed eventually—especially since coal gasification is itself one way to make hydrogen from coal as a transition step to ease into a pure hydrogen-from-water economy, less painful than an abrupt shift that for engineering, economic, and human reasons seems all but impossible anyway.

Coal gasification's beginnings go back more than 100 years. It was first invented in the 1870's to produce so-called city gas, or town gas, to light and heat homes. In the 1920s and 1930s German scientists modified the process to produce a hydrogen-rich "synthesis gas," a basic chemical raw material still used today for making a huge number of organic products. Both the Haber process, combining hydrogen and nitrogen from the atmosphere into synthetic ammonia (the starting point for fertilizers), and the Fischer-Tropsch process for converting brown coal (lignite) into synthetic oil and gasoline are classics of industrial chemistry that had their beginnings in those years.

The process of producing hydrogen via coal gasification was summed-up in a 1976 study, *Hydrogen Tomorrow*,[3] by California's Jet Propulsion Laboratory (JPL), as follows:

> Hydrogen production from coal is basically a partial oxidation process similar to that for heavy oil. The process is complicated by the necessity to handle a relatively unreactive fuel as a solid and to remove large amounts of ash. The solids-handling problem has a severe impact on costs and prevents much of the technology and equipment developed for petroleum from being used in the conversion of coal. Coal, steam, and oxygen react in the basic gasifier processes to produce hydrogen.

Essentially, the hydrocarbon fuel—coal—is made to react with water in the form of steam, requiring considerable extra energy, to produce carbon dioxide and hydrogen.[4]

The two best-known and currently operating commercial coal gasification processes come from Germany, the so-called Lurgi and the Koppers-Totzek processes. Lurgi's process is used mainly for producing synthesis gas for making industrial alcohols and other hydrocarbon products; it has also been used to make town gas. The JPL study says its main drawbacks for making hydrogen are low throughput plus high levels of tar and hydrocarbon gases that must be processed further to make hydrogen. However, it is the only commercial process that operates at relatively high pressures—(300 to 450 pounds per square inch [psi], or 20.5–31 bars)—one of the keys to more efficient production of both SNG and hydrogen.

The Koppers-Totzek process, according to the JPL study, operates at near ambient pressures, which avoids the complexities of processing coal at higher pressures. However, in most applications synthesis gas must be compressed anyway, so this is not a real advantage.

At the March 1976 First World Hydrogen Energy Conference in Miami Beach, three researchers from the Institute of Gas Technology, C. L. Tsaros, J. L. Arora, and K. B. Burnham, presented a paper comparing the characteristics of three main contenders for making hydrogen from coal, the Koppers-Totzek process and the so-called U-Gas and Steam-Iron processes. The latter two are under development at the Chicago-based institute. Included for the purpose of comparison with methane production from coal was the HYGAS process, also being studied at IGT.

The Koppers-Totzek and U-Gas processes are similar inasmuch as they first generate synthesis gas which is then "refined" into hydrogen gas. The Steam-Iron process is based on the decomposition of steam by iron oxide, which, after breaking up the steam, is regenerated by a so-called producer gas made from coal.

Of these three hydrogen-producing methods, IGT's Tsaros, Arora, and Burnham found that the U-Gas process was the most efficient, with a theoretical overall plant efficiency (the plant was assumed to produce 250 million British thermal units [Btus] per day) of 66.4 percent, versus 62.6 percent for the Steam-Iron process and 57.0 percent for Koppers-Totzek method. However, the three also found that the methane-producing HYGAS method was considerably more efficient, with an overall efficiency rating of 74 percent, and that it produced energy at the lowest cost. U-Gas, the most efficient of the three hydrogen producers, produced 1 million Btus[5] at a cost of $2.17. The same energy produced by the HYGAS method cost only $1.77.

In that year, 1976, crude (Arabian light) was selling for $11.51 per barrel, or about $2.00 per million Btus. In the fall of 1978, American coal gasification experts were talking about prices of $3 to $4 per million Btus—around two and a half times the price computed for synthetic gas only two years earlier. Crude was selling for $12.70 a barrel or about $2.17 per million Btus (again, for Arabian light—other grades such as Lybian Es Sider were more expensive), although refining adds enough cost to make the final fuel almost as expensive as ready-to-use synthetic gas. In the spring of 1980, coal gasification experts estimated synthetic gas price as averaging $6.00 per million Btus, using U.S. coal; in West Germany, which is in the forefront of coal gasification technology, the corresponding average was $8-9, based on German coal costs. At the same time energy from crude was still a comparative bargain: Arabian light in the early spring of 1980 was pegged officially at $26.00 a barrel or about $4.48 per million Btus. In sum, energy from coal gasification is still more expensive than energy from oil. The trend is unlikely to change in the decade ahead, and producing and using hydrogen as ultimate clean fuel will probably be even more expensive.

All these coal gasification processes essentially rely on the burning of some of that coal as energy source to drive the gasification process. The next step that is being explored is to tap the heat from a nuclear reactor as a substitute power source for coal gasification.

Efforts to design second-generation, high-temperature nuclear reactors for making process heat, electricity, or both, are being made in most industrial countries—notably the United States, West Germany, and Japan, but also the Soviet Union. Coal gasification via a future high-temperature reactor (conventional boiling water or pressurized water reactors won't work because their operating temperatures—about 220°–320° C. [428°–608° F.]—are too low to be useful as process heat) is attractive both because it stretches coal supplies (no need to burn coal to generate the process heat) and because nuclear heat is potentially less expensive than fossil heat. In principle, the heat is used to force inert coal to react directly with water, with carbon dioxide and hydrogen as the result of the overall reaction.

In the United States, General Atomic was the main promoter of the high-temperature reactor. The company built such a plant at Fort St. Vrain, Colorado. It had several other orders as well but halted the program in the mid-seventies, apparently because it felt that at least at that time there was no commercial future in the concept.

In Germany, the Nuclear Research Center at Jülich is the center for developing the so-called pebble-bed HTR for both electricity production and coal gasification, a joint industry-government project. Researchers at Jülich say commercialization at the HTR has suffered because of General Atomic's decision to pull out, although as far as *process heat* applications are concerned—and coal gasification would be one of them—the overall market situation in Germany at least looks so favorable that development will proceed. Already, a 300-megawatt (electric) (Mwe) HTR for electricity production is nearing completion near Hamm on the edge of the Ruhr area (see Chapter 5).

For this reason, the German government in 1975 approved another prototype 500-Mwe high-temperature reactor, using the Jülich concept. Jülich has been operating a small demonstration plant of 15 Mwe for 10 years, including 4 years of operation at a consistent temperature of 950° C. (1,742° F.), the kind of temperature required for efficient gasification. Under the plan, the government has budgeted some $300 million for making detailed blueprints by 1980. To build the prototype plant, Jülich expects it will have to find additional funds in the range of $400 million. Construction of the prototype HTR, expected to start around 1983, would take at least another six years, meaning the plant would go on stream in 1990.

This suited German energy planners fine because they expected they would be able to meet the country's energy needs until 1985 or thereabouts by imports of natural gas. Coal gasification would not be needed until about 1990, when imports were expected to decline. Under this scenario, nuclear-driven water splitting and major hydrogen fuel usage would not phase in until after the beginning of the twenty-first century.

The significance of the Jülich project is that it drives home the amount of time and money required to bring about a significant advance in what are, after all, relatively well-explored technological fields—coal gasification and reactor technology. It will be at least ten years before the process HTR demonstration plant will start operations and another few years before the first big nuclear coal gasifier cranks up. And given past experience with large-scale technology in general, it would not be too surprising if further delays and more costs crop up en route.

Further down the road is an unusual scheme involving the use of carbon from renewable wastes, leftovers from agriculture and forestry but also industrial and urban refuse, proposed by two researchers from the Battelle-Pacific Northwest Laboratories, C. A. Rohrmann and J. B. Greenborg, at the March 1976 Hydrogen Conference in Miami Beach. The two scientists said that leftovers from corn, wheat, soybeans, and rice straw alone amount to more than 500 million short (454 million metric) tons per year (1975 data). If you count other wastes like forest residues, animal manure, tree bark, wood chippings, and municipal and industrial wastes, the total comes close to 1.5 billion (1.36 billion metric) tons. Somewhat analogous to current methods of hydrogen production from natural gas, coal, and petroleum, in which carbon reacts with water to produce hydrogen, the carbon in these wastes could be utilized, producing hydrogen by partial oxidation—burning it with the air's oxygen together with water. Theoretically, Rohrmann and Greenborg say, 3 pounds (1.3 kilograms) of carbon, or roughly 7.5 pounds (3.4 kilograms) of carbon-carrying waste, could produce one pound (0.45 kilogram) of hydrogen this way.[6]

Rohrmann and Greenborg felt that, given current gross national product (GNP) growth patterns and consequent increased waste production and available efficient agricultural machinery to collect field wastes (even paying a fee to the farmer for the residue), hydrogen could be produced at a cost roughly comparable to electrolysis if the cheapest available electricity (from hydroelectric sources) was used. (At that time the rate was $0.004 per kilowatt hour [kwh].) Furthermore, they say that the 1.5 billion tons of waste generated today would be sufficient to produce the 14 quads (10^{15} Btus) of hydrogen fuel that will be demanded by the U.S. economy in the year 2000. As total waste continues to grow to an estimated 3.7 billion short (3.3. million metric) tons by the year 2000 (more than 8 billion short[7.3 million metric] tons by 2020) less than half of the residues would need to be collected at the turn of the century to meet the hydrogen-as-fuel demand projected for that time period, Rohrmann and Greenborg conclude.

Hydrogen from Water

After burning up a lot of gasified and liquefied coal as fuels, the next step in the broad, decades-spanning scenario would be to gradually increase production of hydrogen from these same hydrocarbons, using more of that hydrogen as fuel. However, hydrogen derived from fossil fuels is at best a stop-gap transitory measure, an "introductory offer," as it were, for a new energy concept. The very idea of switching to hydrogen is to get away from fossil fuels because (1) they pollute—in addition to the various local ground-level pollutants such as unburned hydrocarbons, carbon monoxide, sulfur, and others that make life miserable, the long-term buildup of carbon dioxide in the atmosphere from burned fossil fuels and the feared greenhouse effect causing temperatures to rise worldwide is a global headache; and (2) they will run out sooner or later. Hydrogen from the water molecule is the key component in a benign, environmentally compatible cycle, feeding back into the atmosphere as water vapor, clouds, rain, and again into the earth's water supply—the ideal solution.

Electrolysis, the Proven Method

Electrolysis of water is very simple. Most people remember the principle from their high school chemistry classes: two electrodes, one positive and one negative, are immersed into water that has been made more conductive by the addition of an electrolyte, either acidic or basic, such as potassium hydroxide or sulfuric acid. As direct-current power is applied, hydrogen begins to bubble up at the negatively charged electrode (the cathode), and oxygen rises out of the solution at the positively charged electrode (the anode). Fresh water of high purity—an important criterion because otherwise the accumulating salts would clog up the electrolyzer—is continuously fed to replace the water that has broken down into hydrogen and oxygen.

Commercial electrolysis cells date back to the 1890s, some 55 years after the formulation of Faraday's law in 1835, which stated the basic relation between the chemicals dissolved and the electrical charge and which was regarded as the start of modern electrochemistry.

In industrial practice, an electrolysis plant is considerably more complex than the process just described. In addition to the basic tank arrangements consisting of electrodes, electrolyte, separators (to keep the electrodes from touching and shorting out and to separate the two gases at the source), and a container, all of which can take a number of different configurations, the complete electrolyzer usually requires (1) an electric power converter that changes conventional alternating-current power to direct current at a small but significant loss; (2) equipment to distribute electric power to the various electrodes; (3) a system of pipes to carry oxygen and hydrogen away from the cells; (4) at times, special separation systems to remove the gases from the electrolyte; (5) cooling machinery to remove heat generated during electrolysis; and (6) drying equipment to dry the gases after they have been separated from the electrolyte.

In the United States, industrial-scale electrolysis by tradition has played a relatively small role. As indicated previously, massive users, such as producers of fertilizers and the U.S. space program, have relied on the cheaper method of making hydrogen from natural gas by steam reforming. "Electrolysis has traditionally been considered one of the more expensive methods of hydrogen production, and electrolyzers have been assumed to be inefficient and expensive," according to a 1975 survey of hydrogen production and utilization methods by the Institute of Gas Technology.

This is not quite right, though, and the traditional reasoning was somewhat off base: "On the contrary, it is the electric generation step that is expensive and inefficient," the report continued. "Most commercial electrolyzers available today are capable of electricity-to-hydrogen efficiencies above 75 percent, while their capital-cost potential is far less than that of the power stations that would be required to run them."

Electrochemist Bockris feels electrolysis has acquired a bad name simply because some of the latest insights in electrochemistry have not been incorporated into commercial equipment. In fact, there are even some thermochemical partisans who agree: Two scientists from the chemistry division of Oak Ridge National Laboratory, C. E. Bamberger and D. M. Richardson, reviewing 72 thermochemical cycles in a 1976 paper, acknowledged that "growth in the state of the art and technology of generation of hydrogen by electrolysis may result in improved efficiencies and make it the most likely contender on an economic basis for production of hydrogen from water."

Cesare Marchetti, arguing for thermochemical hydrogen production in a January 1973 article in Japan's *Chemical Economy & Engineering Review*, put the then prevailing view against electrolysis this way:

> Energy is handled many times to make first steam in the boiler, then mechanical energy in the turbine, then electrical energy in the generator which is rectified and then fed to the electrolyzer. All that piles up capital and cascades inefficiency. It is true that industrial electrolyzers looked at as electrical machines are very inefficient (50 percent of the theoretical) . . . and very expensive. Even with unit efficiency and zero capital cost, their potential for producing what, after all, is just a fuel from a sophisticated form of energy like electricity did appear to us very dim.

Nevertheless, electrolyzers do have advantages. Since there are no moving parts they operate trouble-free and more or less automatically, requiring servicing, such as the exchange of corroded electrodes, only once in many years. Electrolysis also lends itself to operation under higher pressures, which in turn aids the efficiency of the process. Finally, electrolysis produces the two gases cleanly sorted out. It yields a very pure hydrogen gas, while hydrogen produced from fossil sources is usually more contaminated.[7] Hydrogen from carbon sources can be cleaned up as well, but it adds another chemical step and, therefore, increases the cost.

The amount of energy needed to decompose water into hydrogen and oxygen by electrolysis is exactly the amount of energy given off in the reverse process when hydrogen burns and recombines with oxygen to reform water vapor. A completely efficient electrolysis cell would require 94 kwh to make 1000 cubic feet (28 cubic meters) of gaseous hydrogen. Not all of the energy needs to be supplied as expensive electricity; only 79 kwh are required in form of electric power and the rest can be brought into the process as heat, a less sophisticated, less expensive energy form.

This duality of energy input—both electric power and heat—as well as the pressure aspect of operating conditions is the basis for more efficient, less expensive, advanced electrolyzer concepts of the future, such as electrolysis with higher temperatures and higher pressures. Researchers both in the United States (General Electric) and in Germany (Dornier System and Lurgi) are investigating electrolysis methods that would, like advanced coal gasification methods, use the heat from a high-temperature reactor to break up water more efficiently. These will be described in the next chapter.

Basic Electrolyzer Types

Essentially there are two types of industrial electrolyzers today, the tank electrolyzer and the filter-press type. Though there have been improvements in materials and details, their basic concept has not changed in about 70 years. An electrolysis landmark was the decision by a Norwegian utility, Norsk Hydro, to install an electrolyzer for making synthetic fertilizer. One of the first truly big installations, it was put up in 1927. The first large electrolyzer in North America was built around 1940 in Trail, British Columbia, by Cominco, and after 1945 many large electrolyzers were built throughout the world. The three biggest current installations, all for the manufacture of fertilizer, are a plant in Nangal, India (built by the Italian company De Nora, of Milan), the Norsk-Hydro plant at Rjakon with a capacity of 284,000 pounds (lbs) (129,000 kilograms) of hydrogen per day, and a plant at the famed Aswan Dam in Egypt, erected by the German machinery builder Demag.

The tank electrolyzer is the older and simpler type. Alternate electrodes are hung into a tank filled with the electrolyte. The electrodes are separated from adjacent opposite-charge electrodes by a diaphragm, usually asbestos, allowing passage of the electrolyte but preventing mixing of the two evolving gases, hydrogen and oxygen. The main advantages of this type are that few and inexpensive parts are needed and that individual cells can be shut down for repair or replacement simply by short-circuiting two adjacent cells while the rest of the cell series continues making hydrogen. The main disadvantages are that it is unsuitable for high-temperature operation because of heat losses due to large surfaces and that it usually requires more floor space than other types.

More recently the second basic type, the filter-press electrolyzer (also called a bipolar cell) has come to the fore. In this type each electrode has both a positive and a negative face, with the positive face in one cell and the negative face in the adjacent cell. Proponents claim that it takes up less floor space and can be adapted more easily to high-pressure and high-temperature operations, making it more efficient. Drawbacks are that it requires much more precise tolerances in construction and that maintenance is more of a problem, because if one cell fails the entire assembly has to be shut down, with attendant loss of production.

The best-known commercial example of the tank cell in North America is the range of so-called Stuart cells, made by the Electrolyser Corporation Ltd., of Toronto. Teledyne Energy Systems, located near Baltimore, Maryland, is one of the best-known makers of filter-press electrolyzers, producing three basic sizes that generate hydrogen at rates ranging from tiny amounts for laboratory purposes to several tons per day. Teledyne got into the business in the late 1960s when it acquired fuel-cell and electrolyzer know-how developed by Allis-Chalmers, mainly for the space program. Teledyne is credited with being one of the few companies in the United States that continues to invest time, money, and resources into improving standard electrolyzer design.

In a 1976 paper two Teledyne researchers, J. B. Laskin and R. D. Feldwick, acknowledged that at that time hydrogen from electrolysis was too expensive compared to other commercial fuels. They also said that the petrochemical industry, which uses hydrogen in large quantities and which is often cited by hydrogen-economy advocates as one of the leverage points where hydrogen could begin phasing into the total energy picture, was not likely to be a large-scale customer of *electrolytically* produced hydrogen.

The overall picture has changed since then due to some advances in technology. One major advance in electrolysis has been the development of the so-called solid-polymer electrolyte (SPE) technology, spearheaded by General Electric. Unlike the conventional liquid electrolyte, the material is a solid sheet that looks and feels somewhat like Teflon. When soaked in water it becomes an excellent conductor, and unlike normal water, it doesn't require any addition of acid or alkalis to propagate the electrolysis process.

Presenting the new development to the international hydrogen community at the 1974 Miami Beach hydrogen conference, GE researcher Leonard J. Nuttall called SPE electrolysis "one of the most promising methods for generating hydrogen from nuclear, solar or other non-fossil sources." At the 1978 hydrogen conference in Zurich, his assessment was essentially unchanged. In a report, Nuttall said that progress was "very encouraging" towards the goals of (1) higher overall efficiency of 85 to 90 percent, compared to the present average of 70 percent, "resulting in lower power consumption per unit of gas generated," and (2) higher current density resulting in lower capital cost of around $100 per kilowatt (current electrolyzers cost two to four times that much). Nuttall said prospects were good for "nearly achieving" the original program goal of producing hydrogen at around $5 per million Btus (1975 dollars), assuming an electricity price of 10 mills per kilowatt hour, and without taking into account the sale price of the automatic by-product, oxygen. A separate IGT study indicated that oxygen sales could cut the hydrogen price in large-scale, advanced-electrolyzer operations of the GE type and in nuclear power by another 64 cents per one million Btus.[8]

GE's electrolyzer program is funded at $1 million annually, with half coming from the Department of Energy and the rest from GE, the Niagara Mohawk Power Company, and the Empire State Electric Energy Research Corporation. GE, which received the original contract in 1975, expects to have a 5-megawatt demonstration unit running by 1983.

At the 1980 3rd World Hydrogen Conference in Tokyo, General Electric reported further progress, claiming a 79 percent hardware cost reduction with improved details such as better current collectors and catalytic electrodes. GE said that, based on a cell module size of 2.5 square meters—future plants would have 10-square-meter modules—such plants would produce slightly more than 200 cubic feet of hydrogen per hour at a cost of about $16 (at 40 percent utilization) and about $22 (90 percent utilization), respectively. This would equal a cost of roughly $23 per million Btus per hour and $32 per million Btus per hour, respectively. This seems high compared to the 1975 assumptions, but the figures represent 1980 dollars, worth roughly 35 percent less than the 1975 dollars on which the 1978 estimates were based. Also, the 1978 Zurich paper assumed electricity costs of 10 mills per kwh, while in the Tokyo paper, the GE researchers assumed 30 mills per kwh as base for their calculations. The GE electrolyzers will get their first commercial trial at a small unused hydropower dam in Potsdam, New York, that had not produced electricity since 1971 (see Chapter 5).

Steam Electrolysis

Beginning in the late sixties, General Electric pioneered work in dissociating high-temperature steam (1,000° C., or 1,832° F.), essentially by operating a high-temperature fuel cell equipped with a solid-electrolyte membrane in reverse. Those original experiments were encouraging. The main advantage of this approach is that with increasing temperatures the requirement for electrical energy is drastically reduced. Overall, the cost for added heat is much less than the cost of the wastefully produced electricity that would be required in electrolysis at normal temperatures, and the overall efficiency is considerably better. Again, the heat from a future nuclear high-temperature reactor or solar power plant is essential for the effectiveness of such a method.

In Germany, Dornier System, a subsidiary of a German aerospace manufacturer, is also investigating steam electrolysis together with Lurgi, the well-known German maker of traditional electrolysis equipment. Their researchers report similarly encouraging findings. Supported by an initial $2.5 million grant from the German Ministry for Science and Technology, the investigation started in the summer of 1975.

At the Zurich conference, Dornier's Wolfgang Dönitz reported that overall efficiencies of 40 to 50 percent "depending on the primary energy source," are feasible for HOT ELLY, the hydrogen economy's first bilingual acronym for the process which stands, in German, for *Hochtemperatur Dampfphase-Elektrolyse* and in English for High Operating Temperature Electrolysis. HOT ELLY also uses solid electrolytes, and because of the elevated temperature (around 1,000° C. [1,832° F.] maximum), special materials are required.

Another interesting approach that surfaced in 1980 is water-splitting by current produced in solar cells. This is being pursued by Texas Instruments in the United States and AEG-Telefunken semiconductor division in Germany. Texas Instruments immerses the cells, small silicon spheres, directly in the water; when exposed to sunlight, the cells produce a current that immediately dissociates the electrolyte into hydrogen and oxygen. Texas Instruments has been rather secretive about the project, a four-year $15 million (some reports put the total at $20 million) program that it shares with the Department of Energy. TI referred to its "solar energy system" briefly in the company's report for the first quarter of 1980, saying "our goal is a 13% array efficiency. We have achieved 10% efficiency with the best 20% of the spheres. We have proved that 13% efficiency can be achieved at the array level with higher quality silicon spheres." Among the team of four inventors is Jack S. Kilby, a former Texas Instruments officer, holder of the U.S. Medal of Science, and inventor of the integrated circuit.

AEG-Telefunken's semiconductor division, which claims to be Europe's biggest manufacturer of solar cells and the only one capable of turning out solar cells for space projects, is drawing up similar plans but with the difference that the solar cell array and electrolysis operations are separated. The electric power generated by the cells is transmitted to the plant, an approach that AEG-Telefunken says makes for more efficient use of the electricity. Reinhard Dahlberg, the division's general manager, says his company has drawn up a ten-year, Deutschmarks 22 billion ($11.5 billion) plan for setting up "solar plantation families" in hot parts of the world; these plantation families would grow in size over decades and would ultimately produce enough hydrogen to replace most or all of the projected future fossil fuel consumption. Dahlberg says the AEG-Telefunken project does not require any new technology but does require society's support in the form of funding: "So far we don't have that large pot of money required for the original spark," he told me in the fall of 1980. He indicated that there is some interest on the part of Arab nations (Saudi Arabian planners have requested and have been sent some of AEG-Telefunken's planning documents) but also elsewhere, making Dahlberg cautiously hopeful that a project along these lines eventually will come off.

Thermochemistry: A Better Way?

One of the earliest proposals for a thermochemical cycle for producing hydrogen from water was formulated and patented in 1924 in England by a scientist working for a company called Synthetic Ammonia and Nitrates Ltd. Emil Collett postulated a two-step cycle, in which water was to react with mercury plus heat to form mercury oxide (HgO) and hydrogen in the first step. In the second step, that HgO was supposed to decompose into the original mercury plus oxygen. It probably wouldn't have worked very efficiently; researchers 30 years later decided that for a number of theoretical reasons, at least three cycles are necessary to break up the water molecule economically and practically by thermochemical means. Also, for thermodynamical reasons, mercury does not react with water.

The interest in thermochemistry flared up again in the 1960s in a military-logistics context in the United States. But it took the dawning of the environmental conscience at the end of that decade, reinforced by the oil shock of 1973, to put steam into the quest for a water-splitting process. An example was Marchetti's idea of producing "high-value biological material" from nuclear power and his subsequent switch to hydrogen as energy carrier prompted him to investigate thermochemistry at Ispra (see Chapter 3).

Another starting point was provided early by the idea that the water molecule could be split simply by heating it: In so-called thermal decomposition, water breaks up into hydrogen and oxygen, but only at temperatures above 2,000° C. (3,600° F.), and temperatures in the 2,500°–3,000° C. (about 4,500°–5,400° F.) range are probably needed for a viable process. The problem is that no nuclear reactors or other more or less conventional heat sources now exist that can deliver that kind of temperature on a sustained basis and none appear to be on the horizon.

Experimental solar furnaces in Odeillo, France, the headquarters of French solar research, have indeed produced temperatures of 3,000° C. (5,400° F.) as well as thermal dissociation of hydrogen and oxygen but so far the conversion efficiency—only a few percent— has been disappointingly low. Nor are there many materials that can withstand those temperatures for long periods of time. A paper presented by General Atomic scientists at the 1978 Zurich hydrogen conference summed up: "Although it is being studied, there are substantial separation [getting hydrogen and oxygen gas out of the superhot steam] and materials obstacles, and it currently appears impractical from an engineering standpoint." In other words, it's very difficult to sort out superhot water vapor, oxygen and hydrogen molecules at 3,000° C., especially in view of the proclivity of hydrogen and oxygen to recombine very rapidly, even at much lower temperatures.

But lower temperatures *plus* chemicals, Marchetti reasoned, was the way to go. In his 1973 article in the Japanese chemical magazine he explained:

> Following the old proverb, 'if you can't carry a load in one journey, make two,' we thought of breaking the water molecule in two steps or more, if necessary with the help of intermediate chemical products, each step requiring heat at temperatures available in commercial reactors.

Other early theoretical considerations included:

- Thermochemical processes tend to be much cheaper than electrochemical ones per unit of energy handled.
- The energy would hopefully be handled only once while in electrolysis it is handled four or five times.
- Processes to make electricity rely on mature technology, and important breakthroughs appear improbable. [This was partially disproved by Dornier-Lurgi's HOT ELLY and General Electric's solid electrolyte approaches.]
- The history of new chemical processes, e.g., in petrochemistry and plastics, shows very steep learning curves.

Marchetti, in effect, argued that even if that first Mark 1 cycle was bad—and criticism was quickly forthcoming for a variety of reasons to be described later—the chances for improvement were much larger than for electrolysis, providing enough justification to carry on research.

Because of its historic significance, a brief description of this cycle is in order. The four-step Mark 1 works with compounds of mercury, bromine, and calcium, using temperatures ranging from a low of 200° C. to a maximum of 730° C. (432° to 1,346° F.). The steps proceed as follows:

1. In the first step the water molecule is split, but not into hydrogen and oxygen; an oxygen-hydrogen group links up with the calcium atom and a hydrogen radical links up with the bromine atom, a process that requires 730° C.:

$$CaBr_2 + 2H_2O \longrightarrow Ca(OH)_2 + 2HBr \text{ (water split)}$$

2. In the next step, which proceeds at 250° C. (432° F.), the hydrogen

is released, with the mercury substituting for the hydrogen atoms in the hydrogen-bromine compound:

$$Hg + 2HBr \longrightarrow HgBr_2 + H_2 \text{ (hydrogen switch)}$$

3. In step three, at 200° C. (392° F.), the calcium-hydrogen-oxygen compound is broken down by shifting the oxygen to again produce water and mercury-oxygen and calcium-bromine compounds:

$$HgBr_2 + Ca (OH)_2 \longrightarrow CaBr_2 + HgO + H_2O \text{ (oxygen shift)}$$

4. In the final, high-temperature step, at 600° C. (1,112° F.), oxygen is released from the mercury-oxygen compound:

$$HgO \longrightarrow Hg + 1/2 \, O_2$$

The sum of these four formulas then can be written as:

$$H_2O \longrightarrow H_2 + 1/2 \, O_2$$

Voilà, there's hydrogen. On paper at least, all three chemicals revert to their original stage to run the cycle time and again.

The main advantages of the cycle are that the heat requirements fall well within the range that can be expected from a future high-temperature nuclear reactor or solar power plant; the system has a single purpose—in other words, all energy is used at maximum efficiency to produce hydrogen; reaction products are supposedly easily separated (although the Ispra team had to start a sizable program to investigate the reactions involved because very little information was available then in the literature); and all by-products can be reinjected at one point or another into the cycles.

The drawbacks—and they are quite serious—include: serious pollution problems with mercury; the need for large amounts of highly corrosive, poisonous compounds—especially hydrobromic acid—in the process and the problem of containment of these corrosive materials; and the disproportionately large amounts of materials that must be circulated in relation to the amount of hydrogen produced.

Mark 1 was essentially a paper concept, but that did not prevent others from taking a closer look. The Futures Group, a private research group in Glastonbury, Connecticut, for example, studied the economics of the Mark 1 cycle two years after the Boston announcement. Their report found that a plant producing 2 million cubic feet (57,000 cubic meters) of hydrogen per hour would cost $74 million at that time, a figure that did not include the cost of the required nuclear reactor. The January 1976 study by the Stanford Research Institute (SRI), "The

Hydrogen Economy—A Preliminary Technology Assessment," extrapolated the cost to be up by almost another third, or $98 million (in 1975 dollars). Total hydrogen cost would be $8.08 per million Btus, the SRI study said—unacceptably high.

European industry sources were also skeptical about these early cycles developed at Ispra. A spokesman for Hoechst, the German chemical company that had a small program going evaluating hydrogen production methods in cooperation with the German lignite producer Rheinbraun, and Interatom, a German nuclear engineering firm, said in 1976 that the Ispra cycles were unlikely candidates because they involved handling solid materials in one or several steps. "Based on our experiences in big-process chemical industry we have the feeling that moving solids around just requires too much energy," he said, adding that cycles utilizing liquids or gases are considered more likely candidates.

In any event, these early efforts inspired a search for thermochemical water-splitting cycles everywhere. A 1974 review of the field by R. E. Chao of the University of Puerto Rico identified four basic cycle families: the so-called halides (very reactive derivatives of the halogen family of chemicals, such as bromine or chlorine); processes based on the "reverse Deacon reaction" (the Deacon reaction is an industrial process for making chlorine from hydrochloric acid and oxygen); iron and carbon oxide processes; and metal and metal-alkali processes. General Atomic, before settling on its present sulfur-iodine cycle, generated some 4,000 four-step cycles in a vast computerized search. Most of them were unusable because of severe material problems, kinetic absurdities, or gross diseconomies.

It seems now that the hybrid cycles involving both thermochemical steps as well as electrolysis are the most promising approach, in close competition with high-temperature electrolysis of steam of the HOT ELLY type. Thus neither camp has been proved totally right, an outcome that was not foreseen at the beginning of the decade. As already indicated, the Mark 13 hybrid in operation at Ispra is the world's first functioning bench-scale thermochemical cycle anywhere. Since May 1978 it has been producing about 100 liters (about 3.5 cubic feet) of hydrogen per hour, which for the time being is merely released into the clear air of Lago Maggiore. The Mark 13 is a three-step cycle in which sulfur dioxide, bromine, and water react together, producing sulfuric acid and hydrobromic acid. Both acids are decomposed—the first thermally at 800° C. (1,472° F.) and the second electrolytically—producing hydrogen and oxygen. The intermediate sulfur dioxide is recirculated, closing the cycle. Giorgio Beghi, project manager of the New Energy Program of the Joint Research Center (the formal name for what is otherwise known as the EURATOM Center), says the purpose of the glass-and-quartz bench-

Figure 4.1. The Mark 13, three-step, closed-circuit cycle at the EURATOM Research Center is the world's first functioning thermochemical water-splitting apparatus. The bench-scale apparatus began operations in spring 1978.

scale setup is "not to optimize conditions or output but to show the feasibility of this particular chemical cycle and to see how our equipment holds up."

Nipping at Ispra's heels is the Westinghouse process, also a hybrid involving sulfuric acid. Westinghouse presented its method with a splash at the 1976 Miami Beach hydrogen conference, taking up an entire morning session with five papers on various aspects. "The product hydrogen and oxygen streams are available under pressure [important for efficient pipeline transmission] and at high purity," said Westinghouse then in a paper. Westinghouse uses electrolysis in the hydrogen-producing step in which sulfurous acid is electrolytically decomposed into hydrogen and sulfuric acid. All other steps are heat-driven, chemically assisted thermochemical cycles. Gerald H. Farbman, Westinghouse manager of advanced technology programs, also set up a bench-scale hydrogen-producing cycle in the fall of 1978, with a hydrogen production rate rather similar to Ispra's. Beghi and Farbman are both convinced that hybrid processes are potentially more efficient than "pure" thermochemical cycles, such as the sulfur dioxide–iodine process under investigation at General Atomic (GA) since 1972. The cost so far has been some $5 million; the project is partially funded by DoE and a group of gas companies. GA claims its cycle is also 45–50 percent efficient, and the company's main hydrogen researcher, John L. Russell, says "there's no question that the process works."

Westinghouse's Farbman said in 1978 that the Westinghouse cycle could produce hydrogen at $7.50 to $9.00 per million Btus (1976 dollars). By comparison, hydrogen produced from natural gas as chemical feedstock costs $2.00 to $3.00 per million Btus. In the next phase, hydrogen from coal, the cost may be around $4.00 to $5.00 per million Btus. Farbman cautions, though, that these "cost estimates are rather speculative. There will still be questions on how to build the systems and what materials are best." Farbman predicts that his company could set up a *pilot* plant by 1988, if funding were available. But he stresses also that *commercial* development depends on the availability of future heat sources—high-temperature nuclear reactor development, which then was practically at a standstill in the United States, but not in Germany—or perhaps a high-temperature solar plant, which is unlikely to be available within the next 10 years. Westinghouse is budgeting half a million dollars annually for its research, with a matching amount from the Department of Energy.

While scientists like Karl-Friedrich Knoche in Germany, James Funk in the United States, Beghi at EURATOM in Italy, and Marchetti in Austria are convinced of the essential validity of the thermochemical water-splitting concept, doubts have been raised in France. Three French scientists working for France's state gas company, Gaz de France, Georges Donat, Bernard Esteve, and Jean-Pierre Roncato, writing in the French energy journal *Revue de L'Energie* in April 1977, said that thermochemical production is inherently uneconomical because it requires processing of such a large amount of chemicals per ton of hydrogen produced. Based on computer analysis of some 2,000 cycles, they claim that "at least 300 tons [330 short tons] of various compounds must be produced per ton of hydrogen produced" and that most cycles would involve the handling and production of some 800 tons [900 short tons] of intermediate, recycled compounds per ton of hydrogen—an uneconomic proposition.

Knoche, a leading European specialist at Aachen Technical University, dismisses the French criticism essentially as rubbish—bad research and faulty chemistry. The French studies were repeats of what he and his team calculated three or four years earlier without taking into account other research results that had become available in the meantime. He claims that some of the equations cited by the French group are wrong and that the data from the promising Westinghouse sulfur-based cycle were simply ignored. Knoche observes that

> the argument that large streams of solids are prohibitive is not new and certainly has to be taken rather seriously. However, the decisive point is what is being done with these streams of solids. The out-of-hand rejection of all processes involving large amounts of solids certainly is not right.

He points out that in a nuclear power plant, for example, the ratio of the amount of water moved around to the production of actual steam is also on the order of 11:1 and nuclear power plants are still the most efficient producers of electricity. "It's a pretty sorry effort," Knoche says of the French attempt to discredit thermochemical processes.

Other scientists say the French charge is essentially politically motivated. France is committed to building a large number of present-generation nuclear power plants as producers of electricity. These scientists guess that France has decided that if it has to produce hydrogen at some future date, it would be easier to go via the electrolysis route with electric power from conventional reactors, eliminating the need for added research into thermochemistry and high-temperature reactors.

Exotic Processes

Electrolysis, thermochemistry, and hybrid cycles are all still in the future. There are a number of more exotic approaches to hydrogen production that are in even earlier stages of experimentation. The established hydrogen community sometimes looks at them the way normal energy specialists looked at hydrogen in the late 1960s and early 1970s, although some have been reported in general-circulation media, like *Fortune* and popular science publications. Researchers in the United States, Japan, and Europe have begun investigating processes involving the direct reaction of sunlight with catalysts or biological organisms such as blue algae, the use of "renewable carbon" sources, and of high-powered lasers that produce hydrogen as a by-product of thermonuclear fusion, an approach pursued by KMS Fusion Inc., of Ann Arbor, Michigan (see Chapter 5).

An approach that is still in the early experimental stage has to do with efforts to "photolyze" water, that is, to split the water molecule by sunlight aided by a catalyst. One approach is to use organic compounds and plant physiology to imitate in one fashion or another the interaction between sunlight and chlorophyll, the ubiquitous green substance that gives most plants their distinctive green color and that sustains plant life-processes. Beyond that, scientists are looking at systems patterned after the light-absorbing capabilities of plants, using synthetic compounds on the theory that they would be more dependable, controllable, and eventually more efficient than organic materials.

One of the first successful photolysis experiments was reported in 1977 by two Japanese scientists, Professors Akira Fujishima of Kanagawa University, Yokohama, and Kenichi Honda of the University of Tokyo. They managed to produce small amounts of hydrogen by shining light on an electrolysis system employing semiconductor electrodes—powered by sunlight only and without any electric voltage. In the Fujishima-Honda cell, a titanium dioxide (TiO_2) electrode was connected to a platinum black electrode through an external circuit. When the TiO_2 electrode was exposed to light, a current flowed from the platinum electrode back to the titanium dioxide electrode through the outside circuit, and Fujishima and Honda observed gas bubbling up from the electrolyte. From the direction of the current they concluded that (1) water can be decomposed by visible light into oxygen and hydrogen without the application of any external voltage and (2) that hydrogen is produced at the platinum black electrode and oxygen at the TiO_2 end.

A research project involving synthetic compounds surfaced with a considerable splash of publicity in 1976, generating articles in *Fortune*, Britain's respected *New Scientist*, and *Der Spiegel* in Germany. This was the discovery by two Austrian scientists working at the University of North Carolina in Chapel Hill, Gerhard and Hertha W. Sprintschnik, that compounds of ruthenium, an exotic, expensive metal, may break up the water molecule. Their discovery was an accident and, in the words of the *Fortune* account by Gene Bylinsky, it "contained all the ingredients of a classic scientific discovery." The North Carolina effort may have triggered research into new and promising avenues of hydrogen production.

Using rather primitive equipment, no lab assistants, and only the counsel of their senior adviser, David G. Whitten, the Sprintschniks did not set out to look for ways to make hydrogen. Rather, they were researching the characteristics of membranes, important in health and disease studies. Their work was not sponsored by an agency interested in energy but by the National Institutes of Health.

In December 1975 Gerhard Sprintschnik was looking for a bright red fluorescence that was supposed to occur when ruthenium powder is dissolved in water and then illuminated. Sprintschnik put a slide with a layer of a ruthenium compound rather than "straight" ruthenium into water and shone a lamp on it but saw no fluorescence. This was the first hint that something unplanned was going on. Later he detected bubbles rising from the water. He collected the gas and an analysis a week later showed that the mixture was in fact *Knallgas*—a hydrogen-oxygen gas mixture in the proper ratio, derived from water.[9]

Although the Sprintschnik-Whitten discoveries created enough of a stir to warrant international coverage, the researchers cautioned against premature hopes of hydrogen production being around the corner. Whitten wrote,

> Although we are certainly very excited about our recent findings, realistically I must say that it will probably be quite some time before any large-scale development of this system is possible. On the molecular scale there will be much research necessary to determine possible compounds . . . as well as determination of the precise mechanism by which this process occurs before we can anticipate any sort of large scale development.

Also, there is the possibility that the Whitten-Sprintschnik results may have been a fluke. At another hydrogen conference in Liege, Belgium, in the fall of 1976 there was hallway talk that other scientists had been unable to duplicate the Chapel Hill results. Walter Klöpffer, a scientist at the German branch of the Battelle Institute in Frankfurt, which is also looking into catalytically assisted hydrogen production, confirmed that those duplication efforts failed but he nevertheless felt that something did happen in the original experiments and that hydrogen was indeed formed. Klöpffer speculated that Whitten and the Sprintschniks had stumbled on some sort of interesting "dirt effect that should be investigated"—some unknown impurities, perhaps, rather than the ruthenium compounds themselves, helped trigger hydrogen production, an effect analogous to the "doping" of crystals with impurities in microcircuitry to achieve certain electronic effects.

Biological processes that seek to utilize the chlorophyll-based means of cleaving the water molecule are also being increasingly investigated. A summary of work in this field was given in Bylinsky's *Fortune* story describing the Whitten-Sprintschnik efforts. The exact process by which chlorophyll extracts energy from sunlight is difficult to describe, but in general it has to do with transfer of the energy contained in a photon (a quantum of light) to an electron embedded in a single molecule, the "reaction center," that forms the heart of the chloroplast, the chlorophyll-carrying chemical structure. This electron is knocked out of the reaction center and then absorbed by another molecule, the so-called acceptor, which carries it away to ultimately help build carbohydrates to nourish the plant.

The interesting part from the point of view of extracting hydrogen from water occurs in the reaction center. The reaction center reaches out to the nearest available "donor" to replace the lost electrons—which turns out to be the water suffusing the plant. Visible sunlight by itself cannot split the water molecule inside the plant. But the activated reaction center, by extracting those electrons from water, overcomes the strong hydrogen-oxygen bond and thus splits the water molecule. The result is molecular oxygen, which escapes into the atmosphere, hydrogen ions and electrons. Hydrogen ions and electrons eventually combine with the air's carbon dioxide to form glucose, a simple carbohydrate.

The trick that researchers are now looking for is to redirect that hydrogen ion. Their aim is to develop a process that instead of winding up with plant hydrocarbons somehow gets the hydrogen out of the plant as a gaseous fuel. According to Bylinsky, scientists introduce the enzyme hydrogenase, extracted from photosynthetic bacteria or from algae. Although the exact mechanism is apparently still unknown, hydrogenase somehow causes the electrons and hydrogen ions to combine into hydrogen gas. As a logical, perhaps promising follow-up, some scientists are trying to duplicate the bare essentials of the photosynthesis mechanism with man-made chemicals that imitate the ability of hydrogenase and chlorophyll to produce hydrogen.

One type of microscopic organism that has drawn the attention of hydrogen researchers is a purple bacterium living in salt flats. In an action somewhat similar to that of chlorophyll, this bacterium's pigment absorbs photons but forms an electric potential along its structure, turning it into something like an ion pump that can electrolyze water, according to a March 1977 article in *Chemical Engineering*. This work is being pursued at the University of California's Lawrence Berkeley Laboratory.

That same lab is also investigating two other biological materials, chloroplasts and cyanobacteria. Chloroplasts produce molecular hydrogen from water when they are coupled to something called a "low-potential electron mediator"—certain proteins—and an enzyme. This approach has yielded high conversion efficiencies of around 80 percent, but the system's life expectancy was only a few hours. Cyanobacteria include microscopically small blue algae able to produce hydrogen under special conditions. These algae normally extract nitrogen from the air for their metabolism, but when nitrogen is not available, they switch to other metabolic methods that involve the release of hydrogen. Growing these algae in an argon atmosphere under artificial sunlight, scientists at the Richmond field station of the University of California have developed a system that produced 2 liters (2.1 quarts) of hydrogen during a 20-day run according to the *Fortune* story—almost laughably small compared to the lab-scale Ispra thermochemical apparatus but the best production rate of any organic setup so far.

Photolysis via a catalyst or via semiconductor electrodes of the Fujishima-Honda type is still very inefficient, with conversion factors of from less than 0.01 percent to 1 percent, and the same holds for biological materials: "The efficiency of such processes is too low to be of practical use at the present stage," concluded a paper reviewing the entire field of hydrogen production via solar radiation in the fall 1976 issue of the *International Journal for Hydrogen Energy*.

This means that one of the "mechanistic" methods of breaking up water molecules—thermochemical water-splitting, advanced electrolysis and/or high-temperature electrolysis, or a combination of both thermochemistry and electrolysis—will be the first to generate hydrogen on a scale necessary for the element's use as a clean chemical fuel. Which of these approaches is likely to be picked is uncertain: after more than a decade of research there is no clear consensus, and both main methods have their advocates. It may well be that all methods eventually will come into use depending on factors other than the relative technical merits—geography, government regulations, a better lobbying effort, availability of capital, or infrastructure or resource peculiarities of a region. The field is wide open, and the race is on.

5

Solar and Nuclear Power: Hydrogen's Primary Energy Sources

"First Large-Scale Solar Energy Project Nears Completion in U.S. Desert" read the headline in the *International Herald Tribune* of November 15, 1977. The story told readers about the progress of an experimental project near Albuquerque, New Mexico, that will collect and focus sun radiation via some 5,500 individually adjustable mirrors on the desert ground to the top of a 200-foot (60-meter) tower where a prototype boiler will be placed.

The Albuquerque project, costing some $21 million, will not produce electricity. Rather, it will serve only to demonstrate the basic validity of the concept of focusing rays into a sharp point on top of a tower, producing steam or superheated air that could be used to produce electricity via more or less conventional turbines. It will also test components, such as the prototype boiler module, that will go into the first actual solar power plant that DoE plans to build, together with Southern California Edison, for an estimated $120 million in Daggett, a small village near Barstow, California, in the Mojave Desert. That plant is expected to go on stream, or, maybe better, "on sun," in 1981 or 1982 to generate 10 megawatts of solar electricity—enough for a small town during daylight hours, and maybe 7 megawatts during periods of cloud cover.

On the other side of the Atlantic, similar but smaller projects are under way. In Sicily, the European Economic Community is completing in 1981 a 1 megawatt solar electric tower that will feed its output directly into the local grid. In Spain, the Paris-based International Energy Agency is putting up two solar energy plants side by side; one is a half-megawatt solar tower plant and the other a "solar farm" plant in which electricity is generated by an array of photovoltaic solar cells. The efficiencies of the two concepts can then be directly compared.

So, what does solar energy have to do with hydrogen? A great deal. A mistake made, even by people with some understanding of energy, is that hydrogen is a primary energy source all by itself. It does exist in miniscule percentages in natural gas and thus is, technically at least, a "source," but in the context of a hydrogen economy it is conceived of as an "energy carrier," the nearest analogy being electricity. Usable electrical power does not exist "raw" in nature but must be manufactured via complicated machinery, drawing on "primary sources" like oil, coal, uranium, and now solar radiation. In similar fashion, hydrogen must be manufactured in a variety of ways, from natural gas now (as shown in Chapter 4), from coal, and eventually from water and both solar and nuclear energy. There are some energy conversion mechanisms that are more intimately linked to hydrogen than others. In the past decade, a number of alternative energy proposals have been suggested that rely on hydrogen produced from water as an essential ingredient in their overall structure. Some of them will be described here to illustrate the link between hydrogen and alternative, environmentally clean "primary sources" of energy. Others are mentioned to illustrate the innovative thinking in the search for new and environmentally acceptable energy sources.

Hydrogen might be loosely compared to the clutch or transmission in an automobile: It does not generate power by itself, but makes it possible to conveniently use the power available from various types of engines—a V-8, a Wankel, a gas turbine, an electric motor, even a steam engine—and to convert it into useful work at the driving wheels. Hydrogen works in much the same way but with some extra advantages. The energy from the various primary sources can be transformed into a uniform storable universal fuel that can be used in a variety of applications. Hydrogen can be conceived of also as a broad river to which many "primary source" tributaries contribute (with obvious political and economic advantages). At the downstream end, the broad river splits again into many different branches, "irrigation canals" sustaining many economic activities of man.

An important implication of this elegant and simple concept (though it is difficult to implement) is that types of primary sources can be utilized for end uses not feasible without the hydrogen intermediary. Atomic or solar energy or hydropower can be converted to chemical energy to propel cars and airplanes, or, ultimately, to make proteins. Without hydrogen, these primary sources are good only for making electricity.

A second very important implication is that hydrogen makes it possible to economically store energy derived from solar or nuclear primary energy sources. Hydrocarbons like crude oil and coal obviously are easily storable, but how do you store sunlight or the heat from a nuclear reactor? Electricity produced from these two sources must be consumed immediately, otherwise it is lost.[1] However, electricity can be indirectly stored by using it to split water into hydrogen and oxygen. Both gases can be stored easily, like any other gas. By burning the hydrogen later with the stored oxygen or oxygen from the atmosphere, electricity or heat only can be produced again when and where it is needed. These aspects will be discussed later in Chapter 8.

Professor John O'M. Bockris, one of the earliest and most active proponents of a hydrogen economy, puts the relationship between primary sources and hydrogen as follows:

> The likely sources of energy for the future are atomic and solar. Atomic reactors can provide electricity which would be cheaper as the reactors increase in size, but with size comes the difficulty of thermal pollution, so that large atomic reactors, which would give relatively cheap electricity at source, would have to be placed either on the ocean, far from population centers, or in remote areas such as Northern Canada, Siberia, or Central Australia.
>
> Correspondingly, massive solar collectors are likely to be far from the population centers which need them, for they would be most advantageously situated in North Africa, Saudi Arabia, and Australia. Hence, the electricity to which they would give rise is liable to have to travel at least 1,000 miles [1,600 kilometers], and, in some situations, as much as 4,000 miles [6,400 kilometers], to go from the site of production to the site of use.
>
> The likelihood of this situation, and the energy loss in conduction, gave rise to the concept of a "Hydrogen Economy." Thus, it could be cheaper to convert electrical energy, which will be a product of solar and atomic reactors, to hydrogen at the energy source. Thereafter, the hydrogen would be transmitted through pipes—the pumping energy being relatively small—and converted back to electricity at the site of use (fuel cells) or used in combustion to provide mechanical power.

Bockris made up a graph showing the relation among distance, cost of production, and voltage. It showed that at distances of between 550 and slightly more than 800 miles (880 and 1300 kilometers) energy transmission by hydrogen is cheaper than high-voltage (700 kv) cable transmission. Thus, he concluded, "For situations in which there are distant energy sources (the typical energy source of the future), hydrogen is likely to be the medium of the energy."[2]

Rather than describe in detail the pros and cons of the various *sources* of energy, fossil, nonfossil, and renewable, the aim here is to sketch briefly how hydrogen ties in to these primary sources.

Solar Energy

Solar energy for home heating is already poised for commercial takeoff both in Europe and the United States, but the relatively simple technology employed is only partially relevant to a hydrogen economy. For the generation of hydrogen on a large industrial scale, solar power requires huge installations with complicated machinery and controls, including computers, on a scale many times that of the upcoming Barstow plant.

The "solar tower" concept was introduced to the hydrogen community at the 1974 THEME conference in Miami Beach. Two physicists from the University of Houston, Alvin F. Hildebrandt and L. L. Vant-Hull, presented their idea of a tower-top point-focus solar energy collector. Hildebrandt, acknowledged as a pioneer of the concept, postulated a tower about 450 meters (1,476 feet) high that would produce 500 megawatts (thermal) (about 250 megawatts [electric]) during sunlight hours. Hildebrandt and Vant-Hull suggested that such towers employing suitable heat transfer cycles "would appear to be well suited for a transfer of solar heat to a hydrogen dissociation process such as the De Beni Mark 1 process" (see Chapter 4).

Hildebrandt's and Vant-Hull's ideas led more or less directly to the Albuquerque and Barstow proposals, albeit minus the hydrogen-making apparatus. "Let's see first whether we can economically generate electricity on a sizable scale and maybe then we can look at hydrogen-making," the reasoning went.

So far, the economics are far from competitive. According to an early *Business Week* story, the electricity to be produced in Barstow will be 12 to 15 times as expensive as power from a new coal or nuclear plant. And Southern California Edison, the project's managing utility, figures that solar power could not supply more than 2 to 3 percent of its total needs by the turn of the century. Utility executives also fear, according to *Business Week*, that after hitting environmentalist roadblocks in almost all other types of new power plants, they may encounter environmental opposition to a solar tower plant as well—perhaps on grounds of using too much land—130 acres (53 hectares). *Business Week* quoted Edison's vice president for advanced engineering as saying, "Just wait and see—there will be a group that opposes it."

Early runs of the partially completed Albuquerque mirror system yielded a significant surprise in terms of a future hydrogen-making capability. The temperature at the focal point was expected to be approximately 1,000°C. (1,800°F.); instead the test crews registered temperatures of about 1,750°C. (3,150°F.)—75 percent more. During a trial run in May 1977, the mirror system effortlessly burned a hole through a quarter-inch steel plate. According to the Associated Press, "seventy-one plates of mirrors concentrated 1,100 suns worth of light intensity," melting through the steel in a little more than a minute. Apparently this test used less than a quarter of the total mirror array; when completed, the system will focus about 300 mirrors.

This bonus is very important. Thermochemical production of hydrogen—breaking up of the water molecule with heat, assisted by recycling chemicals—had proceeded on the assumption that the maximum temperature available from high-temperature nuclear reactors would be about 1,000°C. to 1,100°C. (1,800°F. to 2,012°F.), and thermochemical cycles were designed with that temperature limit in mind. Other more efficient cycles were considered as well but were abandoned because the temperature requirements were deemed too high and practically unattainable.

The Albuquerque data challenged those assumptions. They showed that these temperatures can be reached fairly easily, and it's reasonable to assume that even higher temperatures can be achieved in the future. More efficient cycles may be formulated, according to Norbert Weyss, an Austrian engineer. After his retirement from the Swiss electrical equipment maker, Brown, Boveri & Cie., Weyss went to work for the International Institute for Applied Systems Analysis (IIASA) in Laxenburg, Austria. He visited the Albuquerque facility in 1977. Weyss, who had studied unconventional energy sources at Brown, Boveri and who has developed a solar-energy scenario for his native Austria at IIASA, says that given these new data, the cost of hydrogen production from water via thermochemical means could be "one quarter of what had been thought feasible until now. Obviously, this is very significant and very decisive."

Another promising concept for large-scale production of electricity from solar power is the "solar chimney" proposed by two West German engineers, Jörg Schlaich and Michael Simon, in 1976. Unlike many other proposals, this concept has benefited from Schlaich's vast practical engineering experience in designing and building very high, lightweight structures.

The Schlaich-Simon concept envisions a huge structure that would look like an oversized hybrid of an industrial smokestack and cooling tower, up to one kilometer (3,300 feet) high and 100 meters (330 feet) in diameter. The chimney would be built of lightweight concrete or would

Figure 5.1. An artist's conception of a future 100-megawatt "Solar Chimney." This tower would be 600 meters (1980 feet) high, and the greenhouse would have a diameter of 4.3 kilometers (2.6 miles).

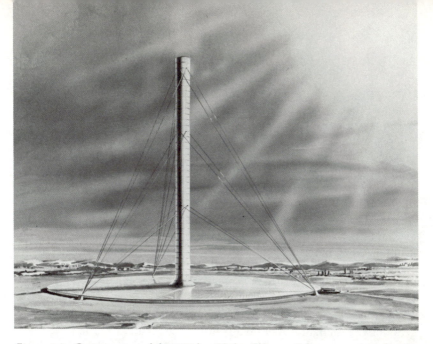

Figure 5.2. Construction of this 100-kw "Solar Chimney" demonstration plant in Spain began in 1980.

be assembled from a ring-shaped cable-mesh system covered with aluminum cladding and hung from a thin, pencil-like concrete pillar in the chimney center. The latter system has already been used in building a 178-meter (587-foot) cooling tower for a high-temperature nuclear reactor under construction in West Germany. On the ground, the chimney would be surrounded by a huge circular greenhouse, a translucent roof 2 meters (6 feet) high and up to 10 kilometers (6.2 miles) in diameter.

The idea is simple: The solar chimney combines the greenhouse effect—air and soil are heated underneath the translucent roof by solar radiation—with the chimney effect, in which a strong upward air current is created by the temperature differential. A giant rotor inside the chimney would drive wind turbines. Such plants, says Schlaich, could produce electricity at costs and amounts comparable to today's nuclear plants: For low-capacity plants from 1 to 10 megawatts, the engineers estimate costs of $1,800 per installed kilowatt, but for large plants of up to 1,000 megawatts the investment might drop to as low as $450 per installed kilowatt. A small 100-kilowatt demonstration plant, funded by the German Ministry for Science and Research, is scheduled to start producing electricity in 1981 at a site in Spain.

A literally further-out concept that has gotten considerable media coverage is to generate solar energy in orbiting solar power stations that would beam huge quantities of electric power via microwave beams to earth. Alternatively, an orbiting system of mirrors would reflect and focus sunlight onto relatively small earthside areas where solar power plants of the type described above would convert solar energy into electricity. Both Boeing Aerospace Co. and Rockwell International Inc. are exploring the first idea.

NASA and the Department of Energy are sharing the cost—$15.6 million—for a four-year feasibility study through 1981 to investigate the engineering, environmental, institutional, and international impacts of huge orbiting solar power plants. In a March 2, 1978, story, *ENR* quoted Peter E. Glaser, vice president for engineering for Arthur D. Little, Inc., of Cambridge, Massachusetts, as saying that such systems could supply as much as 25 percent of the entire planet's energy requirements at the end of the first quarter of the next century. Glaser, who has been pushing the idea since 1968, sees 1996 as a possible target date for the first such satellite.

The second approach, putting up a number of mirrors into space and beaming the sunlight itself into a relatively small area of around 25 miles (40 kilometers) in diameter, was outlined in 1977 by Krafft A. Ehricke, a former NASA space manager. At a Berlin press conference Ehricke dubbed his proposal "An industrial sun for Europe": Reradiating the sun via a system of individually stabilized and controlled mirrors would create a climate in this zone roughly equivalent to Arab or Australian deserts, possibly a bit hotter, but not so hot as to make human existence impossible. Total yield from such an "energy oasis" would be between 35,000 and 50,000 megawatts.

All these solar power plants have in common the capability, in addition to generating electricity on a large scale, of producing hydrogen as a chemical fuel alternative once oil and gas run out.

Nuclear Energy

Despite the fears and the unresolved questions about the safety of nuclear power plants and the sometimes violent opposition to them, a large number of experts, many of them with impeccable credentials attesting to their concern for the environment, remain convinced that nuclear power will remain an important primary power source in the future. They agree that more safeguards are imperative, that nuclear waste disposal looms as a large and unresolved problem, and that nuclear plants may have to be placed in sites far from population centers (a possibility that may actually help speed up the introduction of hydrogen, as noted earlier in this chapter). Regardless of the "Faustian pact" fears about nuclear energy, the power of the atom continues to be regarded as a near-indispensable input at least for the early and medium-term stages of a future hydrogen economy.

Nuclear energy is a potential heat source for thermochemical water-splitting or a source of electricity for electrolysis if that should prove to be economically superior for hydrogen making—a question nobody can now answer with any certainty. For electrolysis, the more or less standard so-called light-water reactors of the types produced now by General Electric, Westinghouse, Kraftwerk-Union of West Germany, and by the Soviets could be used. But the entire chain of inefficiencies—the energy-expensive process of enriching natural uranium, converting enriched uranium to heat to drive turbines to produce electricity to drive the electrolysis apparatus—militates against such a system.

Rather, process heat from a new, largely untried type of reactor called the high-temperature reactor is being advocated as the prime force for making hydrogen—via thermochemistry or electrolysis. One variant of the high-temperature reactor, the so-called pebble-bed reactor being developed by Germany's Jülich Nuclear Research Center together with German industry, has a peculiarity that makes it inherently safer than conventional light-water reactors and thus should go a long way toward removing objections to nuclear power. In a nutshell, the difference is that in a conventional pressurized water reactor (PWR) or boiling water reactor (BWR) of the kind used today, the big concern is not about a nuclear explosion of the Nagasaki-Hiroshima type, but about a loss of coolant together with failure of the emergency core-cooling system. If both were to happen simultaneously, the nuclear fuel core could turn into a white-hot runaway that could melt through the plant's concrete bottom, producing high-pressure radioactive steam from groundwater. This might burst the reinforced concrete containment vessel, releasing radioactive steam and sending radioactive groundwater seeping into fields, rivers and lakes—the "China Syndrome." Although the statistical odds are supposedly against it, a disaster of this type remains a possibility for current reactor types, a possibility that was driven home starkly by the Three Mile Island calamity.

The HTR is immune to that particular danger because it has the characteristic of shutting itself down if the cooling system fails. This remarkable feature was experimentally tested on August 22 and 23, 1970, in the 15 Mwe experimental AVR[3] reactor in Jülich. In the test, the experts simulated an accident in which the four rods controlling the rate of nuclear fission jammed, with the reactor functioning at full power. When cooling was interrupted the reactor shut itself down, remaining "under-critical" (a state in which the nuclear chain reaction is not self-sustaining) for almost a full day and then starting up again slowly. Power output stabilized at about 300 kw, about 2 percent of the reactor's maximum

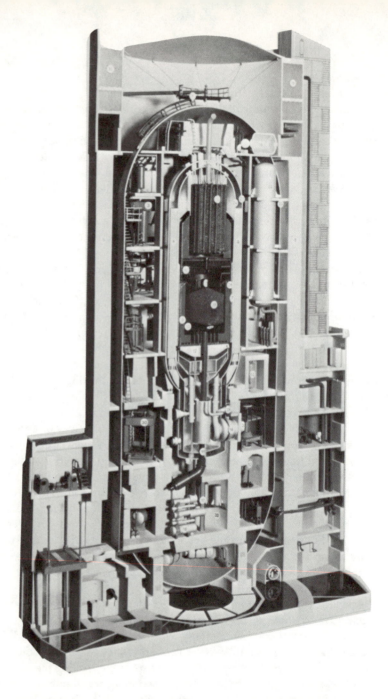

Figure 5.3. A cross section of the experimental 15 MW high-temperature reactor in Jülich, West Germany, that demonstrated the inherent fail-safe feature of this reactor type. The reactor shuts itself down if the cooling system fails and the reactor overheats. Drawing courtesy of Jülich Research Center.

capacity and equal only to the amount of heat that was naturally dissipated to components and equipment surrounding the core. This self-regulating feature depends on complex physical properties of the HTR design, the most important being the so-called negative temperature coefficient. This means that the amount of power produced will always adjust itself to the amount of energy that is being removed from the core: If a lot of energy is removed to drive a turbine and produce electricity, a lot of energy is produced, but if the energy removal rate goes down, the output will go down as well as the reactor chokes on itself. In addition, the HTR has a lower power density than current reactor types, meaning it produces less heat in a given volume. Finally, a great deal of graphite is used in the HTR's construction; graphite is a material that can absorb large amounts of heat without changing physical or chemical properties. All these factors combine to make the HTR, regardless of size, impervious to a core meltdown.

High-temperature reactor research began in the mid-1950s in Britain, culminating in the late 1960s in proposals for a 600-Mw reactor that was never built. Britain did construct on behalf of the OECD (Organisation for Economic Co-operation and Development) a small 20-megawatt (thermal) (Mwth) experimental reactor, the Dragon, matched by Germany's similar AVR reactor in Jülich. While the Dragon was shut down in 1976 after 12 years of operation, the German program grew to the 300-Mw pebble-bed reactor now under construction near Hamm in the Ruhr region, which is scheduled to start power production in 1983. In the United States, General Atomic built a small 40-Mwe HTR at Peach Bottom, Pennsylvania, followed by a larger commercial-sized HTR in Fort St. Vrain, Colorado.

Because of this reactor's typical higher-temperature operations, a few scientists recognized early that HTRs could be used for purposes other than mere electricity production. Rudolf Schulten, head of Jülich's Institute for Reactor Development, noted as early as 1967 that HTRs could provide process heat for chemical and metallurgical purposes, substituting for fossil fuels. Two executives of Dragon, S. B. Hosegood and G. E. Lockett, wrote four years later that the HTR could well supply the high-grade heat needed for a multi-step thermochemical water splitting process for making hydrogen, noting specifically the work then going on at the EURATOM research center in Ispra.

In the United States General Atomic also embarked on a program of developing a line of commercial HTRs for both electricity and process heat generation. As a logical sideline, General Atomic also became very active in developing thermochemical water-splitting cycles, but in 1976 the company halted its entire reactor program because of lacking sales.

This left the Germans alone in the field for several years, although there is now some renewed U.S. interest in participating in a European program. Also, Japan has now embarked on an HTR program of its own.

The German effort is still aimed primarily at developing a cheap heat source for coal gasification. But energy planners all say the HTR will ultimately also serve as a supplier of heat and/or electricity for hydrogen and other chemical industry uses, because in Germany industrial process heat commands a market four times as large as the market for electricity production. For these reasons, in October 1975 the West German government decided to go ahead with the design of a second, larger 500 Mwe HTR. The country has budgeted $500 million for developing blueprints within five years. Construction may start in 1983 and is expected to cost at least another $500 million, with completion expected in the late 1980s. A prototype nuclear-powered coal gasification plant could start operations by 1990, Jülich sources say, but the next step, a HTR-driven hydrogen plant, is not envisioned until after the turn of the century.

Energy From Fusion

Fusion is another great hope for both electricity production and hydrogen generation, but except for one version, laser fusion, it is even further down the road than the HTR. Heiko Barnert, one of the chief researchers at Jülich working on the HTR-hydrogen complex, predicts that neither fusion nor solar energy plants would be any real help towards resolving the general energy dilemma within the next thirty years or so.

Fusion methods all have to wrestle with the problem of how to confine a plasma, a hydrogen gas heated to about 100 million degrees centigrade (180 million degrees Fahrenheit), duplicating the conditions inside the sun under which positively charged hydrogen nuclei overcome their mutual repulsion to merge into a helium atom, thus producing and releasing an excess of energy—sunshine. So far the problems of confining this inferno and of attaining the necessary temperatures and pressures on an industrial scale and producing a net energy gain have not been solved. One scientist at the 1974 THEME conference in Miami Beach likened the problem of fusion containment to "the imprisonment of a gorilla in a cage fashioned of rubber bands." In theory, fusion is the ultimate, clean primary energy source because in addition to creating energy it produces largely chemically inert, nonradioactive helium as an end product.[4] Once fusion is commercial, today's urgent unresolved questions of how to store the mushrooming quantities of toxic nuclear waste and safeguard against the abuse of weapons-grade plutonium, a by-product in current nuclear power plants, would become largely academic.

A promising fusion variant of special relevance to a hydrogen economy is the laser fusion research pursued by KMS Fusion Inc., of Ann Arbor, Michigan. KMS Fusion's history is a fascinating tale with a David-and-Goliath flavor, in which a small company with an unusual concept is not taken seriously at first, struggles against great odds to survive, and in the end emerges in the forefront of a scientific field generally thought to be the province of the big-science organizations like Los Alamos, Sandia, and the state-run laboratories in Europe and the Soviet Union.

In most fusion research, plasma confinement and heating is attempted by some sort of magnetic technique. In laser fusion, the idea is to bombard tiny glass pellets filled with the rare hydrogen isotopes tritium and deuterium with very intense laser beams from all sides. This bombardment compresses the pellets to extreme densities and pressures to achieve the same fusion effect and energy production. Rather than approaching fusion as a means of producing electricity, the late Keeve M. Siegel, founder and former president of KMS, argued that laser fusion should be used to produce hydrogen as an intermediate. Siegel reasoned that nuclear fusion, which produces mostly neutrons and alpha particles in an approximate 80:20 ratio, can be used to break up water. KMS claims to have invented several cycles in which the water molecule is broken up in a two-step process. Essentially, the KMS radiolytic-thermochemical cycles involve first the dissociation of carbon dioxide (CO_2) via radiation—the difficult step—into carbon monoxide plus oxygen. The carbon monoxide then reacts with water thermochemically at around 500°C. (932°F.) to produce molecular hydrogen and, again, carbon dioxide. In a second step, methane would be produced from that hydrogen as a means of keeping standard natural gas pipelines filled and working, a notion that produced financial support from Texas Gas Transmission Corporation.

Siegel believed a pure hydrogen economy would entail too many and too expensive technical changes in pipeline, storage, and burner equipment. However, hydrogen would be basic to large-scale coal gasification, and substitute natural gas (SNG) would combine the benefits of hydrogen as an inexhaustible fuel with the economics of leaving the existing national and international natural gas distribution structure intact, saving untold billions. Siegel, a mathematician and entrepreneur whose initials formed the company's name, claimed as early as 1974 to be making hydrogen "by the thimbleful and bucketful," according to a December 1974 story in *Fortune* magazine. At one time he almost persuaded Saudi Arabia's oil minister, Sheikh Yamani, to back his approach to making hydrogen. Yamani told me in an interview in Riyadh in October 1975 that Saudi Arabia was planning for the days when oil would run out and was interested in investigating alternative energy sources. Yamani also said he and some of his advisers had discussed Arab funding for the KMS program with Siegel earlier that year. Siegel suffered a fatal stroke while proposing a much larger laser fusion program to a subcommittee of the congressional Joint Committee on Atomic Energy in March 1975, and the Saudi interest apparently ended with Siegel's death.

For a while KMS Fusion was in peril, and the parent company, KMS Industries, had to sell off various corporate properties to keep fusion work funded. At one point it looked to outsiders as if KMS Fusion would go out of business altogether, but the company was rescued by a new government contract in 1977 to produce those miniscule pellets used by other laboratories in laser fusion research. The precariousness of its position in the mid-seventies was due to the prevailing scepticism about laser fusion in general and the KMS objective of making hydrogen via that route in particular. "A bit offbeat," commented one prominent hydrogen advocate at the time.

However, since then, the KMS fortunes have turned, in part because of a growing belief in Washington that laser fusion may in fact be better than other fusion techniques, in part because the government thought that more fusion funding should go to private companies like KMS rather than exclusively to the big super-labs. A year after the life-saving pellet contract, Siegel was posthumously vindicated and KMS was fully back in the laser fusion research business. In early 1978, *Business Week* reported that laser fusion "may well emerge as the preferred technique over competing [fusion] approaches, such as magnetic confinement," and KMS is right in the forefront, according to the magazine. Henry J. Gomberg, the company's chairman, told a meeting of the American Institute of Chemical Engineers in November 1977 that hydrogen production from laser fusion is relatively simple compared to other methods:

> Our objective with combination radiolytic-thermochemical cycles is 40 percent conversion to chemical energy, and capital investment and operating cost low enough so that the cost of hydrogen is in the $3.00-4.00 per million Btus range. We believe the lower capital investment possible through direct chemical conversion will hold the edge over other methods, including high-temperature electrolysis, and is definitely the preferred method for laser-fusion applications.

KMS always has been much more optimistic than others as to when—many scientists still say "whether"—laser fusion will become a reality; hydrogen/methane production is tied to that. "By the late

1980s we could have demonstration plants, not just small pilots but plants producing at the equivalent of 100 megawatts electric power," says Dr. Wayne Meinke, KMS Fusion executive. He feels the pellet-to-pipeline approach will be much cheaper and simpler than an electricity-generating fusion plant.

Derivatives of Solar Energy

Other sources of energy—wind power and ocean-thermal energy—are often not recognized as derivatives of solar energy. The oceans trap vast amounts of solar radiation, with higher temperatures near the surface and colder deeper layers. Solar influx drives the global wind patterns.

Ocean-Thermal Energy

In order to tap ocean-thermal energy, the idea is to exploit the temperature differences between the various layers, which is not very large—about 20-25°C.—but which is inexhaustible. Heat stored in the warm water layers near the surface is used to turn a liquid with a very low boiling point—ammonia, for instance—into vapor, which drives an electricity-producing turbine. Cold water pumped up from the ocean's deep layers is then used to recool the ammonia back into its liquid phase in a closed cycle. The ammonia is then reheated to produce vapor again to drive the turbines. A French physicist, Jacques d'Arsonval, first made suggestions along those lines almost a century ago. In the late 1920s or early 1930s a French engineer, Georges Claude, actually built a shore-sited ocean-thermal plant at Matanzas, about 50 miles (80 kilometers) west of Havana, in Cuba. Somehow, it never became quite clear whether the plant had a net energy output or a deficit; tropical storms ravaged the cold-water inlet pipe and there were mechanical problems. Cheap fossil fuels spelled the end of Claude's scheme.

Ocean-thermal power was introduced to the hydrogen community at the 1974 Miami Beach THEME conference, not so much as a specific hardware proposal describing a particular type of ocean-thermal power plant, but rather as a general recommendation for ocean siting of future solar-to-hydrogen facilities. The concept, described by William Escher and Joe A. Hanson, then at the Oceanic Institute, Waimanalo, Hawaii, envisioned both direct solar conversion via photovoltaic collectors and ocean-thermal plants to be mounted on large floating platforms for large-scale hydrogen production. These platforms—models of so-called super-stable platforms have been tested by the institute in a Hawaiian bay under a "floating city development" program—would also house facilities for exploiting other sea resources such as shellfish and magnesium and potash from the sea, plus some offshore manufacturing.

Two years later at the 1976 First World Hydrogen Conference, two Johns Hopkins scientists presented a much more detailed proposal for making fertilizer offshore via hydrogen from ocean-thermal energy. Gordon L. Dugger and E. J. Francis outlined the design of an ocean-thermal energy plant ship to produce ammonia, raw stock for fertilizers, drawing on ocean-thermal energy to produce hydrogen and combining it with the nitrogen in the atmosphere. The study, conducted with the help of the Department of Commerce's Maritime Administration, several private companies, and other research institutes, resulted in a baseline design for a 100-Mwe plant ship capable of turning out 313 short tons (283 metric tons) of ammonia per day. The authors, extrapolating their cost data to a bigger, more efficient (500 Mwe) ship producing 1,697 short tons (1,539 metric tons) of ammonia per day, came up with an ammonia cost of $90 per ton (1975 dollars) for the early to mid-eighties when such a ship might become operational. This, the authors say, would be profitable, because fertilizer costs may go as high as $180 per ton or more by the mid-eighties. The total cost of such a ship might be $383 million (1975 dollars), including a hull made of concrete, electrolysis and ammonia plants, and deploying the ship to its site.

To Australia's Bockris, ocean-thermal exploitation is attractive because it represents "energy mining" that, next to mirror concentration methods of the type tried in Albuquerque and Barstow, is "the most promising method of collecting massive solar energy." In a paper written in the early seventies, Bockris observed,

> oil has been cheap because it represents the products of millions of years of insolation and photosynthesis used to give back energy in the one century. Solar thermal gradient mining represents the withdrawal not of the heat stored in a surface layer or of the input *rate* from the sun in one day, but that arising from long insolation and which has caused the gradient over 2,000 feet. As the collecting platform moves onwards, it is mining this heat store, which is then renewed in succeeding months.

The Department of Energy has been funding an OTEC (Ocean Thermal Energy Conversion) program since 1974. Initially, DoE spent money rather cautiously—in 1976, the total was $8 million spread over 30 contracts—because of the uncertainties involved: One staffer of the congressional Office of Technology Assessment that year called OTEC a "wacky, improbable technology," according to an article in *Chemical Engineering*. Two early contracts turned out to be most important, one with TRW Inc.'s energy group at Redondo Beach, California, and the other with Lockheed Missile and Space Co.'s ocean energy systems group in Sunnyvale, California. Both companies pursued the concept because they believe such plants would find early market niches as power sources for off-shore chemical plants, to produce ammonia hydrogen, or for aluminum processing, a belief borne out by events in 1980. Both companies propose to build huge buoy-like structures floating in the ocean with long pipes reaching down about one kilometer (more than half a mile) to pump up cold water needed to cool the working fluid. Lockheed's early design envisioned a power output of 360 Mw but one-third would be consumed on board, mostly for pumping the cooling water.

As the primary energy is virtually free, renewable, and inexhaustible, and given considerable enthusiasm in Congress for the idea right from the start, OTEC was at least assured of a reasonable trial. In mid-1978 the Office of Technology Assessment reported to Congress that OTEC plants were unlikely to become a "viable part of the U.S. energy supply in this century" but nevertheless recommended continued funding in the range of tens of millions of dollars until the mid-1980's. As it happened, in 1980 OTEC turned out to be one of the first alternative energy systems to begin the transition from the experimental to the commercial stage, according to an October 6, 1980, story in *Business Week.* Following the success of a small 60-kilowatt Lockheed demonstration plant that churned out electricity off Hawaii in a three-month trial, Congress passed legislation committing the Department of Energy to put up 10,000 Mw of OTEC capacity by the year 2000, including a $2 billion loan-guarantee program. DoE was looking for design proposals to construct up to three 40-Mw pilot plants by 1986, estimated to cost about $2,000 per kilowatt hour, twice the cost of nuclear plants ($1,000/kwh) and more than twice the cost of coal-fired plants ($900/kwh). Nevertheless, DoE officials estimated that OTECs moored off Puerto Rico or Hawaii could produce power for less than 10 cents/kwh compared to an expected average cost of up to 20 cents/kwh on the continental United States by 1990.

Not only utilities, but also chemical and aluminum producers are beginning to pick up on the idea first outlined at the 1974 and 1976 Miami Beach hydrogen conferences: *Business Week* reported that a consortium of seven ammonia producers led by Devco International Inc., of Tulsa, Oklahoma, planned to apply to DoE to design a $200 million, 40-Mw plant ship to be stationed off the coast of Brazil to produce 140 metric (154 short) tons of ammonia a day. Scaled up later to an output of 1,250 metric (1,380 short) tons per day, Devco executives believed that production costs in 1990 would be about $230 per metric ton ($209 per short ton), competitive with Gulf Coast prices expected by then. According to *Business Week*, Reynolds Metals Co. is also very interested in utilizing OTEC-generated electricity for aluminum production.

But the obstacles in scaling-up OTEC barges remain formidable. Plant and barge have to survive for at least 30 years in harsh ocean conditions; the deep-water pipes reaching far below the surface must be just about unbreakable; and methods will have to be developed to keep water intakes and heat exchangers free from slime and marine growth such as barnacles. But given the prospect of free primary energy plus a financial assist from the U.S. government, a number of companies were expected to jump on the OTEC bandwagon.

Wind Power

Another variant of solar energy is wind power, and the beginning of 1978 marked the advent of the first major new wind-power installation in recent years, a 200-kilowatt, 100-foot- (31-meter-) high experimental machine in Clayton, New Mexico, that cost $1.2 million. At $6,250 per kilowatt, that's roughly six times the per-kilowatt investment cost of a nuclear plant, even though the "fuel" is free (but it is also of negligible cost in nuclear plants). In Denmark, a 2,000-kilowatt unit with a wind generator 54 meters (177 feet) in diameter began operations on the western coast also in 1978. In Britain, a 30-kilowatt, three-bladed "aerogenerator" with a 17-meter (55.8-foot) diameter is churning out electricity for the local grid in Aldborough, North Yorkshire, at reportedly rock-bottom investment costs—about £100 or $190 per kilowatt, according to European news accounts. Sandia Laboratories in the United States and the German aerospace firm VFW in Europe experimented with smaller, lighter "troposkien"[5] wind generators that resemble oversized eggbeaters. In 1980, DoE was supporting the construction of wind turbine systems ranging in size from 100 kilowatts to 2.5 Mw to collect data for future commercial wind farms, according to a November 6, 1980, report in *Engineering News Record.*

An engineering professor at the Amherst campus of the University of Massachusetts, William Heronemus, is probably America's Mr. Wind Power. Heronemus has developed a concept of rows of huge wind generator towers far off New England's shore that would electrolyze hydrogen from sea water to transport energy to shore. As early as 1968 Heronemus began investigating eight different ways of generating energy without pollution. Wind power was one of them, and it attracted him in part at least for personal reasons. "I was a Naval officer, and I'm quite a sailor," he told a utility newsletter reporter. Heronemus has been intrigued by boats and the wind to the extent that he even designed a catamaran in which a windmill powered the ship's propeller. His research led in 1971 to his first proposal for a floating windmill system that would produce electricity to split seawater into hydrogen and oxygen, piping the hydrogen to shore for power production. Heronemus claims that these early figures showed the system was economical, even "before the . . . oil cost increases."

For massive hydrogen production from the sea, Heronemus proposes an awesome array of 700-foot (213-meter) aluminum towers grouped in clusters, with each tower carrying 34 wind turbines, 60 feet (18 meters) in diameter, off the Maine shore. The central masts would rest on submerged flotation bodies counterweighted by concrete ballast further down in the water. Heronemus has also worked on other, smaller tower designs that could be implanted into the sands of Georges Bank or Nantucket or New York shoals. To be economical each station must produce at least 2 megawatts peak power, 3.4 megawatts for the biggest tower. Heronemus has designed one such grid that would comprise almost 14,000 units aligned in a north-south pattern that would begin 10 miles off Cape Cod—far enough to minimize visual pollution, he says— and stretching as far as 100 miles (160 kilometers). Such a grid could supply almost all of the 159 million megawatt hours per year required by New England, Heronemus claims.

Central to Heronemus's concepts is the use of hydrogen as an energy storage and transport medium. Each tower cluster is equipped with machinery, first, to distill pure water from sea water. The pure water, essential for the electrolyzing process, would then be broken down into hydrogen and oxygen by pressure electrolyzers, and the high-pressure hydrogen would be fed to shore through submerged concrete pipes. At the far sea end of the main trunk, Heronemus would place a submerged deepwater hydrogen storage system capable of holding up to 40 percent of the system's annual hydrogen production. The storage system consists of cylindrical concrete hulls ballasted with sand and gravel to provide neutral buoyancy capable of holding hydrogen at pressures of up to 3,000 psi (207 bars). During strong winds (meaning more hydrogen output) the storage tanks will take up excess hydrogen and will release it into the lower-pressure trunk pipe during calm periods when production is low or zero. On shore, the energy system would consist mostly of fuel cell–powered mini substations to provide pollution-free electricity in the New England area.

Ever the true salt, Heronemus gives short shrift to the objection that his strings of wind-power derricks extending for miles out to sea would hamper navigation. "Hogwash!" he wrote in one of his papers.

If there were a proper level of navigation in New England waters, some of us wouldn't be concerned about our economic future. Navigation as practiced by the typical New England fisherman would *profit* from this scheme—they have always wanted streetmarkers and signs to compensate for their inoperative compasses.

As to damage to fish and the fishing industry, Heronemus says disturbance would be slight during construction of the system and zero afterwards. Oxygen produced as a by-product, if bubbled through the water, would result only in enrichment of fish life. There might be interference with fishing operations as such, Heronemus concedes, but he says in view of overfishing of these offshore waters by (mostly foreign) fishing fleets, "honor and acclaim should go to *any* process which would slow down even somewhat the deliberate rape of our shelf fisheries which is now systematically being conducted by our friends from overseas."

Until now, none of Heronemus's ideas have been put into practice, and because of the sheer size of his projects, there is doubt that they will be carried out in the near future. It's a long way from the 200-kilowatt Clayton generator to an offshore wind-power system rated at tens of thousands of megawatts.

Those put off by Heronemus's technological gigantism, even though the technology—wind and hydrogen—is essentially benign, can find comfort in small-scale residential wind-power systems that rely on relatively small amounts of hydrogen as an energy-storage "buffer" for windless days. One early system utilizing off-the-shelf components was suggested at the 1974 THEME conference by Professor L. W. Zelby, an electrical engineering specialist at the University of Oklahoma at Norman. Basing his assumptions on a minimum wind speed of about 6 miles (10 kilometers) per hour, which occurs about 80 percent of the time in central Oklahoma and also in other parts of the country, and energy requirements of about 30,000 kwh for a home of about 200 square meters (2,200 square feet) with normal utilities and insulation, Zelby calculated an energy storage need of at least 6,000 kwh annually. But since it would be desirable to draw off the hydrogen gas under pressure, pressurizing equipment would require another 1,500 kwh, bringing the total annual storage requirement to about 7,500 kwh. In terms of storage tank size, this would be less than 2 cubic meters (71 cubic feet). Peak load demands would require about 15 kw but this could be relaxed considerably "by not running the washer, dryer, and dishwasher concurrently," Zelby said. To convert the available wind energy, Zelby figures that a relatively simple windmill with a 14-meter (46-foot) blade diameter would be sufficient, and the total setup, using commercially available components, would have cost about $5,000 at the time. Simplicity is the key: The engine needed to power the generator on no-wind days would be a 9-horsepower lawnmower engine, easily modified to burn hydrogen.

Zelby is convinced that the wind conditions of Oklahoma hold true for much of the continental United States, and he says his down-home system could work well in about 50 percent of the country.

Similarly, a wind-power system providing up to 100 percent of the total energy required for a 100-head dairy farm, using hydrogen and also hot water as storage mediums, was suggested two years later at the 1976 Miami Beach hydrogen conference by two researchers from the Institute of Gas Technology, Raymond Tison and Nicholas P. Biederman, as part of a study for ERDA and the National Science Foundation. Tison and Biederman found that, given the present state of technology, using hydrogen was not economically feasible for cash grain operations such as corn and soybeans because of the need for large amounts of energy storage for crop drying. It does look attractive for confinement-type mass animal husbandry operations because of the relatively even, flat pattern of energy needed throughout the year to run electric motors, lights, and space heaters. Like Zelby's Oklahoma domestic system, the farm system would rely on compressed gaseous hydrogen for storage. Unlike Zelby, who suggested using a lawnmower engine to drive an electric generator, the IGT scientists would produce electricity from hydrogen- and air-fed fuel cells; adding a bank of more or less normal batteries as additional "buffer" would permit them to use smaller, less expensive fuel cells for peak demand. Tison and Biederman, who ran their assumptions and data through a computer, believe an optimum wind-energy system for a dairy farm of the size mentioned, using both hydrogen and hot water for storage and employing current technology, could be had for less than $100,000 and would produce energy at costs of 10–15 cents per kilowatt hour. This is a high figure; at the time U.S. domestic electricity cost about 5 cents per kilowatt hour.

Geothermal Energy

Geothermal energy was first exploited in Italy in 1904 in fields near Pisa. According to a survey by an American team, the Futures Group of Glastonbury, Connecticut, the total output of installed geothermal power plants around the world was only about 1,000 Mwe in the mid-seventies—less than the output of a single modern nuclear power plant.

In 1975, the U.S. Geological Survey (USGS) released the first comprehensive assessment of national geothermal resources. As reported in an industry publication, the *Engineering Mining Journal*, the survey concluded that there is a great deal of geothermal energy in all 50 states, but only a small percentage can be tapped with existing technology. In all, the USGS estimated that the United States has geothermal resources potentially capable of producing about 42,000 Mw-centuries—a Mw-century is equal to 1,000 kilowatts of electricity produced continuously for 100 years—at costs ranging from then current levels to about twice that much. Adding *estimates* of as yet undiscovered geothermal resources would bring the total to 150,000 Mw-centuries, according to the USGS, which termed the potential as extremely important—although it will not solve the country's energy problem by itself.

More recently, Sandia Laboratories in Albuquerque, New Mexico, has developed an as yet theoretical hydrogen production method that combines elements of the chemistry of thermochemical water-splitting with heat input from geothermal sources. According to a report in *Science News* of January 7, 1978, the idea is to have water react with hot magma in the earth's crust, a method that sounds "a bit futuristic" but that the Sandia group of four scientists says will work. In this approach, iron contained in the magma would combine under high-temperature conditions—best results were obtained at about 1,200°C. (2,190°F.)—with the water's oxygen, freeing the hydrogen at a rate of about 500 pounds (227 kilograms) of hydrogen per hour when coupled to an injection rate of 20,000 gallons (76,000 liters) of water per hour. An addition of 10 percent biomass—refuse like organic garbage, sewage sludge, straw and stalks, seaweed—would produce gases containing 10 percent hydrogen, 4 percent carbon dioxide, 1 percent carbon monoxide, and a trace of methane. At roughly half that temperature much more methane would be produced but less hydrogen and carbon monoxide.

As to practicality, the Sandia team admits that drilling far down to reach such temperatures is a big obstacle, but they say there are some magma chambers within two or three kilometers of the ocean floor that would be reachable with an extension of present drilling techniques.

Variations on Water Power

A coldly exotic source of primary energy suggested by Swiss researchers is "glacier power" in Greenland. Ulrich La Roche, a scientist working for Swiss power equipment–maker Brown, Boveri & Cie, proposed tapping Greenland's enormous hydroelectric potential, which he estimates amounts to between 100 gigawatts (a gigawatt is 1,000 megawatts; a terawatt is 1,000 gigawatts) and one terawatt. This is far in excess of what the population in the ice-free coastal range would need for itself and is therefore exportable. La Roche suggests that this energy export could take the form of ammonia, synthesized from hydrogen, which in turn would be produced by "glacier power plants." La Roche, who also presented his ideas at the 1976 Miami Beach hydrogen conference, said water collects inland on Greenland's high plateau and then drops to the sea as water or icebergs through the ice-free coastal zone—a drop that would permit construction of large hydro plants. La Roche mentions the possibility of changing the albedo—the degree of reflection—of the Greenland ice to increase the water flow: If the starkly reflecting white of the ice surface could be darkened, more ice would melt and more water would flow. La Roche himself is apparently a bit awed by the idea: "Only gradually will the full potential be available as realization of hydropower systems has to go hand in hand with more detailed knowledge of the hydrology and glaciology to exploit it further," he said in Miami Beach.

An interesting "small is beautiful" variant of hydropower-for-hydrogen schemes is a 1978 proposal by the Institute of Gas Technology to convert small water-storage dams and waterfalls too uneconomical for large-scale hydroelectricity production to local hydrogen production. A study sponsored by the Department of Energy estimated that there are some 50,000 falling-water sites in the United States that, using advanced low-capital-cost electrolyzer technology, could produce up to 240 trillion Btus worth of hydrogen fuel annually, according to an account in *Engineering News Record.* The hydrogen could be sold as a blend to local natural gas networks, stretching supplies by up to 20 percent with current pipeline, metering and end-users' combustion equipment. It could also be sold together with by-product oxygen as an industrial chemical commodity. The study estimates production costs at between $5 and $30 per million Btus, depending on the reservoir's capacity and head. At the low end of the price range, this hydrogen would be competitive with natural gas supplements that utilities have to buy occasionally when demand exceeds supply. Even the most expensive price would be competitive with industrial "commodity" hydrogen today, the study asserts.

In 1979 DoE funded first-year contracts for a demonstrator project in the village of Potsdam, in upstate New York, that will use the General Electric–developed advanced electrolyzers. Under a $2.9 million joint program of DoE, the New York State Energy and Research Development Authority (NYSERDA) and the village of Potsdam, the half-century-old dam will be revived and upgraded to generate 700 kilowatts instead of the original 150 kilowatts to produce electricity as well as hydrogen for the village: slightly less than one-third of the electric power will be used for production of 1.5 million cubic feet of commercial-grade hydrogen a month worth about $90,000, according to preliminary estimates.

6

Water Vapor from the Tailpipe: Hydrogen as Automotive Fuel

First Attempts

Back in 1966, three years before Buckminster Fuller was telling college audiences how to use the world's energy "current account" instead of robbing the global energy "savings account," a devout Mormon high school student piloted a wildly backfiring Model A Ford truck—license plate "Utah 1576, Horseless Carriage"—through the quiet residential streets of Provo. With the help of his father, a teacher and some friends, 16-year-old Roger Billings had spent some three months and 800 working hours, not just to refurbish another copy of the all-American automotive classic, but to make technological history. That Model A truck, which delivered little power but "an amazing repertoire of noises," according to Roger, was the first internal combustion-engine car in the United States fueled by hydrogen. For Roger, who had started tinkering with hydrogen as a fuel two years earlier, it was a momentous event: "Those were the proudest days of my life," he recalled later, "driving that truck on a fuel they said would never work."

Billings was not the only auto buff then fascinated by the possibilities of hydrogen. Enthusiastic amateurs as well as professionals were beginning to think about clean fuels, picking up where Erren and his contemporaries had left off three decades earlier.

Most representative of the hydrogen enthusiasts who, stimulated by the environmental movement, wanted to exploit the unique properties of the element, were four members of the Perris Smogless Automobile Association, a group of residents of Perris, a small California town a dozen miles south of Riverside. The four—a civil engineer, a newspaper publisher, and two aerospace engineers—were among the earliest to share a commitment to ridding the environment of what they considered its worst enemy, automotive pollution, years before it became the

Figure 6.1. The first U.S. car to run on hydrogen, a Model A Ford truck converted in the mid-sixties by Roger Billings. Photo courtesy Billings Energy Corp.

nemesis word in advanced energy circles and long before that first 1973 oil shock. Patrick Lee Underwood, one of the aerospace engineers, had worked for Lockheed in various research programs, and had thought about hydrogen as aviation fuel in the late sixties; he had heard about the hydrogen-fueled experimental B-57 bomber that the U.S. National Advisory Committee for Aeronautics had test-flown successfully back in 1957. The *First Annual Report of the Perris Smogless Automobile Association*, published in 1971, stated that the idea

> of using hydrogen and oxygen in a standard reciprocating automobile engine had occurred to Mr. Underwood several years ago but no constructive effort had been expended; indeed, the idea was not very well developed, generally because it was thought to be under development as a natural course by the aerospace industry.

The actual project got its start in December 1969 when Underwood challenged an editorial written by Dwight B. Minnich in his paper, *The Perris Progress*, asserting that there was no solution to the emission prob-

lem of the internal combustion engine. A month later Minnich, Underwood, and Fredric F. Nardecchia got together in Minnich's office to
sketch out the outline of a hydrogen test program; they were joined
shortly after that meeting by Paul B. Dieges. The first test vehicle was a
1950 Studebaker, "thought to have a working engine" and bought for
$10 from a junk dealer. Several attempts with various hydrogen-oxygen
and hydrogen-air mixtures failed, but finally the group succeeded in starting the engine. They fed gaseous hydrogen into the manifold intake, by-
passing assorted piping and valve arrangements. The tests were run by "remote control from behind a large rock." After adjusting gas pressures and
carrying out some other tests, the group established that the engine could be
made to run quietly, start easily, and respond rapidly to control changes,
that it did not knock or display "any other disturbing sounds," but that
it used an unexpectedly large amount of hydrogen. The Studebaker
project was abandoned after the engine failed to restart following a final
test in which the engine grossly overrevved on too much hydrogen.

In their next project the group converted a 1930 Model A Ford pickup
truck for road trials, again burning hydrogen with oxygen. The arrangement also included a condenser to cool the exhaust vapor back to water,
with excess hydrogen to be recirculated to the combustion process. The
truck, licensed as an antique, made its first run in February 1970, covering about a mile, followed later by several trips through and around Perris, plus some demonstration runs for officials of the California Air
Resources Board. In a paper presented at the 1971 Intersociety Energy
Conversion Engineering Conference, Underwood and Dieges reported
that the Model A truck worked fine. The exhaust water vapor was continuously accumulated and drained off and "the water was found to be
potable but somewhat oily and rusty tasting."

Next, the Perris group planned to convert a 1952 Cadillac that had
been donated for experimenting with hydrogen operation, but those
plans were aborted with the announcement of the 1970 Clean Air Race,
sponsored both by the California and Massachusetts Institutes of Technology. This was a coast-to-coast event from Cambridge, Massachusetts,
to Pasadena, California, that would pit all types of non- or low-polluting
cars against each other. The Perris project had obtained one of several
assistance grants from General Motors to help prepare a Ford pickup
truck to operate on liquid hydrogen and liquid oxygen for the race. Unfortunately, the project was stopped by a variety of logistical and mana-
gerial problems. For example, they could not get enough small vacuum-
jacketed dewars (thermos bottle–like, double-walled containers) to carry
adequate liquid hydrogen to propel the car from one major refueling
place to the next (Linde, a commercial hydrogen manufacturer, had of-

fered whatever liquid hydrogen was required but the problem was to bridge the large gaps between the various Linde distributorships). In the course of race preparations, the team developed such novel hardware items as a so-called "oxyburetor," analogous to a carburetor in which hydrogen takes the place of air, drawing in a proportionally metered amount of oxygen instead of hydrocarbons as second gas.

The truck eventually did run in preliminary trials with top speeds of about 40 miles (64 kilometers) per hour, but its ability to climb hills was "poor" due to an insufficient oxygen flow rate limited by inherent restraints of the oxygen cylinders and the flow-rate regulators.

The most poignant and revealing part of that *First Annual Report*—as far as is known, there was no other—was the balance sheet. Expenditures totalled $8,038 for a whole year of work, with major individual contributions of $2,465.68 by Underwood, $1,828.68 from Minnich, and close to $400 each from Dieges and Nardecchia. General Motors chipped in $2,180, and the California Society of Professional Engineers contributed $300. The biggest single expenditure items were $1,429.01 for patent fees, $1142.46 in travel costs for the Clean Air Car Race, and $877.72 for exotic parts for the noncompeting Ford pickup truck. Hydrogen cost $241.84 (Linde did contribute some hydrogen free of charge). The oxygen bill ran to $50.20.

The very name of the Perris group evoked pioneering associations: The "smogless automobile" recalled the "horseless carriage" days of a bygone era, transposed to the dawn of the hydrogen era. The language of the group's annual report testifies to a sense of humility but also of mission and excitement. In the preface, the four describe themselves as

> average business and professional men with average means and the usual family and personal obligations. We have, of necessity, pursued our regular livelihoods during the course of this effort. These remarkable results, which have vastly exceeded even our own expectations, have thus far been elicited by a commitment of only somewhat higher order than we might have otherwise directed toward civic, social, church or hobby activities, plus our vacations which all of us devoted to this project.

Their sense of outrage at the ravages upon the environment became clear in the report's opening words:

> Future historians, if there are any, may well record that the private automobile and not the nuclear bomb was the most disastrous invention of a society so obsessed with technology that it never recognized the failures of engineering run rampant until too late. For the automobile-freeway

system is surely the most inefficient, dangerous, costly, and environmentally damaging transportation ever conceived; about the only real plus is flexibility, and the actual popularizing features are frighteningly Freudian. . . . survival demands that the air pollution caused by the automobile be eliminated almost immediately.

Strong words from three engineers and a small-town newspaper publisher.

Industry and Science Take a Look

As time went on, industry began to take more interest. Just about nine years after Roger Billings rattled through the streets of Provo, West German car maker Daimler-Benz unveiled a hydrogen-powered minibus at the 1975 International Auto Show in Frankfurt, the first ever shown publicly by a major manufacturer. A second version was shown at the 1977 show, followed by a hydrogen city bus in 1979.

In that first Daimler-Benz bus, some 50,000 liters (13,200 gallons) of hydrogen were stored at room temperature under pressure of 25 to 30 bars (363 to 435 psi) in a tank containing titanium-iron hydride, one of a number of chemical compounds that can store hydrogen gas under certain pressure and temperature conditions and that release the gas when heated (more on storage technology in Chapter 8). Daimler-Benz said with average speeds of up to 60 kilometers (37 miles) per hour, one tankload of hydrogen was enough for a range of 100 to 120 kilometers (60 to 75 miles)—a five- to six-fold range increase compared to an electric-powered vehicle with a storage battery weighing roughly the same as the hydride tank. To avoid the backfiring so typical of early hydrogen-fueled engines, Daimler-Benz simply recycled about one quarter of the exhaust into the engine, a trick that completely eliminates engine knock as well but results in a loss of power. Heat required to release the hydrogen from the hydride is provided by the hot water from the radiator and engine cooling jacket, which is fed via a heat exchanger into the hydride tank.

Daimler-Benz figures that storage capacity of the hydride tank could be increased relatively easily two to three times within the next 10 years. This would make hydrogen fuel ideal for smog-plagued urban areas, provided that somebody like the oil companies would be willing to set up the required network of hydrogen "gas" stations—a big if. The harmlessness of the hydrogen "exhaust" was driven home to German TV viewers in a film clip, loaned by Jet Propulsion Laboratory in Pasadena, California, for a news feature on the 1976 Frankfurt show. The camera focused first

Figure 6.2. A staff member of the Jet Propulsion Laboratory demonstrated graphically that the exhaust of a hydrogen-powered car consists of almost pure water. He drank the water that condensed out of steam from the tailpipe of the car. (Section of a 16-mm movie made by the JPL)

on the exhaust pipe of an idling car emitting white vapors. Next, a man held a drinking glass against the exhaust tube allowing the vapors to cool and condense into a colorless liquid. In the startling final shot, the man lifted the glass to his lips and drank it down—almost pure water.

Between the early Billings effort and the Daimler-Benz prototype lies a decade of research, most of it by university scientists. Whatever Roger's reasons for choosing a Model A were, the choice was curiously appropriate: The Model A had begun the era of automotive mass mobility, which in the end threatened to choke to death on its own pollution, giving rise to the electric car as an environmentally acceptable alternative. However, mated to clean-burning hydrogen as fuel, the conventional Otto engine, pronounced dead or dying in some quarters, again looks like the most promising power plant for many decades to come. Hydrogen proponents argue that the electric car, while elegant in conception, is uneconomical and cumbersome unless somebody comes up with an ultra-light battery holding much more energy than current types. Driving ranges of 30 to 40 miles (48 to 64 kilometers) at low speeds (otherwise the battery discharges current too quickly) and the need to recharge the heavy batteries for hours make the electric urban vehicle a rather hopeless concept for metropolitan areas like Los Angeles, for example, with its hundreds of miles of freeway.

At the same time, automotive engine technology, the know-how of manufacturing reasonably efficient, long-lasting internal combustion engines—both the gasoline-burning Otto engine and the sparkplug-less diesel—is mature. Given the billions of dollars car manufacturers have invested in engine plants, the hydrogen community believes it would be economic folly on the grandest scale to discard all those plants, machine tools, transfer lines, know-how, and expertise laboriously acquired in roughly three quarters of a century. Instead of throwing the baby out with the bathwater and coming up with new and largely untried propulsion systems we should switch the fuel.

"It is not the internal combustion engine that pollutes our air, but its present fuels," declared Kurt Weil, professor emeritus at Stevens Institute of Technology, Hoboken, New Jersey, at the landmark 1972 Energy Conversion Conference held in San Diego, California. Weil, who is German-born, has experience with hydrogen going back to the 1930s when he and Erren suggested a scheme to use excess capacity in Germany's electric power grid to produce hydrogen through electrolysis (see Chapter 3). Suggesting a similar system for the United States, Weil told his fellow researchers at San Diego:

> the central element of such a system is the hydrogen-burning internal combustion engine which already exists in practical and proven models. Its multi-fuel and mixed-fuel version offers not only complete adaptation of all existing internal combustion engines (about 150 million engines in the USA alone) but it also allows complete flexibility in
>
> - phasing out hydrocarbon fuels when, to what degree, and at which rate desired, and geographic adaptation to various available fuels and mixtures;
> - reducing or eliminating air pollution from internal combustion engines, including carbon dioxide, nitric oxides and particulate matter to any degree, at any time of danger and at any region.

It was this lure of the clean-burning engine that prompted Roger Billings, today one of the prime movers in hydrogen applications, to get involved. Billings had not taken any formal chemistry or physics courses until he read a book that told how water could be broken down into hydrogen and oxygen by electrolysis and that hydrogen, burned in air, turns into water vapor again. He studied chemistry, and as public interest in pollution began to stir, he started experimenting with hydrogen-burning engines. One of his first machines, a modified lawnmower engine, ran on hydrogen for 20 seconds. In another attempt he nearly blew up his kid brother, who was watching the mixture control in a glass flask that was part of the experimental carburetor. The highly volatile hydrogen-air mixture promptly backfired into the glass flask, which exploded. Fortunately, Roger had the foresight—he attributes it to divine guidance—to cover the flask with a heavy coat beforehand. He once told a reporter for a Mormon magazine:

> I did this before most of my experiments because I didn't know exactly what I was doing. In the prayer I asked that we be protected and given inspiration to know what we should and shouldn't do.
>
> Immediately I had a very strong feeling that I should cover the flask, so I took my father's heavy canvas trench coat, zippered and buttoned it and put it over the flask. When I started the engine it backfired. The fire followed the perfect mixture of hydrogen and air into the flask. There was a tremendous explosion and the coat was ripped to shreds, but neither I nor my little brother who had been kneeling close to the flask was hurt. I have a collection of experiences like that when God has helped me.

A few years later, as a graduate student in chemistry at Brigham Young University, he entered and won the antipollution category of the 1972 Urban Vehicle Design Competition with a hydrogen-fueled Volkswagen, far exceeding then existing federal clean air standards. Billings's VW exhaust was said to be even cleaner than the air the carburetor was taking in to burn the hydrogen, but that may have been hyperbole.

Runner-up in the antipollution category but winner of the overall design category in the competition was a student team from UCLA that had entered a hydrogen-burning American Motors Gremlin. The UCLA team captain was a student named Frank E. Lynch, and right after the results were announced, Billings and Lynch decided to team up to tackle the problem of building the pollution-free car of the future. The result of that resolve was the Billings Energy Corporation of Provo, established to promote and eventually make money off the hydrogen-fueled automobile. (Lynch left the Billings group a few years later.) Since then Billings and his staff have converted a Japanese Mazda with a rotary Wankel engine, a Ford Falcon, a Chevrolet Monte Carlo, a Winnebago Motor Home, and most recently, in 1978, a small city bus to hydrogen. The Winnebago was a kind of demonstrator for "hydrogen in the home": In addition to fueling the car's 440-cubic-inch (7.2-liter) V-8 engine, gaseous hydrogen was used to run on-board appliances such as the space

Figure 6.3. Roger Billings's hydrogen-fueled minibus linking the cities of Provo and Orem in Utah. A prime reason for using hydrogen in cars is to combat air pollution. Photo courtesy of Billings Energy Corp.

heater, cooking range, refrigerator, air conditioner, and power generator.

In addition to Billings, the Perris group, and Daimler-Benz, there were at least a dozen attempts in the 1960s and 1970s by institutions or private companies to use hydrogen, either alone or as a supplement to regular gasoline to improve emissions performance—fewer unburned hydrocarbons, carbon monoxide and NOX emissions, the last being the group name given to various nitrogen oxides that occur in any combustion process because of the nitrogen in air.

While the general feasibility of burning hydrogen had been pretty well established, initially researchers were plagued by the backfiring problem, and there was no agreement how best to meter the fuel flow—by fuel injection or by more or less conventional carburetion. Some, like Bill Escher, suggested a completely closed, cycle system carrying both liquid hydrogen and oxygen on board a Model A truck; the condensed water vapor was to be used as cooling water in the radiator! Others proposed and tried what amounted to a kind of micro-refinery under the hood of the car, breaking down conventional gasoline or kerosene into hydrogen

Figure 6.4. Roger Billings and one of his hydrogen-fueled engines.

and other components before shooting it into the engine. The idea was to clean up emissions and also to ease the transition into the hydrogen economy.

Two scientists from the University of Oklahoma, Roger J. Schoeppel and Richard G. Murray, were also among the first to begin mating hydrogen to the internal combustion engine, three years after Billings's experiment. Working as a team, Schoeppel and Murray converted a single cylinder 4-horsepower lawnmower engine to hydrogen.

In 1970, Murray and Schoeppel received a contract from the Environmental Protection Agency and adapted a 3.5-horsepower, 4-cycle engine to hydrogen by injection—a significant change, as will be explained later. Modifications included installing a second camshaft system to operate the hydrogen injection valve and installation of a water cooling system to improve cooling characteristics of cast iron cylinders. Tests were encouraging, Murray and Schoeppel said in a paper. Fuel flow was only one-third that of normal gasoline, torque was fairly constant over a wide speed range, and power could be boosted beyond the manufacturer's rating simply by injecting more hydrogen because exhaust temperatures were relatively low.[1] The two scientists believed that hydrocarbon, carbon monoxide and dioxide, sulfur, lead, and organic compound emissions were negligible. As to NOX emissions, they claimed that the engine produced "far less concentrated" emissions than gasoline-powered engines, but these claims were not sustained by other hydrogen researchers.

In another significant early test, two University of Miami researchers, Michael R. Swain and Robert R. Adt, Jr., reported the successful conversion of a Toyota 1600-cc (97.6-cubic-inch) station wagon, lent by a Miami Toyota dealer, to hydrogen. Swain and Adt devised a new fuel admission system dubbed HIT, for hydrogen induction technique, which took advantage of specific hydrogen characteristics of high flame speeds and wide range of fuel-to-air ratios: The two reasoned that instead of changing the total amount of fuel and air for different power output—stepping on the gas increases the amount of both fuel and air going through the carburetor into the engine—the fuel-to-air ratio itself was changed. In other words, low power meant less hydrogen but the same amount of air. For more power, more hydrogen but the same amount of air—a richer mixture—was injected. It is similar to the diesel principle; in a diesel engine the amount of fuel is also varied with the same amount of air.

Swain and Adt reported fuel consumption very roughly equivalent to 42 miles per gallon of gasoline—a 50 percent improvement in brake thermal efficiency—at 40 miles (64 kilometers) per hour, but the number may have been somewhat on the high side. The car was driven only up to a speed of 60 miles (96 kilometers) per hour, not because it wouldn't go any faster but because of speed limits.

Another tack was described at the 1972 San Diego conference by Harold Sorensen, of the International Materials Corporation, of Boston, Massachusetts. Sorensen proposed to fuel a conventional car with standard unleaded gasoline but in effect burn only hydrogen in the engine, with carbon dioxide and water vapor as the only emission vapors. His trick was to "reform" or break down the gasoline aboard the test car (a 1971 Ford Torino with a 305 cu. in. V-8 engine) via heated steam into hydrogen and carbon dioxide in a multi-stage process. The Boston Reformed Fuel Car, as it was known, was also developed in part under a contract with the Environmental Protection Agency (EPA). Sorensen said the only effects on the engine in early tests were that spark plugs and exhaust valves were slightly rusted after 50 hours of operation because of high-temperature water vapor, a problem Sorensen felt could be licked by metallurgical changes. *Business Week* reported in March 1973 that the company had not come up with a test car it had contracted for delivery to the EPA in November 1972. In 1976, scientists at the First World Hydrogen Conference reported that the Boston fuel car effort was terminated when the IMC corporation folded.

Siemens, the German maker of electrical equipment, also announced in 1973 that it had developed a "crack carburetor" using a catalytic process to break down gasoline into methane, hydrogen, and carbon monoxide, but the project was dropped two years later because Siemens couldn't find any takers.

Another project receiving considerable publicity in early 1974 was conducted by the Jet Propulsion Laboratory of the California Institute of Technology and sponsored by NASA. It involved burning hydrogen together with conventional gasoline in car engines at ultralean conditions. Hydrogen is generated aboard the car from gasoline using hot air at 1,500° to 2,000°F. (815° to 1,100°C.). Unlike the Boston car, in which all gasoline would be converted into hydrogen, only small amounts would be produced. Hydrogen would have the effect of extending the flammability limits of the fuel-air mixture downwards, requiring even less fuel with the same amount of air. This was expected to lead to "a striking improvement in thermal efficiency" and very significant reduction in the emission level. The Caltech car did turn out to be more efficient and produce less NOX, but at a power loss, and other emissions were still high.

In similar tests evaluating hydrogen injection into commercially unleaded gasoline, two General Motors engineers found that the lean limits could be reduced further and NOX emissions cut drastically, but at a cost. R. F. Stebar and F. B. Parks said at a Society of Automotive Engineers conference in Detroit in February-March 1974 that by adding about 10 percent hydrogen, the lean limit went down by almost one-third, NOX emissions were reduced to one seventy-fifth, and carbon monoxide levels stayed about the same, but hydrocarbon emissions went up dramatically. Although operating somewhat more efficiently, the engine produced only about two-thirds of its normal-fuel power. Stebar and Parks concluded that most of the fuel apparently must be reformed but "because of [hydrogen] generator inefficiencies, overall fuel economy will suffer. Accordingly, future applications of the hydrogen supplemental fuel concept will depend largely on the development of a satisfactory, on-board generator." In other words, Sorensen's idea of converting *all*, not just a small portion, of the fuel was basically right in terms of emission control, but an efficient way of cracking the gasoline is still needed.

In Europe, Renault, the French car manufacturer, announced in 1972 that it was planning to build a hydrogen-powered car, a modified Renault T-4 propelled by burning hydrogen in sophisticated fuel cells. Nothing ever came of it other than studies on paper, apparently, because of the absence of active government support.

Carrying the Fuel on Board: The Key Problem

In the gasoline-powered or diesel-powered car, storing the fuel is easy. Conventional designs with engines up front usually have the gas tank underneath the trunk, close to rear axle. The classic VW beetle with its rear-mounted engine simply reversed the arrangement. With hydrogen, the situation is different: on-board fuel storage represents one of the key obstacles to the automotive "clean machine." The solution most people think of—storing the gas in steel-walled pressure tanks similar to those used in welding—is out because of excessive weight, although it poses the least design problems. One researcher, Larry Williams of Martin Marietta Aerospace, Denver, Colorado, calculated once that a hydrogen pressure tank capable of holding roughly the same amount of energy as a 80-liter (17.6-gallon) fuel tank for a standard-sized car would have to weigh about one and a half metric tons (1.7 short tons) and would require a pressure of 800 atmospheres as well as steel wall thickness of 7 centimeters (almost 3 inches). Exotic materials such as titanium, carbon, boron, glass composites, or cryogenically formed steels could cut the weight by a maximum factor of about five to maybe 300 kilograms (660 lbs.)—still far too heavy. Even if a pressurized-gas container of acceptable weight, comparable to the 50 kilograms (110 lbs.) of a conventional gas tank, could be developed, pressure containers represent a serious hazard in case of a collision: "These tanks would explode as if they contained high explosives, causing great blast damage and greatly increasing the danger of fire," Williams warned.

The two main storage methods seriously considered, then, are either storing hydrogen cryogenically (i.e., at temperatures of minus 252°C. [minus 421.6°F.], close to the absolute freezing point of minus 273.96°C. [minus 459.69°F.]) or bound within the structures of certain alloys as hydrides.

Cryogenic Hydrogen Storage

Williams, a strong advocate of cryogenic storage for car, truck, and aircraft applications, lists the following main advantages of this storage method:

- lowest cost per unit energy
- lowest weight per unit energy
- simple supply logistics
- normal refuel time required
- no unsurmountable safety problems

The disadvantages are:

- loss of fuel when vehicle is not in operation (the supercold liquid evaporates)
- large tank size
- cryogenic liquid engineering problems

Williams says liquid storage will require the development of highly reliable, low-heat-leak, low-cost storage vessels. Vessels of this type—dewars—have been developed in large sizes for trucks and rail cars, and there have been some models with extremely low evaporation losses.

Apart from the high cost of hydrogen liquefaction, another main argument against this method is the extremely high cost of the storage tanks. A 1972 study by the Oak Ridge National Laboratory said that compared to the roughly $30 expenditure for a conventional car gasoline tank, a liquid-hydrogen storage tank with roughly the same energy equivalent would cost about $2,000, with mass production cutting the cost insignificantly to between $1,200–$1,800—still far too much. Comparable liquid natural gas (LNG) tanks would cost $700 in prototype and $300–$500 in series (Beech Aircraft Corp., of Boulder, Colorado, developed and showed an experimental 18-gallon (68-liter) LNG tank for car use in 1973). A tank for methanol, a liquid synthetic fuel used by Volkswagen in an experimental fleet, would cost only about $35, the report said. (Storage and handling problems and experience are described in more detail in Chapter 10.)

Use of such ultracold fuels poses many problems needing technical solutions, such as simpler methods of metering and measuring vessel content (a new type of gas gauge); small-scale pumps and pressure equipment (the common gasoline pistol-type nozzle won't do; a tightly coupled connection between the liquid-hydrogen pump and the car tank is required); disposal of vented hydrogen; and design optimization for mass production.

Hydride Storage Systems

Hydrides may be the answer to the problem of how to store hydrogen aboard the automobile. Hydrides are compounds originally developed for nuclear power plants to slow down fast electrons, providing a means of controlling nuclear reactions and thus output of a nuclear power plant.

Titanium-iron hydride, for example, the material used in the Billings and Daimler-Benz cars, looks and feels like any ordinary metal—tiny silvery granules without any hint of the unusual. However, they have the remarkable characteristic of absorbing hydrogen like a sponge, with different hydrides soaking up and releasing the gas at different pressure and temperature conditions. Heat is given off when the hydride is formed by the reaction of hydrogen with the metal (heat of formation); the same amount of heat must be added to the hydride to release the hydrogen (heat of decomposition). Hydrides bind the hydrogen atom atomically; the hydrogen atom is integrated into the crystalline structure of the hydride, with the hydrogen atom's electron transferred to the hydride.

Integrated in this way into the storage material, hydrogen does not take up any additional volume as a gas or a liquid would. For this reason, any hydride can carry much more hydrogen energy in terms of space volume than liquid hydrogen, but there is a weight penalty attached. For example, a 100-liter (26.4-gallon) tank of titanium-iron hydride carries 1.2 to 1.5 times as much energy as a 100-liter tank of liquid hydrogen but it weighs about 25 times as much.

Most of the basic research having to do with storing hydrogen in hydride alloys was done for more than a decade by a team at Brookhaven National Laboratory. The first papers were presented in 1966, and as early as 1969, a team of six scientists presented a study, "Metal Hydrides as a Source of Fuel for Vehicular Propulsion," at the International Automotive Engineering Congress in Detroit.

Billings and Daimler-Benz were the first to use hydrides in cars. Billings and his crew converted a Chevrolet Monte Carlo in 1974 to hydrogen, using both a cryogenic dewar-type tank designed by Beech Aircraft Corp. to store liquid hydrogen and a titanium-iron hydride storage tank developed by Billings. The hydride itself was held in a bundle of tubes inside the container, which, said a press release at the time, "resembles a steam boiler." The tank was located where the normal gas tank usually is, below the trunk and behind the rear axle, but it was big and bulky and together with the dewar took up most of the trunk space. Both systems combined gave a range of about 145 miles (230 kilometers). Tank developer Beech said its double-walled steel tank had been vibration-tested for an equivalent of about 200,000 miles (320,000 kilometers) and claimed it was safer than a conventional gas tank in a crash.

After converting dozens of automobiles to hydrogen, Billings had discarded the idea of storing hydrogen as an ultracold liquid on board his cars. Both his 1977 Cadillac, which operates alternatively on hydrogen and gasoline, and his converted garden tractor use titanium-iron hydride tanks. Billings also plans to convert a forklift truck and a lawnmower to hydrogen use, and there is apparently potential for hydrogen-powered mining equipment—examples of special marketing niches where hydrogen, because of its special properties, has an edge on conventional systems.

Take forklifts, for example. There are two basic types, the electric, battery-powered forklift of relatively low power requiring frequent recharging and the conventional gasoline- or diesel-powered machines with more power. "Most of these operate in closed warehouses where pollution is a serious, life-threatening problem," Billings said in a fall 1977 story in the quarterly, Hydrogen Progress, which is published by his firm. "Hydrogen-powered forklifts are the answer. They would eliminate the need for those huge, expensive warehouse exhaust fans." Similar considerations hold for underground mining equipment. Either mines must be equipped with complex ventilation equipment to cope with exhaust fumes from diesel-powered equipment or electrically powered mining equipment must be spark-proofed to eliminate any chance of setting off a mine gas explosion; this generally entails a loss of power. "The advantages of non-polluting but efficient power equipment in the closed environment of an underground mine are obvious," Billings observed.

The Daimler-Benz hydrogen van that was unveiled at the 1975 Frankfurt show also used hydride storage. Daimler-Benz doesn't think that liquid hydrogen is the way to go for cars, mostly because of high liquefaction costs. Liquid hydrogen because of its extreme cold is dangerous to passengers and it burns easily. If it is spilled on tires, they may become brittle and burst. At the 1976 Miami Beach and 1978 Zurich conferences, almost all researchers discussed car applications in terms of hydride storage except for one Japanese and two Germans, who since then have presented a very interesting liquid hydrogen fuel system for cars, described later in this chapter.

Like Billings, Daimler-Benz initially used a titanium-iron storage

Figure 6.5. Daimler-Benz's first hydrogen-powered minibus shown first at the 1975 Frankfurt Auto Show.

hydride, developed at Brookhaven, mainly because their engineers were in a hurry to show the general feasibility of hydride storage and hydrogen as car fuel to a wide public—the press, lay people, and plain car nuts coming to the 1975 Frankfurt Auto Show. "We completed the engine in about two weeks," says Dr. Helmut Buchner, who runs the Daimler-Benz hydrogen-hydride program.

Except for a number of test gauges mounted on the dashboard, the first Daimler-Benz hydrogen bus was indistinguishable from the production model. One had to look very hard to notice anything different on the outside. The gas filler cap was replaced by a small hydrogen intake valve mounted on the right side underneath the body, just behind the front wheel. And when you put your hand in the exhaust it felt lukewarm—almost like the steam from a tea kettle that's just warming up. This was the water exhaust vapor, which is partially recycled through the engine to prevent backfire—a method that also cuts power by about one-third.

(Daimler-Benz acknowledged that the idea of recycling some of the

Figure 6.6. The hydride storage tank in Daimler-Benz's first hydrogen-powered minibus was stored under a seat bench behind the driver.

water vapor from the exhaust to cool the engine and eliminate backfire came from a paper written by Joe Finegold, one of the winners of the original Urban Vehicle Design Competition of 1972. Finegold told me at the 1976 Miami conference that he and his fellow students at UCLA more or less played a hunch when they decided to reroute the exhaust vapors back into the engine. After some early trials on an engine dynamometer, "we towed the car down to the muffler shop to weld on the necessary piping." First, they connected only two of the eight cylinders with so-so results, "but then we connected three cylinders, and it worked great," Finegold recalled.)

Riding the bus around the Daimler-Benz test track at the plant in Stuttgart was not noticeably different from riding an ordinary bus. Engine noise was the same, and the bus swung at a steady 100 kilometers (60 miles) per hour through the banked turns. Once the driver stopped the bus completely on a ten-degree incline, and the vehicle climbed away smoothly in first gear. The 65-liter (17-gallon) tank carrying 200 kilograms (440 lbs.) of titanium-iron hydride was stored under a passenger seat bench. To release the hydrogen, heat from the engine radiator is cycled via a heat exchanger through the hydride tank. The conventional carburetor is absent. Instead a so-called *gasmischer* (gas mixer) mixes air and hydrogen, which is then sucked through the manifold into the engine for normal combustion.

The goal of Daimler-Benz, and of other researchers elsewhere, is to find better hydrides that can store more hydrogen fuel for greater range, cut the still considerable weight of the hydride tank, or do both in some optimum tradeoff. Gasoline, with a low tank-weight of 50 kilograms (110 lbs.) is most efficient when it comes to range versus weight. Methanol, another synthetic fuel, comes off second best, with about half the range of gasoline (more on that later). Both hydrogen and the electric battery are faced with much increased "fuel tank" weights. For comparison purposes, Daimler-Benz settled on a hypothetical tank weighing 500 kilograms (1,100 lbs.), ten times the weight of the standard gas tank.

The result: the currently used titanium-iron hydrides are best, giving a range of around 240 kilometers (150 miles). (As mentioned, the tank used in the actual Daimler-Benz hydrogen bus was only about half that weight, about 250 kilograms [550 lbs.], giving half the range.) The electric car batteries are hopelessly outclassed: With the same "tank"—lead batteries, that is—the range is only 40 kilometers (25 miles)—one-fifth or one-sixth of the titanium-iron value.

Some organizations, such as Ford Motor Co. and British Railways, have been attempting to improve the economics of the electric car by working on high-temperature batteries with temperatures of roughly 400°C. (752°F.) and employing highly corrosive materials such as sulfur, natrium, and sodium. Theoretically, such batteries could quadruple the lead-battery range (always assuming the same basic weight criterion of 500 kilograms) to close to 200 kilometers (125 miles). That would be still considerably less than the range *already achieved* via titanium-iron storage of hydrogen, and it is speculative, hazardous, and so far unsuitable for cars. According to Daimler-Benz scientists, the lifetimes of these experimental high-temperature batteries are still being measured in minutes; heating such a battery to the required temperature before it releases power takes a long time; and the combination of high temperatures plus such volatile materials as natrium and sodium doesn't make for anxiety-free driving.

In 1977, Daimler-Benz unveiled two further refinements of the hydrogen-hydride concepts. One was a passenger car, a 2.8-liter (170-cubic-inch) sedan fueled by both hydrogen and normal gasoline in infinitely variable ratios from pure hydrogen during idling; mostly hydrogen for low-load, low-emission city driving; and switching increasingly to gasoline for maximum power at the car's top speed of 190 kilometers (118 miles) per hour. At low power, the hydrogen acts as an ignition agent—the gasoline-air mixture was so lean that it wouldn't combust, but adding hydrogen made the mixture burn. Two very desirable results were, Buchner said at the 1978 hydrogen conference in Zurich, that "on the one hand, 25 percent less gasoline is consumed because of the much more favorable combustion of the very lean mixture

Figure 6.7. Two recent Daimler-Benz developments, a sedan that runs both on hydrogen and gasoline, and an advanced version of a hydrogen-powered city bus that uses hydrides as storage elements. Both vehicles were shown to the international hydrogen community at the 1978 hydrogen conference in Zurich.

while on the other hand . . . the pollutants CO [carbon monoxide], NOX, and CH [unburned hydrocarbons] are at a minimum." Daimler-Benz cooperated with the University of Kaiserslautern in this project.

The second, more exciting project was the hydride city bus burning hydrogen only but with a more advanced storage system. This bus contained two hydride systems, one a low-temperature titanium-iron tank of the type used in previous test vehicles, the other a high-temperature magnesium-nickel system. The two complement each other. The low-temperature system works well at ambient and low temperatures, assuring easy start-up of the engine as little heat is required to release hydrogen to fuel the engine. The drawback is that low-temperature hydrides can store only limited amounts of hydrogen. The high-temperature magnesium-nickel hydride can store larger amounts, but it requires higher temperatures (200°-300°C., or 390°-572°F.) to release the hydrogen from the hydride state. In mirror-image fashion, both hydrides release heat when being charged with hydrogen—less heat for the low-temperature material, more for the high-temperature hydride.

The dual-tank system provides a number of unexpected and startling advantages. In addition to serving as a heat "primer" for the high-temperature, high-energy storage tank, the low-temperature tank functions as an air-conditioning unit simply by absorbing heat from the bus interior, releasing hydrogen to the engine. Even if the engine is shut down, the air-conditioning effect can be obtained by blowing air over the cold (0°C. or 32°F.) titanium-iron tank until the tank warms up.

Differences in temperature and pressure in the two hydride systems permit heating the vehicle's interior with the engine switched off simply by shunting the hydrogen gas from one reservoir to the other. After a trip, when both reservoirs are partially empty, there is a pronounced pressure difference—20–30 bars (290–435 psi) for the low-temperature hydride vessel versus 1–3 bars (14.5–43.5 psi) for the high-temperature one. Obviously a gas will flow from a high-pressure to a low-pressure tank. The high-temperature magnesium-nickel alloy releases proportionately much more heat than the low-temperature titanium-iron alloy absorbs from the ambient air during its discharge process. Result: a surplus of heat to warm the passenger compartment, a system that Daimler-Benz says works as long as 24 hours after the engine has been shut off. This heat essentially represents the heat content of the exhaust gas necessary to release hydrogen from the high-temperature hydride. In effect, the total system works as a waste-heat storage unit recovering energy that would otherwise be lost. Daimler-Benz says total energy savings can be as high as 30 percent (of the lower heating value of the hydrogen consumed). During operation of the car, the exhaust—water vapor—is condensed back into water while helping to release the hydrogen. Part of this water is injected into the engine's cylinders to avoid mis- or backfiring.

At the Zurich conference Buchner said that the overall weight of this bus was still higher than that of a comparable gasoline-powered model despite the fact that all these auxiliary functions were in effect performed by the gas-tank arrangement. Nor are there any adequate infrastructures on the horizon to permit sales of such cars or buses to the average consumer. Still, Buchner thinks local bus transport, city taxis, delivery vans, and mine vehicles—in short, fleet operations of one sort or another—"might be envisaged . . . in the near future." The gasoline-hydrogen car version, he commented in Zurich, "might conceivably be used as an intermediate solution between petroleum and hydrogen technology."

The Soviets, meanwhile, seem bent on catching up in this area. At the 1976 Miami Beach hydrogen conference, observing Soviet scientists said in hallway conversations that they had experimentally converted a couple of Soviet-built Fiats to hydrogen use. Two years later, a Moskovich sedan was also modified to run on gaseous hydrogen, according to a report in a March 1978 issue of *Eastwest Markets*, a now defunct trade publication specializing in East-West business developments. The report said that "the vehicle worked well on a test track and emitted pure water vapor as exhaust," but the Soviets felt that it was essentially dangerous to store hydrogen in the car. A November 1978 article in the newspaper *Socialist Industry* said Soviet scientists had also successfully tested another car, a Volga, on a mixture of gasoline and hydride-stored hydrogen. *Socialist Industry* reported that by year-end a number of taxis and a bus would be put on the streets of Kharkov, in the Ukraine, for testing.

Like the Mercedes-Benz sedan, the experimental Volga used 80 kilograms (176 lbs) of titanium-iron hydride as a hydrogen storage medium capable of holding 2.4 kilograms (5.3 lbs) of hydrogen. The car's range was given as 350 kilometers (217 miles), with top speeds of 90 kilometers (56 miles) per hour, and it gave off no carbon dioxide and only minimal amounts of nitrogen oxide.[2] Hydrogen accounted for only 5 percent of the total fuel supply, but overall fuel efficiency was also increased by 25 percent. Also, like the Daimler-Benz car, the Volga's hydrogen-gasoline ratio was apparently variable, with the car running almost entirely on hydrogen at low speeds when pollution normally is highest.

Daimler-Benz and Billings initially settled on the titanium-iron hydride as storage medium to demonstrate to the public what hydrogen fuel in a car was all about. The material absorbed and released the gas easily at room temperatures and below, and modifications could be held to a minimum. The research job ahead will be mainly metallurgical—looking for new and better hydrides and engineering ways of putting them to work.

Nevertheless, Daimler-Benz thinks work is needed on the mechanical side as well to improve the internal-combustion engine. While hydrogen can be burned in internal-combustion engines with only minimal engineering changes, this does not mean that the present state of the art, the result of more than 70 years of gasoline-based experience, is necessarily best for hydrogen as well. Daimler-Benz has a new engine research program to optimize engine performance, financed in part by the German Ministry for Research and Technology. Starting from the standard 2.3-liter (140-cubic-inch) passenger-car engine, Daimler-Benz plans to develop a much improved motor. This will entail changed configuration of the burning chamber in each cylinder, changes in valve timing, and a smoother method of recycling the exhaust water vapor into the engine. Also, for comparable performance Daimler-Benz expects that hydrogen engines will have to have bigger displacements to compensate for the power loss caused by recycling of the exhaust water vapors. Compression may be lowered somewhat and the carburetor may be replaced by a gas mixer but, says Helmut Säufferer, another scientist, "that's about it," at least for the present.

Säufferer and Buchner indicate that Daimler-Benz will probably also investigate different combustion processes, such as the one pioneered by Schoeppel of Oklahoma University and by Erren in the thirties, which promised to provide full power without knock or detonation. Unlike conventional engines, which "inhale" a fuel-air mixture for combustion, *only air* is compressed in the Schoeppel engine during the intake stroke. Hydrogen gas is injected at the last moment just before the piston reaches its highest point. The result is a smoothly working engine with fairly constant torque over a wide speed range, with a small increase in fuel consumption, increased power, and no pre-ignition. Absence of detonation and knock was due to closing the intake valve before hydrogen is admitted, precluding manifold backfire. Schoeppel said in early papers that by using air as the sole working medium, no explosive mixtures could accumulate in the intake manifold or crankcase. The result: full power, no excessive temperatures or pressures, and still very low emissions. In fact, said Schoeppel, just by increasing the flow of hydrogen, more power could be extracted from the engine than specified by the manufacturer.

Much of the reasoning behind the decisions by Billings and Daimler-Benz to opt for heavy-hydride storage for automotive use had to do with safety. Ever mindful of the "Hindenburg syndrome," researchers generally consider hydrides safer all around because they cannot spill liquid hydrogen, vent it, or burn in a crash. Nevertheless, two German scientists, Walter Peschka and Constantin Carpetis of the Energy Conversion Division of the German Aerospace Research and Testing Institute in Stuttgart, are still convinced that liquid hydrogen is the way to go for cars, if the ideas propounded by Larry Williams a few years earlier are updated with near-practical hardware.

At the 1976 Miami Beach conference, Peschka and Carpetis discussed and showed pictures of the world's first liquid-hydrogen fuel tank specifically designed for passenger cars, a round flat stainless steel design incorporating two separate shells—one inside the other with a vacuum in between—and capable of holding about 110 liters (29 gallons) of liquid hydrogen laid out for a normal, low operating pressure of 4.5 bars (65.3 psi). The tank has only two connections—LH_2 supply and tank vent—to the "gas" station. The liquid hydrogen is heated up by hot water from the radiator and transformed into the gaseous phase for combustion. Peschka and Carpetis say that as far as the "gas station" side is concerned, "standardized reliable quick-disconnect type fillings activated by compressed air and controlled by the vacuum system can be developed or are available." The two scientists found that refilling time for a tank of this size, which gives a range comparable to a conventional gasoline tank, can be kept short, probably "on the order of a few minutes." Cooldown of the tank from room temperature to supercold cryogenic temperatures, often described as a problem mitigating against liquid hydrogen in cars, took less than 30 minutes, requiring the vaporization of about 20 liters (5.2 gallons) of liquid hydrogen. To recover these and other boil-off losses sustained when the car stands idle for a longer period of time, they suggest incorporation of a small hydride tank alongside the main liquid hydrogen tank to soak up the gasified "cooldown" hydrogen. They figure that with only 10 kilograms (22 pounds) of magnesium in this secondary reservoir and a low filling level, a car can store the boil-off over a period of 50 hours. They conclude that "the weight advantage of the cryogenic liquid hydrogen system guarantees the same range achieved from gasoline-powered cars," in contrast to present hydride storage methods.

Secondly, while safety is the standard objection to liquid hydrogen for cars, "gasoline—widely used over a time period of about 100 years—is also a hazardous fuel, in many respects similar to hydrogen." They say that, based on their experience, a compact LH_2 tank for cars can be made "at moderate cost." Carpetis said the original tank cost about DM 8,500 ($4,230 at 1978 exchange rates) to fabricate, but mass production of around 100,000 units would bring the cost down to DM 1,800–2,000 ($895–995)—a lot, but not more than the cost of a hydride tank and hydride material or of current exhaust cleanup equipment such as catalytic converters.

In a sequel two years later, Peschka and Carpetis unveiled the lab model of a semiautomatic liquid-hydrogen service-station pump, so simple to operate that it might be feasible even in a self-service station. As described at the 1978 hydrogen conference in Zurich, the Peschka-Carpetis device can pump between 120 and 150 liters (31 and 39 gallons) of liquid hydrogen in around five minutes without previously needed precautions. "Handling and comfort of the refueling unit is comparable to that of self-service stations," Peschka and Carpetis said, and "no expensive parts or elements are necessary." One of the main differences between this and ordinary gasoline pumps is the twin-hose arrangement, one for the actual pumping of the fuel and the other for ventilation and removal of gaseous hydrogen in the tank, similar to aircraft procedures where a second ventilation line is also used.

The twin hoses have a joint plug for insertion in a matching filler in the car. If the connection between the two is not accurate, sensors indicate that via blinking lights. After completing the procedure, the hoses—double-walled, insulated, and highly flexible—are flushed with dry nitrogen to prevent the buildup of explosive hydrogen-air mixtures. Technically, the entire operation is rather complex, but actually only a few steps are necessary, the two said: "Connection between the twin-hose plug and the tank, opening of the tank valves, closing of the tank valves, and removal of the twin hoses."

Peschka and Carpetis concluded that hydrogen as ultimate fuel requires a long period of introduction in view of the long-standing prejudices against it as being "especially dangerous." If similar objections against gasoline had prevailed a century ago, "we still should be using horses."

In 1979, Peschka began work on a liquid hydrogen–fueled car, a used BMW 518 with 60,000 kilometers (37,500 miles) on the odometer when conversion began. Adapted to liquid hydrogen at a cost of approximately Deutschmarks 120,000 ($64,000)—cheap as far as most research projects go—the BMW is Europe's only LH₂-powered car in 1980. It is not licensed for over-the-road driving, but it has logged about 1,200 kilometers (750 miles) without a hitch on a test track belonging to the institute near Stuttgart. Compared to the original 90 horsepower when it was gasoline-driven, the BMW's 60 horsepower is rather lame; the loss was incurred mostly because of water injection for engine cooling. Peschka is confident, though, that with time, experience, and adaptation of other fuel-feeding methods, such as direct injection, the power loss can be eliminated. Peschka is fond of pointing out that his liquid hydrogen–fueled BMW has just about the same range and weight as a conventional gasoline-fueled vehicle, unlike hydride-tank-equipped hydrogen machines, which usually weigh more and have a shorter range. "The tank is heavier than a normal gas tank but the liquid hydrogen is much lighter than gasoline," he says. Peschka's institute is collaborating with the Los Alamos Scientific Laboratory in the United States, which is also operating a liquid hydrogen–powered passenger car, a Buick Century V-6; the vehicle's hydrogen tank and the liquid-hydrogen service pump were supplied by Peschka's institute.

Further proof that the liquid-hydrogen route has not been discarded altogether comes from Japan. In 1979 a team from the Musashi Institute of Technology, Tokyo, demonstrated a cute little fastback sports car fueled by liquid hydrogen, the culmination of ten years of work with hydrogen and cars. The car was powered by a two-stroke, three-cylinder, 550-cc (33.5-cubic-inch) engine that produced roughly 23 percent more power on hydrogen than when fueled with gasoline (35 hp. compared to the original 28 hp.), whizzing along at a top speed of 118 kilometers (74 miles) per hour. Team leader S. Furuhama reported in the *International Journal of Hydrogen Energy* that the car had a range of 300–400 kilometers (185–200 miles) with a tank capacity of 60 liters (15.8 gallons), never suffered from flashbacks or backfires, and had very low nitric oxide emissions.

Furuhama and his coworkers, reporting in more detail on their efforts at the 1980 Third World Hydrogen Conference, said the main differences between their project and similar projects were that (1) they injected cold liquid hydrogen directly into the two-stroke engine, obtaining NOX emissions that were lower than with a four-stroke engine, without aids such as simultaneous water injection, and (2) they developed a very small LH_2 pump for that purpose. Previous injection setups always had to rely on fairly large, power-hungry compressors to pressurize gaseous or liquid hydrogen sufficiently to permit injection. Given the small size of the car and its engine, development of such a small pump with a bore of 15 millimeters (0.55 inches) and stroke of 70 millimeters (2.13 inches) driven by a 70-watt motor was essential.

Methanol: Alternative or Forerunner?

Although hydrides are promising as a means of storing hydrogen, they are far from perfect. In a 1978 paper describing hydrogen research, Daimler-Benz acknowledged that "the key problem, storage of hydrogen aboard the vehicle, at the moment has not been satisfactorily solved." Short-term application (meaning in the next 10 years or so) would consist at best of urban fleet vehicles—taxis, trucks, buses—but this again would entail the setting up of a large-scale hydrogen manufacturing and pipeline distribution network, which unfortunately doesn't exist. Säuf-ferer recalls the nineteenth century "gas factories" that produced town gas from coal for cooking and heating, forerunners of a hydrogen economy inasmuch as they produced a gas that consisted of 50 to 80 percent hydrogen.[3]

For these reasons, a lot of people think that hydrogen is not the preferred type of fuel for automotive use at all and that perhaps some other synthetic, but *liquid* fuel is much preferable. At the 1974 THEME conference in Miami, a group of researchers from the Stanford Research Institute said that replacing the gasoline-based fuel system with something else was very difficult because the "distribution network proves to be a dominant component of the total private vehicle transportation system." They noted that "once established, the infrastructure networks of a system become very resistant to change. . . . institutional change is often less readily accomplished than technical change" and that society becomes locked in to a given system. Examples, other than gas stations, abound: the standard gauge of railroad track; the 60-Hertz, 110-volt electrical system in the United States (in Europe, a 50-Hertz, 220-Volt system is used); the number of lines in a TV screen. The paper concluded:

> Compared to several alternatives, especially the use of methanol in vehicles, a transition to hydrogen would appear to be needlessly disruptive. . . . it is our present conclusion that it is very unlikely that the transportation system will evolve of its own accord in the direction of using hydrogen as a fuel for private vehicles; moreover, government intervention to alter this state of affairs in favor of the hydrogen system is unlikely to be warranted.

Methanol, a particular type of alcohol, is being advocated by some as the clean, liquid fuel for cars of the future. The company that has pursued the concept most vigorously to date is Germany's Volkswagen (VW). Daimler-Benz has also converted some cars to methanol use, but as one Daimler-Benz scientist put it, "we feel that methanol is too close already to introduction to warrant a major research effort." Volkswagen began thinking about a large-scale methanol test in 1973. In 1975 the company equipped a fleet of 40 cars to burn methanol instead of gasoline. Some of the cars were maintained at VW headquarters in Wolfsburg, but others were in the field, being operated by the German automobile club ADAC in Munich, Hamburg, and Berlin.

Ernst Fiala, the genial, Austrian-born research chief of VW, once explained the philosophy that led to the methanol tests: "We started by trying to figure out what the total degree of efficiency is in a car. We tried to figure out how much energy is needed to transport, say, one ton of freight over 100 kilometers." These "energy chains" took into account the energy losses at each stage of the chain—energy lost in transporting crude oil from the Persian Gulf to Europe, refining the crude, distributing fuel to gas stations, burning the fuel in the car, and transporting the weight of the car itself in addition to the freight.

The overall efficiency for a standard gasoline-powered car was found to be about 4 percent, i.e., only 4 percent of the initial energy stored in the crude oil was actually used to move the goods. For a diesel engine it was somewhat higher, but for an electric-powered car the figure was only 2 percent (it is highly inefficient to mine coal, burn it in inefficient power plants, lose more energy in power lines, and charge and transport the heavy battery).

"We then asked what are the requirements for a good fuel," Fiala continued.

We said it should be liquid for ease of distribution and handling, it should have a good efficiency, must be knock-resistant, and the emissions should be clean. When you weigh all these factors it becomes evident that methanol is a very good fuel. Methanol has a knock rating of more than 100. You can therefore raise the compression to 1:10 and obtain high performance, good specific fuel consumption, and relatively clean exhaust.

Based on our knowledge today, it is probable that in 50 years we'll be driving on methanol, more probably than any other fuel. I mean, even in 100 years it will be more reasonable to drive with a liquid fuel rather than a gaseous fuel, even as far as the gas station problem is concerned. There are these titanium storage units, but all this is pretty complicated at the gas station level. The gas must be under pressure, or you have to exchange the entire tank. I think, therefore, the ideal fuel simply is a liquid fuel.

Methanol is a synthetic liquid fuel closest to hydrogen in terms of environmental cleanliness. It has only one carbon atom in its structure; in the words of two Massachusetts Institute of Technology (MIT) scientists, T. B. Reed and R. M. Lerner, it "can be thought of as two molecules of hydrogen gas made liquid by one molecule of carbon monoxide," and "it thus shares many of the virtues of pure hydrogen." Also called methyl alcohol, wood alcohol, or methylated spirits, methanol (CH_3OH) is a clear, non-smelling liquid fuel[4] that freezes at—97.8°C. (—144°F.), boils at 64.6°C. (148°F.), and mixes easily with water. In fact, it attracts water, which is one of the drawbacks when it comes to burning it in auto engines. Methanol can be made from many sources—natural gas, petroleum, coal, oil shale, wood, farm and municipal wastes, and even from limestone together with coal, using waste-heat from current-generation nuclear power plants.

One of the chief drawbacks of methanol is that though it produces more specific power—about 10 percent more than gasoline—it has only a little more than half the energy content of gasoline—64,700 Btus per gallon compared to 120,000 Btus for gasoline. In practical terms, this means a methanol-fueled car gets only 55 to 60 percent of the mileage of a conventional car. Another problem is that methanol is hard to start in cold weather because it lacks the volatile components found in gasoline that help in ignition. Also, the high latent heat (methanol requires 473 Btus to convert a pound of liquid methanol into its gas stage, versus only 130 Btus for one pound of gasoline) makes ignition with a cold engine more difficult. A third drawback is that methanol is toxic, both as a vapor or liquid.

After a year of operating its methanol fleet, Volkswagen reported in October 1975 at a General Motors research symposium in Warren,

Michigan, that cold starts became problematical below 8°C. (46°F.). VW and other researchers say that the most practical solutions are volatile additives that help ignition, such as butane, methyl ether, or even normal gasoline, sprayed into the intake air during the start procedure, or installation of a flame preheater, fueled by methanol, in the intake manifold. "A conclusive and ideal solution has not been found so far," reported VW. Improved atomization of the fuel—a more even, finer distribution of methanol in the gas mixture—is the key to warm-up and smooth cold-weather running, and VW says it may require modified fuel injection systems or a special methanol carburetor.

As to range, VW's paper didn't mention any prospects for improvements, although it said the high antiknock rating of methanol makes it possible to raise compression, possibly as high as 14:1, which in addition to even more power may make possible "a simultaneous improvement" in fuel consumption. How much, VW didn't say, but most likely it would be only a few percentage points, a long way from the mileage achieved with gasoline.

Volkswagen reported that in cold-start tests using European criteria carbon monoxide was reduced by 25 percent compared to gasoline but output of hydrocarbons was up 22 percent. However, in hot-start tests the CO emissions were down more than two-thirds—68 percent—and hydrocarbon emissions were down by 28 percent. In both tests, the output of nitrogen oxides was down 20 percent.

Another disadvantage of the straight methanol engine is that it produces twice as many aldehydes, a very reactive form of hydrocarbons, as does gasoline. But, says VW, once the engine compression ratio is raised to 14:1 (a normal ratio is 9.7:1), aldehyde levels fall back to those of straight gasoline. Furthermore, if water is added to methanol, a normal occurrence since methanol is hydroscopic (water-attracting), aldehyde levels go down by 40 percent and nitrogen oxide levels are reduced by 50 percent.

Burning methanol fuel also reduces the output of polynuclear aromatic hydrocarbons to less than one-tenth of the levels recorded with gasoline. The significance of this, according to VW, lies in the fact that some of these compounds are regarded as "severely carcinogenic." With methanol, then, there would be less of that poison in the air.

VW does not operate all of its test fleet on straight methanol; some cars operate on a gasoline-methanol mixture (85 percent gasoline and 15 percent methanol) called M-15. With the blessings of the German government and cooperation of the giant German chemical company BASF, VW hopes to use this to promote methanol and introduce it gradually into the fuel market place. In Germany, "we are using 20 million tons of gasoline but only 4 million tons of methanol annually," noted Fiala.

> The question is how can you tickle the system, stimulate its use and pro-
> duction? One method is to mix both. Gradually you mix more methanol
> and less gasoline. With M-15 we could increase methanol sales. While you
> can't mix more than 15 percent methanol in gasoline, it may be sufficient to
> gradually promote the setting up of a pure methanol plant parallel to
> gasoline, just like you sell premium today. You could gradually introduce
> methanol pumps alongside regular and premium pumps, and in 20 years we
> may have pure methanol cars.

In the United States, the leader of the automobile industry, General Motors, is taking what amounts to a wait-and-see attitude to alternative fuels in general and seems to have made only limited efforts in this area, especially when measured against the scope of the Volkswagen and Daimler-Benz studies. GM has experimentally converted several cars to methanol operations, including a 1974 Chevelle with a modified carburetor and a 1975 Oldsmobile Cutlass with electronic fuel injection that works much better with methanol. GM has also run V-8-equipped cars on combinations of gasoline and hydrogen but has restricted pure-hydrogen testing to single-cylinder laboratory engines.

In general, GM agrees with Volkswagen that methanol is likely to be the alternative fuel in the medium-term automotive future and that straight methanol is preferable to gasoline-methanol blends, although GM has many doubts on technical as well as economical and political grounds. Joseph Colucci, head of the Fuels and Lubricants Department at GM Research Laboratories, commented in early 1977:

> The research we're doing on methanol is aimed at increasing our
> knowledge of the fuel so that we'll be ready if the government should
> legislate its use in automobiles. But we feel that methanol would be better
> used as a fuel in industrial and utility gas turbine engines for stationary
> power plants. This will release hydrocarbon fuels for automotive use and
> thus avoid the modification of cars required for methanol. . . . But if we
> have to, we're confident we can build cars compatible with this alternative
> fuel.

Colucci repeated this view in a statement on alcohol fuels to the Senate Appropriations Committee in January 1978:

> Use of alcohol as fuel in automobiles is technically feasible, although the

result in the case of an alcohol-gasoline blend would be some degradation in driveability. Methanol appears to us to be the most practical alcohol fuel for automotive use in the United States since it can be readily produced from coal. . . . Development of a production and distribution system for alcohol fuels would take a large investment and long lead times. During this lead time period any necessary vehicle modifications could be accomplished.

Clearly, alcohol *could* be used as a strategy to reduce petroleum consumption in the U.S. But questions of *availability* and usage priorities are of paramount importance.

GM is even more sceptical about hydrogen: "We view the production prospects of hydrogen-powered cars and trucks as being in the very distant future, if at all," said a paper prepared by the Fuels and Lubricants Department in 1977, a position that in 1980 was still the official stance of GM, which is betting much more on the electric car as a viable alternative. At a time when world petroleum reserves are beginning to vanish "we believe the prospects are better for the volume production of methanol or hydrocarbon automotive fuels from coal, for example," the paper said. Electrolytically produced hydrogen should rather be used for space heating or in industry rather than in cars. "GM Research Laboratories engineers and scientists have been looking at hydrogen and will continue to do so because we can't afford not to," but "at present there doesn't seem to be very much incentive for operating experimental vehicles on 'straight hydrogen.'"

A compromise in the hydrogen-versus-methanol debate seemed to be shaping up in a report presented in 1980 at the Tokyo hydrogen conference by two scientists from the Jet Propulsion Laboratory in California, John Houseman and G. E. Voecks. After reviewing a number of projects involving total or partial conversion of gasoline and methanol into hydrogen on board a car, Houseman and Voecks concluded there are "no significant incentives" to convert gasoline into hydrogen—unless emission standards cannot be met any other way. Fuel efficiency of converted gasoline is about the same as for current engine types fitted with three-way catalytic exhaust converters, giving no real advantage either in terms of emissions or economy. However, the picture changes when methanol is converted into hydrogen, the two JPL scientists said. Methanol decomposed into hydrogen and carbon monoxide with an assist from engine heat gives most of the advantages of a pure hydrogen engine and few of the drawbacks such as heavy hydride tanks. Tests, especially those by Nissan, showed a 20 to 40 percent increase in fuel economy and no need for catalytic converters: "Such a system may well be better than a straight hydrogen engine, running on pure hydrogen," their report concluded; "a lot depends on what kind of hydrogen storage device will be developed," adding, "it appears that it will be difficult to find a better storage device for hydrogen than liquid methanol for automotive applications." Houseman and Voecks presented a phasing-in scenario for hydrogen engines that envisions retrofitting current engine types by around 1985 with on-board hydrogen converters using methanol as fuel, followed by the introduction of engines optimized for hydrogen combustion, but still using methanol, by about 1990, to be followed by the replacement of methanol by pure hydrogen carried on board in improved hydride systems or other storage methods, possibly by 1990. "It appears that we can enjoy the benefits of [the] hydrogen engine in the not too distant future by storing hydrogen onboard in the form of methanol," they concluded.

The Fuel-Cell Car

Some companies—General Motors and Union Carbide in particular—have been experimenting with hydrogen-powered fuel cells for automotive propulsion. Back in 1967, when the electric car was considered a hot possibility, both companies came up with prototypes that combined fuel cells and an electric motor. General Motors at one point developed the electric battery-operated Electrovair, an electric version of its air-cooled Corvair, as well as a fuel-cell-powered van, called the Electrovan.

Fuel cells are devices in which hydrogen recombines with oxygen to produce electricity and water—a reversal of electrolysis, which splits water into hydrogen and oxygen. Though fuel cells have worked well to supply spacecraft with both electric power and drinking water and research is under way using large fuel cells in utilities operations, these devices still are too expensive for cars. Even if they were perfected and cheap, fuel-cell cars still would face the number-one problem shared by the conventional internal-combustion engine—how to carry hydrogen. Until that problem is solved, fuel cells are running a distant third behind hydrogen and methanol as fuels for conventional internal combustion engines.

A hydrogen-methanol survey, published by the German Ministry for Science and Technology in the mid-seventies, said fuel-cell-powered cars are likely to perform better than battery-powered cars, which isn't saying very much in view of the electric car–hydrogen car comparison drawn up by Daimler-Benz that was mentioned earlier. The survey also cited the following drawbacks:

Figure 6.8. One of the first methanol-fueled VW "Rabbits" being turned over to their owners in Berlin in early 1979 in the world's first mass trials of alternative fuels—methanol/gasoline blends, hydrogen, and electricity.

- High thermic and corrosive demands on the fuel cell's auxiliary systems.
- High investment costs.
- Uncertain lifetimes and operational safety.
- Lack of an air electrode, free of noble metals, that meets all demands of traction operation regarding lifetime and load capacity (a key problem of the hydrogen-air fuel cell).
- Long heating-up times to reach operating temperatures; this means limiting use of the fuel cells to scheduled line operations (bus lines, maybe taxis).
- Possible risk to individuals (high degree of danger from acid burns) and to the environment (spills of caustic lye, pollution of ground water).

Since that report, government and industry in West Germany have moved ahead consistently on the alternative fuels front. Following Volkswagen's methanol and Daimler-Benz's hydrogen experiments, the government, in January 1979, started the world's first mass trials in a major urban environment, involving 1,000 test vehicles testing methanol-gasoline blends and hydrogen as well as electrical vehicle operations in West Berlin. The four-year trial is expected to cost as much as DM 200 million ($100 million), of which the government will pick up DM 135 million ($68 million). Because the methanol option is regarded by the Germans as the most likely near-term possibility, methanol will get the lion's share of funding, with roughly 65 percent of the total. Hydrogen, regarded as a promising farther-term option, will be allocated roughly 25 percent, and 10 percent will be spent on testing electrical vehicles in short-range special applications.

The methanol-gasoline passenger cars—Volkswagen alone plans to make available at least 1,000 models—will be offered to ordinary drivers who have to agree to check in for periodic examination and testing. Hydrogen operations will be limited to city buses, and battery-powered pickup trucks will most likely be tested as service vehicles for West Berlin's public transport authority or in similar applications. "We figure it's all right to let ordinary drivers handle methanol cars, but with hydrogen there are too many unsolved technical problems, and it's better to let professionals drive the buses," commented a government official involved in coordinating the program. In addition to testing the vehicles as such, the program also involves the development and testing of infrastructure components such as refueling stations, storage facilities, but also cost-benefit analyses, systems analyses, and hardware development.

In the same year in the United States, Roger Billings presented the first hydrogen-powered cars for sale to the general public. The first 10 copies were priced at $30,000. Billings offered the Dodge Omni converted to operate on both hydrogen and gasoline. The price, which Billings hopes will go down after the initial 10, also includes an electrolyzer to make hydrogen at home. Billings said the hydrogen-powered version achieved the equivalent of 44 mpg (5.5 liters per 100 kilometers), compared to 30 mpg (7.8 liters per 100 kilometers) for the standard gasoline version. Thus, it looks as if things are moving, if slowly.

7

Clean Contrails over Lake Erie:
Hydrogen as Aircraft Fuel

Early Efforts

Twenty years ago, the B-57 twin-engine jet bomber was one of the workhorses of the U.S. Air Force. Therefore the wing-tip tank-equipped version that lolled at some 50,000 feet (15,000 meters) over Lake Erie in 1957, at speeds of Mach 0.75 or thereabouts, never warranted a second glance by the residents of the Cleveland area. The plane just looked like any other B-57, except perhaps for the wing-tip tanks: the one on the left side was slightly thinner and looked a bit makeshift, less smoothly rounded than the one on the right. Another, almost unnoticeable difference was a small boxlike structure mounted outboard of the left engine underneath the wing, an air-hydrogen heat exchanger. Nevertheless, this plane was destined to become a maker of aviation history and a pacesetter for the hydrogen economy. Based at the NACA Lewis Research Center near Cleveland, Ohio, this B-57 was the first plane ever to fly, partially at least, on liquid hydrogen. While the twin-engine jet was fueled conventionally by normal kerosene at takeoff, the pilot could switch one engine over to hydrogen in flight, drawing liquid hydrogen under pressure from the left wing-tip tank (pressure was provided by helium, which was carried in the right wing-tip tank) and pushing the cryogenic liquid to the heat exchanger. There, heat from the inrushing air served to warm up the cold and liquid hydrogen, which reverted to gas. The hydrogen gas then burned quite normally in the left jet engine.

The plane flew for about two years, burning hydrogen in flights as long as 17 minutes, always at high altitudes and cruising speed, with no fuss and no problems. It's unlikely that any ground observer could see the difference between the two engines at that height, when both produced the typical white vapor contrails—except that the left contrail was cleaner. Had the plane operated closer to the ground while burning

Figure 7.1. A B-57 airplane with a hydrogen system.

hydrogen on one engine, possibly there might have been a visible difference, with the kerosene-burner on the right streaming black exhaust smoke, and the hydrogen-fueled engine on the left emitting only a slight amount of whitish water vapor. But as it was, the B-57 switched to hydrogen operation only at high altitude because that was the objective of the program: to determine hydrogen's potential for increasing a plane's maximum operating altitude.

Hydrogen was very much in the air, as it were, in those days. In addition to the engineering studies at the Lewis Center that led to the B-57 hydrogen high-flyer, Lockheed, on the West Coast, was doing studies of its own in collaboration with engine maker Pratt & Whitney and a division of AiResearch. This led directly to one of the truly sensational episodes in this area, the initiation in 1956–1957 of a liquid hydrogen–fueled, supersonic spy plane called the CL-400. Before anybody starts looking for remnant pieces or claims to have actually seen the plane, it should be said that the program was terminated, for reasons to be discussed later, before the plane reached the prototype stage.

The story of this almost-airplane was secret until only a few years ago when the former project engineer for the CL-400, Ben R. Rich, later a Lockheed vice president, described the plane to a select group of some 120 aviation and hydrogen experts at a working symposium on liquid hydrogen–fueled aircraft held at NASA's Research Center in Langley, Virginia, May 15 and 16, 1973. Some of the detailed work that went into a Pratt & Whitney Model 304 jet engine designed for liquid hydrogen had

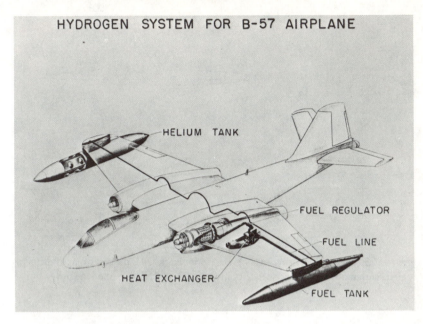

Figure 7.2. Hydrogen system for a B-57 airplane.

been reported earlier. But that meeting marked the first time that anything about this project, which led later to the famed supersonic SR-71 reconnaissance plane, was described to outsiders.

According to Rich's report, the twin-jet CL-400s were supposed to fly at close to 100,000 feet (30,500 meters) altitude and cruise at Mach 2.5—two-and-a-half times the speed of sound and with a range of 1,100 miles (1,770 kilometers). Lockheed planned to produce six planes, with delivery of the first of two prototypes to take place only a year and a half after go-ahead was given. That plane didn't look like any of the sleek, delta-winged or swing-winged supersonic jets of today. The general shape of the CL-400 was similar to the F-104 Starfighter, with wings sticking out at right angles from the fuselage. "During those days, concepts like blended wings, double-delta etc., were not known," Rich told his fascinated audience. "Because of the accelerated schedule it was necessary to utilize established aerodynamic configurations."

Considering the fact that the plane was supposed to carry a crew of two and a payload (mostly aerial cameras and other reconnaissance equipment) of only 1,500 pounds (680 kilograms), it was too large, measuring more than 164 feet (50 meters) in length, standing 30 feet (9.1 meters) high, and having a wingspan of almost 84 feet (25 meters). The

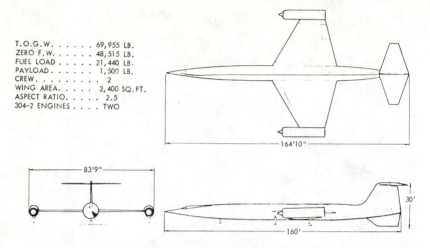

```
T.O.G.W. . . . . . 69,955 LB.
ZERO F.W. . . . . . 48,515 LB.
FUEL LOAD . . . . . 21,440 LB.
PAYLOAD . . . . . .  1,500 LB.
CREW . . . . . . . . 2
WING AREA. . . . . 2,400 SQ.FT.
ASPECT RATIO. . . . 2.5
304-2 ENGINES . . . . TWO
```

Figure 7.3. Schematic drawings of the 1956 Lockheed design of a hydrogen-fueled, supersonic, reconnaissance plane, the CL-400. The plane was never built.

fuselage had a diameter of 10 feet (3 meters). The plane's two engines, each delivering 9,500 lbs. (4,300 kg.) of thrust, were located at the wing tips where in other planes auxiliary fuel tanks are located. Small outrigger landing gears at the wingtips stabilized the plane on the ground, with most of the weight borne by centerline-mounted main and nose landing gears. "The low density of the cryogenic fuel necessitated a large fuel volume, in effect a supersonic widebody jet," Rich recalled. Total fuel was 21,404 pounds (9,708 kg) of liquid hydrogen and at takeoff the plane would have weighed 69,955 pounds (31,731 kg, more than 31 tons)—a big bird at that time.

To appreciate the importance of the project it should be remembered that not a great deal was known then about liquid hydrogen. "Liquid hydrogen in those pre-Sputnik, pre-space race and pre-Apollo days wasn't much more than a laboratory curiosity," as hydrogen consultant Bill Escher once put it. "There was very little knowledge of liquid hydrogen or cryogenic handling, other than that related to the hydrogen bomb experience," Rich reported at Langley. "Consequently it was necessary for us at Burbank to set up a test facility to learn how to handle liquid hydrogen in a fashion no different from hydrocarbon fuel. It was our feeling that if you could not handle liquid hydrogen like gasoline, you did not have a practical vehicle."

An old World War II bomb-shelter revetment in Burbank was converted into the test site, with instrumentation, laboratory, and cryogenic equipment housed in three wooden barracks put up for that purpose. Rich and his crew, under the overall direction of Lockheed's famous Clarence L. (Kelly) Johnson—director of the "Skunk Works," Lockheed's advanced projects organization, father of both the U-2 and the big twin-engined SR-71 Blackbird supersonic reconnaissance plane—set up scale hydrogen tanks and fuel supply systems to get the hang of handling the stuff. Much effort was spent on, among other things, discovering how to run supercold liquid hydrogen at −425°F. (−254°C.) through a hot wing-structure with an average temperature of 325°F. (162°C.), induced by air friction at supersonic speeds.

A great deal of work also went into studying the much-feared, but largely unknown, hazards of the fuel, including a large number of deliberate attempts to explode hydrogen. "The deflagrations were generally mild due to the high hydrogen flame velocity," Rich said. "The fireball was much less than a comparable kerosene fire. . . . Only 2 of 61 liquid hydrogen tests produced bona fide explosions. In both cases oxygen was deliberately mixed with liquid hydrogen," just about the most dangerous situation and one not very likely to occur in normal operations. Said Rich: "We showed that a hydrogen aircraft was feasible. Liquid hydrogen could be handled, with the proper procedures and care, as easily as hydrocarbon fuel."

The plane got as far as wind-tunnel testing, and component development and procurement of the basic materials for building the plane had begun. But in 1957 the program was cancelled for both technical and logistical reasons after a conference between then Secretary of the Air Force James H. Douglas and executives from Lockheed and Pratt & Whitney. One reason was that once the overall design was fixed there was not much room left to improve the plane's range, mainly because of the peculiar characteristics of liquid hydrogen. "First, the airplane was too short-legged and had not more than 5 percent potential range performance stretch," according to Rich, the result of the inherently low supersonic lift-to-drag ratio of a liquid hydrogen–fueled aircraft. Hydrogen's large volume and the resulting large fuselage in relation to the small wing area meant a disproportionately large amount of aerodynamic drag, which could be compensated for only by using a lot of energy just to keep the plane aloft, something that was not helped by the relatively crude aerodynamics that Rich mentioned.

The second reason had to do with the logistics of carrying such an exotic fuel to planes that might be stationed at distant airbases, presumably on the periphery of the Soviet Union and of China, although Rich did not say that outright in his presentation. "How do you justify hauling enough LH$_2$ around the world to exploit a short-range airplane?" he asked rhetorically. Another fundamental reason for the lack of success of this design was the fact that the engine was very heavy and suffered from high fuel consumption.

In the course of the CL-400 program Lockheed played around with the concept, varying size, weight ratio, lift-drag ratios, Mach number, and other variables that produced such outsized, exotic machines as reconnaissance planes up to 290 feet (88 meters) long, with ranges of 4,000 miles (6,400 kilometers) and takeoff gross weights of 358,000 pounds (162 metric tons), half of which was due to liquid hydrogen. Other studies showed that if airplane designers switched to hydrocarbon fuels, the range of 1,100 miles (1,700 kilometers) for the CL-400 could be doubled, flying at somewhat lower altitudes and without the handling and logistics problems of LH$_2$. These considerations ultimately led to the development of the supersonic SR-71 Blackbird high-altitude reconnaissance plane.

Lockheed turned its liquid hydrogen data over to Convair, which was then starting to develop the Centaur rocket, the first space rocket fueled with liquid hydrogen. This ultimately led to the Apollo man-on-the-moon programs, which are now continuing with the space shuttle effort.

Hydrogen's Advantages

What exactly is it that makes liquid hydrogen so attractive as an aviation fuel? The answer is, quite simply, energy—more exactly, energy per weight basis. Some far-sighted scientists perceived this very early in this century, as, for example, Britain's J.B.S. Haldane in his famous 1923 "Heretics" lecture in Cambridge (see Chapter 3). Liquid (as opposed to gaseous) hydrogen stores more energy—about 2.8 times as much, pound for pound—than conventional jet-grade kerosene.

At the same time, however, liquid hydrogen requires three to four times the volume of conventional jet fuel, given the same weight. More precisely, one pound of liquid hydrogen contains 51,500 Btus (113,500 Btus/kg). Jet-A, the most common jet fuel, on the other hand, has only 18,600 Btus per pound (41,000 Btus/kg). But per cubic foot of volume, liquid hydrogen contains only 227,700 Btus (8 million Btus per cubic meter), while Jet-A has 906,000 Btus (32 million Btus per cubic meter). Put another way, to obtain the same heating value contained in one cubic foot of Jet-A, almost four times that volume of liquid hydrogen, 3.97 cubic feet, is needed. The result is that hydrogen-fueled aircrafts will be fatter, with a thicker fuselage to carry all that fuel, but will be lighter as well.

Quite apart from the environmental advantages of burning hydrogen in jet engines, which are basically the same as burning hydrogen in car engines—no smoke, no unburned hydrocarbons, no CO_2 and CO, and low NOX emissions—there are economic advantages to using liquid hydrogen as aviation fuel.

At that same 1973 NASA hydrogen symposium, two NASA scientists, Cornelius Driver and Tom F. Bonner, Jr., presented first rough estimates of what hydrogen usage would mean in terms of a practical design goal, a jet-freighter capable of carrying a payload of 265,000 pounds (120,000 kilograms, or 120 tons) over 5,000 nautical miles (9,260 kilometers). Their study did not assume any design advantages that might come about as the result of using hydrogen—an important factor, as will be seen later. They merely cranked in liquid hydrogen numbers instead of kerosene data into airplane design computations. Even those initial, once-over-lightly figures that took only the improved heating value into account were startling. Based on the general formula that provides a measure of an airplane's overall flight efficiency

$$\frac{M\,(L/D)}{SFC}$$

in which M, the Mach number or the plane's speed, is multiplied by the lift-drag ratio, L/D, and divided by the specific fuel consumption (SFC), Driver and Bonner said the fuel flight efficiency for planes such as the Boeing 707, DC-8, Boeing 747, DC-10, and L-1011 would roughly double "if no serious problem is encountered in providing the necessary hydrogen volume."

With then available technology, the use of hydrogen fuel on this hypothetical 265,000-pound- (120-ton-) payload jet freighter with a range of 5,000 miles (8,000 kilometers), would have resulted in a plane with a gross weight of 950,000 pounds (431 tons), while the Jet-A plane would have weighed more than one-third more, around 1.5 million pounds (680 tons). Both planes would have been about the same length, 375 feet (114 meters) for the LH_2 plane versus 371 feet (113 meters) for the kerosene-fueled plane, but the hydrogen plane would have had a fatter fuselage and smaller wings because all the hydrogen would be carried in the fuselage[1] instead of the wings, as is the practice now.

The result would be that the payload-to-gross-weight ratio would be much more favorable, increasing from an average of 18 percent to roughly 29 percent. In other words, while planes in this general category—DC-8s, 747s, and Tri-Stars—can carry less than one-fifth of their total weight as freight, with a hydrogen plane the payload would amount to almost one-third—an improvement of supreme importance to

Figure 7.4. Daniel Brewer of the Lockheed Corporation.

airline operators. It also means that, despite higher costs for liquid hydrogen, use of the fuel would be economically justifiable, assuming, of course, that the entire complicated airport infrastructure, such as cryogenic tanks, hydrogen generators, pipelines—in other words, the entire fuel equipment—is installed and written off. Estimates of the cost of coal-based liquid hydrogen in the late seventies ranged from $6 to $8 per million Btus, compared to Jet-A prices of 40 cents per gallon or $3.15 per million Btus. Since then, aviation-grade kerosene prices have doubled in the United States to about $0.94 per gallon in the fall of 1980; in West Germany they were even higher, about $1.35 a gallon. Obviously they are going to go up even more in line with other fuels, given OPEC's price policies. In the not-too-distant future Jet-A and other fuels may reach parity with the cost of liquid hydrogen. When that point will be reached is uncertain, but it seems inevitable. In fact, some experts contend that on an equal heating value basis, it may already have been reached.

At the same NASA conference a Lockheed engineer, Daniel Brewer, came up with similar numbers in what he called a 'cursory investigation" of the switch from fossil fuels to liquid hydrogen, using state-of-the-art technology of a commercial Lockheed Tri-Star as the basis for comparison. This hypothetical plane, with the same payload of 56,000 pounds (25 tons), flying at subsonic speeds of Mach 0.82 and with a range of 3,400 nautical miles (6,300 kilometers), would weigh only

318,000 pounds (144 tons), compared to 430,000 pounds (195 tons) for the current Jet-A–fueled Tri-Star. Brewer figured that smaller and lighter engines exploiting liquid hydrogen's cooling properties would reduce specific fuel consumption by another 5 to 10 percent. "Also, something like a 25 percent reduction in engine maintenance and a 25 percent increase in engine life is forecast as a result of using the clean, smooth-burning fuel," he said. "In view of these potential cost savings, airline operators could afford to switch to hydrogen fuel long before the relative costs of kerosene and LH_2 reach parity on the basis of cost per Btu."

Three years later, Brewer presented more refined data on hydrogen-fueled airplanes, both supersonic and subsonic, the result of his work under NASA contracts. These much more detailed analyses of aircraft, which NASA specified should become operational between 1990 and 1995, confirmed the earlier estimates. As far as was possible in theoretical studies, they concluded that hydrogen-fueled aircraft would be more economical, less polluting (in terms of both hydrocarbon emissions and noise) and generally more acceptable to humans.

NASA had asked Brewer and his team to:

- assess the feasibility of using hydrogen fuel in commercial transport planes;
- determine the advantages and/or disadvantages of hydrogen as compared to conventional Jet-A fuel;
- pinpoint problems and technology needs that would occur with liquid hydrogen;
- present an outline for the development of needed technology.

Of 24 designs studied, Brewer discussed a long-range passenger plane (400 passengers, 5,500-nautical-mile [10,000-kilometer] range) as a representative sample. In a report on his team's findings in the first edition of the new quarterly *International Journal of Hydrogen Energy* in early 1976, he said that the 24 subsonic designs included both cargo and passenger variations with ranges of 3,000 and 5,500 nautical miles (5,600 and 10,000 kilometers), cruise speeds of Mach 0.8 to Mach 0.95, and payloads ranging from 88,000 pounds (40 tons) (for a 400-seat jumbo passenger liner) to 250,000 pounds (113 tons) for the 5,500-mile-range cargo plane (similar in size to the huge Galaxy C-5 military transport craft).

The overall data were roughly as previously predicted, but with some important refinements. Gross weight was more than one-third less (391,700 pounds, or 177 tons, for the hydrogen plane versus 523,200 pounds, or 237 tons, for the Jet-A plane). Fuel weight for the H_2 plane

Figure 7.5. Early Lockheed designs of liquid-hydrogen-fueled transports with a capacity of 400 passengers over 5,500 nautical miles. The idea of carrying LH_2 tanks on top of the wings was abandoned because such a design would entail too much aerodynamic drag.

was one-third and the engines needed to deliver 11 percent less thrust with resultant weight and size savings. The wing area was reduced by about one-fourth because of the lighter loads, but the hydrogen plane was about 10 percent longer (219 feet versus 197 feet; 66.7 versus 60 meters).

The plane again would carry liquid hydrogen tanks inside the fuselage structure fore and aft. Early designs that envisioned hydrogen carried in tanks mounted on top of each wing were abandoned. Initially, there was concern that H_2 fuel tanks should be accessible from the outside for ease of repair and to minimize leak hazards, but Lockheed analyses later indicated that these advantages were too slight to outweigh the penalty of much reduced performance due to more drag. In fuselage tanks, rigid plastic foam envelopes the outside of the aluminum tank, and the foam in turn is covered with a multi-layer vapor barrier consisting of a plastic sheet and aluminum foil. The entire system is wrapped in fiberglass or some other, more advanced composite material for mechanical protection.

One design difference was that there would no longer be any direct ac-

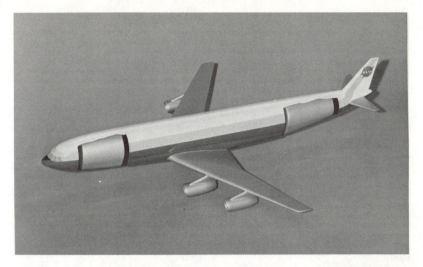

Figure 7.6. A NASA rendering showing the locations of the liquid-hydrogen tanks inside the fuselage.

cess from the passenger compartment to the cockpit because the forward hydrogen tank would be in the way. A potential hijacker would be unable to reach the cockpit in flight.

In terms of noise pollution, the hydrogen-fueled subsonic transport would be considerably quieter during takeoff and cruise but not during landing. Using standard yardsticks, the so-called sideline measurement (taken about one-third of a nautical mile from the runway centerline) and flyover (measured three and a half miles from the point of brake release during takeoff), hydrogen planes are potentially quieter. For flyover noise, measured in so-called EPNdB (Effective Perceived Noise Level in terms of decibels), the long-range hydrogen plane would create 104.9 EPNdB while the Jet-A plane would register at 107 EPNdB. The difference in sideline noise is less pronounced, with only about 0.8 EPNdB difference between the two designs. On approach, the LH_2 plane would be somewhat noisier because of a combination of factors. First of all, the empty hydrogen plane weighs about the same as the Jet-A plane, but because it has smaller engines and smaller wings with a lower lift-to-drag ratio, the engines have to run at a higher power setting during the approach to maintain the same glide angle—the pilot has to "step on the gas" harder, which obviously makes more noise. Taking all these values together, Brewer says the future LH_2 plane would affect a smaller area with high noise—the so-called 90-EPNdB contour, the area around the runway in which these noise levels are registered during takeoff and landing—than an equivalent kerosene-fueled plane. Compared to a current L-1011 Tri-Star, this 90-EPNdB "footprint" is one-third less for the bigger, heavier 5,500-mile-range craft, and only a little more than half for a lighter, passenger plane with a short (3,000 miles) range.

For purposes of this study, NASA laid down guidelines on emissions of carbon monoxide, unburned hydrocarbons, nitrogen oxides, water vapor, smoke, and odors for a future aircraft with presumably more advanced engine technology. These hypothetical kerosene-burning engines of advanced turbofan design produced twice the allowable amount of CO, unburned hydrocarbons, and "objectionable" odors during idling on the ground, but performed under the limit in terms of smoke and NOX during takeoff. As expected, the hydrogen plane produced none of these objectionable emissions. In cruise conditions, hydrogen engines will produce about twice the amount of water vapor—82.4 pounds (37.3 kg) per nautical mile compared to 41.9 pounds (19 kg) for the kerosene plane.

Wouldn't these bigger-than-normal water-vapor emissions drastically change the weather? skeptics have asked. In the absence of real experimental data, it's hard to say. Lockheed's Brewer doesn't think so, though, and apparently feels the meteorological impact would be minimal or nonexistent. By way of illustration, Brewer says that if the water vapor coming out of the plane's four jet engines is visualized as a thin film of water the width of the engine's exhaust nozzle, the thickness of this water film would be only 0.00008 inch (0.00003 centimeters); 82.4 pounds (37.3 kg) of water spread over one nautical mile doesn't seem to warrant many worries.

What about nitrogen oxides, the by-product of any burning process in the atmosphere? With hydrogen, chances are that the problem, if not licked, can at least be diminished. At the 1973 NASA symposium, two scientists from New York University, Antonio Ferri and Anthony Agnone, said that *existing* types of turbojet engines burning hydrogen would actually produce more nitrogen oxides. But, they added, the situation would change completely if different combustion schemes, such as vaporizing the hydrogen, premixing it with air, and injecting it into the combustor before burning were introduced. This works for both hydrocarbon fuels and hydrogen, but hydrogen is especially suitable because it mixes more easily and therefore a simpler combustor design can be utilized. Ferri and Agnone concluded that for future subsonic planes the formation of nitric oxides can be much reduced by combustor designs of this type because "the fuel can be mixed early and does not need to be vaporized." The same point was made by another scientist, Jack Grobman of the NASA Lewis Research Center, who said that considerably more potential exists for reducing nitrogen oxides with hydrogen than with kerosene. Advanced engine component concepts such as a "swirl-can" combustor or a "flower-pot" combustor should have "considerable potential for minimizing nitrogen oxide emissions in jet aircraft using hydrogen."

If hydrogen makes subsonic transport look good, it makes a future supersonic transport (SST) positively glow with economic promise and environmental health, although studies are needed to determine whether and how increased water vapor, in itself harmless, might change weather dynamics in the high stratosphere, the dwelling place of future SSTs.[2]

The proposed American SST, which Boeing was supposed to build after winning a design competition against Lockheed, was killed by environmentalists in the Senate in 1971. In retrospect this was a good thing. Aside from pollution concerns, the plane's marginal economics might have sounded its death-knell a couple of years later following the Arab oil embargo and the energy crisis of 1973.

The French-British SST, the Concorde, has so far been less than a resounding commercial and economic success. In the Soviet Union, the TU-144, the Russian SST that looks so much like the Concorde, has been withdrawn because of technical problems. According to European press reports, the Concordes operated by British Airways to the Middle East are flying with low load factors and are in the red. In early 1979 Air France was reporting average load factors of 65.1 percent in transatlantic runs but wasn't making any money either.

So, except for airplane buffs like Senator Barry Goldwater, who needs an SST anyway? The SST has been a dirty word in Congress ever since Senator William Proxmire spearheaded the drive to kill it on environmental grounds. The fact that former President Richard Nixon was a strong supporter of a supersonic transport program at the time didn't help matters either. There is little evidence that the feelings in Congress have changed since then.

However, the environmental objections to an SST become largely pointless once hydrogen enters the picture. When it comes to emissions, hydrogen-fueled SSTs would have the same advantages as subsonic airplanes that burn hydrogen—no CO_2, CO, or unburned hydrocarbons at all, and, as already pointed out, the potential exists to lick the nitrogen oxide problem with advanced combustion technologies. There are indications that sonic booms can be reduced by some design changes. Also, advanced supersonic transports with increasing Mach numbers will fly higher—a future Mach 6 plane may cruise at 100,000 feet (30,000 meters), three times as high as today's planes—and less of the sonic boom shock wave will reach the ground.

Quick-turn-around aircraft have become almost a necessity, given passenger growth projections, if congestion in the air, especially around airports, is to be minimized. NASA's Witcofski reports that by 1990 international air traffic, most of it long-range, will have grown to the point that some 6.5 million passengers will be crossing the Atlantic annually in both directions, requiring 325 flights a day (assuming 200 passengers per plane). To relieve that aerial congestion, the obvious answer is faster as well as bigger planes that can make more trips per day and carry more passengers.[3]

Time savings can be quite enormous. The Mach 2 Concorde does the one-way trip between Paris and New York in 3 3/4 hours. A second-generation Mach 2.2 advanced supersonic transport (AST) would make the 3,500-mile (5,600-kilometer) trip in about three and a half hours. Future Mach 6 vehicles (such aircraft are being studied) would cut the trip to 2 1/4 hours, although some analyses predict that, beyond Mach 3, the total gains would not be very large because more time is needed for acceleration and deceleration and the actual Mach 6 flight portion is relatively short.

Still, all three major U.S. airplane makers have continued work on SSTs with marginal funding because, as former NASA administrator James C. Fletcher once put it, "if some day the Congress and the country decide to go ahead [with an American SST], we have to be in the best position we know with current technology for such a program."

Former astronaut Frank Borman was quoted in *Aviation Week & Space Technology* some years ago as saying that with fuel costs going almost straight up, the SST is an economic impossibility unless it is fueled by hydrogen. Borman was already a senior vice president at Eastern Airlines when he made that comment.

Lockheed's Brewer is firmly convinced a hydrogen-powered AST is certainly technically feasible today and environmentally desirable. And compared to an equivalent Jet-A–fueled AST, the hydrogen-fueled version would be economically advantageous. For several years, even before the 1973 energy crisis, Brewer, in a number of papers that press the point in their titles—"The Case for a Hydrogen-Fueled Supersonic Transport" (1972) and "Hydrogen: Make-Sense Fuel for an American Supersonic Transport" (1974, coauthored with Bill Escher)—has been putting his case before his peers with Lockheed's corporate approval.

Just as he did for subsonic airplanes, Brewer outlined the findings of the NASA-commissioned investigation of hydrogen for supersonic aircraft in the *International Journal of Hydrogen Energy* in 1976. Generally, the same characteristics that made liquid hydrogen superior to kerosene for subsonic planes apply to the AST, only more so. Using the Mach 2.7,

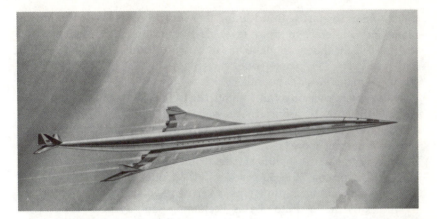

Figure 7.7. Lockheed's version of a Mach 2.7, 234-passenger advanced super-sonic transport, fueled by liquid hydrogen.

234-passenger, 4,200-nautical-mile (7,700-kilometer) range design, Lockheed squared off against Boeing in the U.S. design competition. The hydrogen-fueled version was again fatter and longer, but also lower and almost one-third narrower in wingspan terms, facilitating taxiing in congested airport areas.

The weight savings for the LH_2 plane were stupendous: At 368,000 pounds (167 tons) gross weight, the plane would weigh only half of the Jet-A equivalent craft (750,000 pounds, or 340 tons). It would need only one-fourth the fuel weight of the kerosene plane to fly the same distance, and the engines had to provide only little more than half of the thrust—46,900 pounds (22,200 kg) per LH_2 engine versus 89,500 pounds (40,600 kg) per Jet-A engine—of the kerosene-powered equivalent.

Comparing the two designs represents a fascinating study in trade-offs. Under cruise conditions, specific fuel consumption for the Jet-A plane (pounds of fuel consumed per hour, divided by engine thrust, i.e., power) is 2.69 times that of the hydrogen-fueled plane—basically, the difference in heating values of the two fuels. However, because the liquid-hydrogen plane must also have a larger fuselage to store the more voluminous fuel, it would be penalized by more drag and a lower lift-to-drag (L/D) ratio—more energy would be required to keep the plane aloft. The difference in L/D ratio is 21 percent, meaning that for the same weight, the Jet-A plane would have about one-fifth less drag and would require less engine power (thrust). Lower power in turn means lower fuel flow, which would compensate to some extent for the Jet-A plane's less favorable specific fuel consumption. But the liquid-hydrogen plane is much lighter to start with, meaning that less power is needed to lift the plane and accelerate to cruise level. The final difference is expressed in the fuel weight that each plane has to carry to identical payload, range, and speed: The LH_2 plane would carry 81,440 pounds (37 tons) of fuel, the Jet-A plane 326,000 pounds (148 tons).

Thus, given lower overall weight, the LH_2 AST would also be more energy-efficient: According to Brewer's calculations, it would require 4,272 Btus per seat per mile. The Jet-A design would require 6,102 Btus—43 percent more.

Brewer came to the slightly startling conclusion that, based on the then current cost of coal ($17.50 per ton in the United States), a LH_2-fueled AST was almost competitive with a kerosene-powered AST. According to studies by the Institute of Gas Technology and by Linde for NASA, liquid hydrogen could be produced from coal for $6.00 per million Btus. At that fuel price the liquid-hydrogen–fueled AST could operate at a direct operating cost (DOC) of 3.4 cents per seat per nautical mile. A corresponding Jet-A–fueled AST could afford to pay 52 cents per gallon ($4.12 per million Btus) to provide equal DOC, an increase of only about 10 cents per gallon above 1978 prices. Assuming that both fuels, synthetic Jet-A as well as liquid hydrogen, must be produced from coal, the LH_2-fueled version would have offered cost advantages as early as the mid-seventies.

Beyond economics, the environmental aspects that made the hydrogen-fueled subsonic transport plane attractive also apply to the LH_2-fueled AST. Both sideline and flyover noise are expected to be lower—105.9 EPNdB versus 108.0 for the Jet-A version, and 104.3 EPNdB versus 108.0, respectively—because the plane is considerably lighter.

Sonic boom pressures are likely to be down as well, because of the LH_2 plane's reduced weight and smaller wing area, and further pressure reduction may become possible with advanced designs. Brewer projects a maximum sonic-boom pressure of 1.32 pounds per square foot (psf) (6.4 kg per square meter) for the LH_2 version at the start of supersonic cruise compared to 1.87 psf (9.1 kg per square meter) for the Jet-A model at the same point. At the end of flight, the corresponding figures would be 1.19 and 1.40 psf (6.9 and 6.8 kg per square meter), respectively, and maximum pressure encountered during climbout would be 2.08 psf (10.2 kg per square meter) for the LH_2 plane compared to 2.50 psf (12.2 kg per square meter) for the Jet-A design.

As to emissions, the supersonic hydrogen engine would have low NOX emissions, no CO, no unburned hydrocarbons, and no odor emissions. On the other hand, the LH_2 plane would produce almost twice as much water vapor as the Jet-A–fueled SST—146 pounds (66.2 kg) per nautical mile compared with 75.3 pounds (24 kg)—for all four engines.

A peculiarity of liquid hydrogen is its ability to absorb large amounts of heat. While of no particular importance in the design of future ASTs with speeds of around 2.7 times the speed of sound, it becomes crucial when looking beyond the AST toward future hypersonic transports (HSTs) that may cruise three, six, or even eight times the speed of sound. Aircraft and components of this type have already been studied at Langley and elsewhere. Airplane concepts like this are beginning to seep into the design offices of commercial plane makers and are no longer confined to science fiction as evidenced by a fall 1977 announcement from Lockheed that it had received a $250,000, 15-month contract from NASA to study a liquid hydrogen–fueled, liquid hydrogen–cooled, arrowhead-shaped transport plane cruising at 4,000 mph (6,400 kilometers per hour), six times the speed of sound. The idea was not to build an actual plane or components, but to refine the concept on paper—to improve aerodynamics and lift, reduce sonic boom shock, and so on with computer studies and model testing. At present, NASA does not anticipate building such a plane until the beginning of the next century.

At these tremendous speeds, the vast cooling capability of liquid hydrogen becomes an additional asset, quite independent of the fuel's energetic and environmental advantages. One main problem with aircraft of this type is that the friction of the hypersonic airstream builds up tremendous temperatures at the leading edges of fuselage, wings, and control surfaces, up to 2,500°F. (1,370°C.) at the nose of a Mach 6 plane zooming along at 90,000 feet (27,000 meters). Temperatures of this magnitude can be handled by installing special heat shields made of superalloys and refractory metals to protect the primary structure. But such intricate designs involving thin heat shields, protective sliding joints, and flexible bellows are delicate, and it is uncertain how they would stand up to the rough treatment of commercial aviation.

A way out is to employ the cold hydrogen fuel as a coolant for the HST, funneling the liquid through carefully spaced cooling tubes in all the critical areas where heat buildup occurs, but also cooling the flight deck and the passenger compartment. As described by NASA's Witcofski in various papers, LH_2 would be used indirectly. The coolant circulating through airframe and skin would be a secondary fluid—a water-ethylene-glycol solution for cooling aluminum or a silicone-based liquid for titanium parts—that would carry the heat away from these critical areas and transmit it via a heat exchanger to the liquid hydrogen, which then is burned in the engines as fuel. The friction heat thus transferred imparts an extra "push," an extra amount of energy, into the fuel.

Figure 7.8. British Aircraft Corporation's "notional concept" of a liquid-hydrogen-fueled Mach 3 to 3.5, 500-passenger airliner for the 21st century. This rendering of a possible future hypersonic transport was displayed at the 1976 Farnborough Air Show.

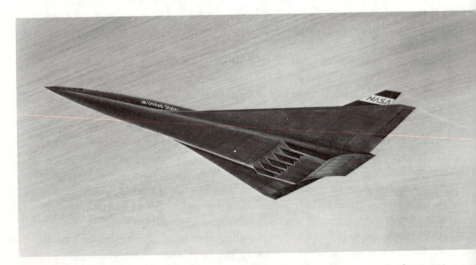

Figure 7.9. A design sketch released with Lockheed's announcement of a $250,000 paper study for a liquid-hydrogen–fueled Mach 6, 200-passenger airliner. NASA awarded the study in 1977.

This "actively cooled" design has the advantage over "hot structures" in that the metallurgical requirements are much simpler. Instead of superalloys and refractory metals, more conventional materials that fall within the existing metallurgical experience of airplane manufacturers can be used. If it were possible to cool the skin and primary structure of the aircraft to around 500°F. (260°C.) in a Mach 6 airliner, the aircraft could be constructed of titanium, using current materials and construction technologies, Witcofski said in a report at the 1972 San Diego conference. With minimal heat shielding it would be feasible to cool the airframe to 200°F. (93.3°C.), making possible the use of aluminum and even opening the door to the use of boron-aluminum composites. Significantly, "the weight of the entire cooling system was found to be more than offset by the weight savings accomplished by reductions in the weight of the airframe, heat shields and insulation," Witcofski said.

The verdict regarding the use of liquid hydrogen for long-range commercial aircraft, both subsonic and supersonic, is, in Brewer's words, "an enthusiastic yes!"[4] Said Brewer:

Technically, there is no question concerning its superiority. The use of LH_2 as fuel for transport aircraft in both speed categories results in designs which are lighter, quieter, use smaller engines, are able to operate from smaller airports,[5] minimize pollution of the environment, and expend less energy in performing their missions than equivalent designs fueled with Jet-A. In addition, the hydrogen aircraft are physically smaller in span and wing area, but characteristically have larger fuselages.

At prices currently being paid by international air carriers for Jet-A fuel, and using recent estimates of the price for which liquid hydrogen could be manufactured from lignite or coal, pipelined to the airport site and there liquefied and stored, LH_2-fueled aircraft could be operated by the airlines at significant saving in direct operating cost.

Criticism of Hydrogen and Countercriticism

Other studies have disputed that last judgment, though. Witcofski, whose credentials as an ardent advocate of hydrogen are beyond doubt, reported at the 1976 First World Hydrogen Conference in Miami Beach that in terms of total cost, including the expense of making, transporting, and storing aviation fuel, liquid methane may be less expensive and therefore preferable from the standpoint of economics in the next 15 to 20 years; but this prediction leaves out the entire range of environmental questions.

To be sure, hydrogen, in Witcofski's view, is still the ultimate chemical energy carrier, once nuclear energy and sun power can be tied *economically* to hydrogen production. But meanwhile, coal is probably the most plentiful energy resource for the next decades. To make coal usable for a wider range of energy applications than exist now, including the production of synthetic fuels via coal gasification and liquefaction, is the aim of energy policy planners on both sides of the Atlantic. Witcofski, reporting on various coal utilization studies conducted for NASA by the Linde Division of Union Carbide and the Institute of Gas Technology, said that in the total energy production chains for synthetic aviation kerosene, liquid hydrogen, and methane, the last fuel emerges as the most efficient when the total cost of production, transport, storage, and combustion in the airplane are taken into account.

Witcofski cautioned, though, that coal was the only source of energy considered in his paper, and "conclusions drawn from this paper with regard to the viability of hydrogen-fueled aircraft in the future of aviation should be done so with that fact in mind. Emerging hydrogen production technologies, based on other energy sources and improved liquefaction techniques, may greatly change the perspective of hydrogen-fueled aircraft in the future."

Others also doubt that liquid hydrogen derived from coal liquefaction or gasification would be an economical proposition, arguing that some sort of synthetic hydrocarbon fuel is more practicable. Two Rand Corporation researchers, William Mikolowsky and William Stanley, said at the 1976 Miami conference that liquid hydrogen would be about three times as expensive as synthetic jet fuel, using the same ground rules such as coal price and financing. Mikolowsky said that with coal as the primary energy source, synthetic jet fuel probably would run about $3.20 (in 1975 dollars) per million Btus, while liquid hydrogen would cost about $9.50 for the same amount of energy—a much wider cost gap between the two fuels than the one in the NASA-commissioned studies.

Mikolowsky limited his report to a study of liquid hydrogen as used in military aircraft. He further narrowed his remarks to the fueling requirements of very large planes, 330 to 375 feet (100 to 114 meters) in length and weighing 1.275 million pounds (578 tons) for the LH₂ version to 1.84 million pounds (834 tons) for the synthetic jet fuel version, the type of plane required for global airlifts of military equipment or as an airborne missile-launch station.

Mikolowsky found that over a plane's typical 20-year life cycle and given the unusual air force requirements, fuel costs would outweigh the lower production, development, and nonfuel operating and support costs of a liquid hydrogen–fueled supertransport. This is based also on low utilization typical of air force practices in times of peace, when large transports are flown only two hours a day on the average. If the plane flew more frequently the fuel costs would go up sharply and the hydrogen plane would be even less attractive—assuming that the Mikolowsky numbers are correct, a point disputed by Brewer and others.

Mikolowsky assumed that liquid hydrogen would not be widely available at airfields around the world in the time frame under study (1985–2000), affecting refueling prospects and routing. In a 10-point assessment, Mikolowsky gives 5 "most attractive" points to the syn-jet plane (basing flexibility, routing flexibility, in-flight vulnerability, prelaunch survivability, and crew safety) while the LH_2 version gets only 3 "most attractive" points (public safety, air pollution, noise pollution). In two areas, technical risk and development potentials, the two models are rated as comparable. Again, Brewer disagrees sharply as far as technical risk is concerned, pointing to air force tests in which both incendiary and fragmentation bullets were fired into tanks containing liquid hydrogen and JP-4, a type of kerosene aviation fuel (see Chapter 10). Liquid hydrogen was much more benign and forgiving, providing greater crew safety.

In terms of economics, Mikolowsky reported on a variety of projected missions. In the strategic airlift category, the syn-jet plane wins in almost all categories as being more *energy effective* in all missions (e.g., North Atlantic Treaty Organization [NATO] range and NATO radius, Middle East and Far East range and radius) and as being also more *cost effective* in all but the Middle East radius assignment (radius meaning there is no fuel available at the unloading point and the plane must carry enough fuel when starting out to permit return to base in the United States). For station-keeping missions (the missile-carrying plane takes off, flies to a certain point where it loiters in readiness to launch missiles or other hardware such as microfighters, and returns to base later), the syn-jet plane was more cost effective in all categories with station radii to 6,000 nautical miles (11,000 kilometers). In terms of relative energy effectiveness the LH_2 plane was rated "most attractive" only for long-range missions with radii of 4,500 and 6,000 nautical miles (8,200 and 11,000 kilometers), respectively. "In summary, then, we believe that there is little, if any, potential for liquid hydrogen as a fuel for aircraft entering the Air Force inventory between now and the turn of the century," Mikolowsky concluded.

Here too, the Mikolowsky numbers are disputed. The Rand data, in effect, represent the complete reverse of what Witcofski calculated about process thermal efficiency and cost, based on the NASA-commissioned IGT-Linde studies. Brewer, in fact, has compared both approaches[6] and concluded that hydrogen is the preferred fuel in terms of a plane's life cycle and the total process energy required.

Lockheed's studies for NASA, which have focused entirely on commercial aircraft, examined the use of synthetic jet fuel and also of liquid methane. Brewer dismisses liquid methane as being an inferior choice for reasons such as safety and availability as well as environmental considerations, the main factor that killed the earlier U.S. SST program.

Brewer argues that since civil commercial aviation is a truly international business, with airplanes refueling in New York as well as Rome, Tokyo, Jeddah, Warsaw, and Karachi, a future synthetic aviation fuel must be equally international—locally producible, with uniform characteristics everywhere.

This is no problem when petroleum is cheap, with kerosene as well as other hydrocarbon fuels available at low cost all over the world. But petroleum isn't cheap any longer and it's going to be more expensive. More importantly, the percentage of the total energy consumption used in commercial aviation in industrial nations such as the United States is going to quintuple in the last 30 years of this century, according to a 1971 article by E. Cook in *Scientific American*, cited by Brewer.[7] In 1970, only about 2 percent of the total energy used in the United States was used in commercial aviation; this figure may reach 10 percent by the year 2000. These growth estimates are based on pre–oil shock data and assumptions and though total growth projections are being scaled down, the ratio of aviation to nonaviation energy use may still be indicative of future trends. Brewer now provides a striking example to illustrate the dilemma airlines will face if they still have to rely on petroleum-based aviation fuel in 2000: The recoverable oil in the Alaskan North Slope is estimated at 9.6 billion barrels. With current refinery practices, only about 5 percent of a barrel of oil is converted into fuel with commercial aviation specs, but the yield can be maximized to 17 percent at the expense of gasoline and other products. If that 10 percent estimate is accurate, the entire crude deemed recoverable from the North Slope would supply the minimum aviation needs forecast for 2000 for only two and a half months. If refining production is really cranked up to the 17 percent level, an unlikely assumption, the North Slope yield would last for eight months, Brewer said.

And even if future aviation were stifled to the extent that actual energy usage turns out to be only one-tenth of what the 1970 forecast predicted, the figures wouldn't be all that much better—20 and 80 months, respectively—not a great deal of jet fuel from the North Slope.

The point of this digression is to illustrate Brewer's contention that there is no way around the development of a new generation of synthetic aviation fuels—synthetic kerosene, methane, or hydrogen—even if total demand rises only slowly.

The capitals mentioned as international refueling points were picked with a purpose. If methane were to become the future preferred aviation fuel, that would be all right for, say, New York and Warsaw. The United States and Poland have plenty of coal, and coal gasification plants, the source of any future liquid methane, are being studied in both places and will probably be built.

But what about Rome? Tokyo? Karachi? Jeddah? Italy has no coal; neither have Japan, Pakistan, and Saudi Arabia. However, Italy could produce hydrogen from solar power; so could Pakistan and Saudi Arabia.[8] Japan could make hydrogen from offshore floating nuclear and solar "energy islands" that the country plans to build under its far-sighted, comprehensive national energy plan, Project Sunshine.

The point is quite clear: While local utilities and power plants can employ any type of primary energy or carrier that is locally most advantageous, international air travel has to use the same energy carrier everywhere. Says Brewer:

> If international air travel is to continue to flourish and expand as projected in the face of definite prospects that some countries may be unable to obtain adequate supplies of petroleum at all times, it becomes mandatory either that all nations agree to share their petroleum fuel supplies or that they adopt an alternate fuel that can be commonly produced without hazard of control by a cartel.
>
> Hydrogen offers many potential advantages for this application including the facts that (1) it can be manufactured from coal and water, or from water directly, using any of several processes and a wide variety of possible energy sources, and therefore can be considered to be free of the dangers of cartelization and (2) used as a fuel for aircraft it has been shown to provide significant improvements in vehicle weight, performance, and cost and to result in reduced pollution of the environment. Recognition of these advantages has, as a result of NASA-sponsored conceptual design studies, led to consideration of hydrogen as a leading candidate to replace Jet-A as the fuel for commercial aircraft of the future.

Among airplane manufacturers, Lockheed seems to be alone right now in promoting hydrogen as an aviation fuel for subsonic planes, although nobody questions the need for liquid hydrogen for a future hypersonic transport of the type that Lockheed was exploring under its 1977 NASA contract. Speaking for the skeptics, G. J. Schott, chief engineer in Boeing's Office of Energy and Emissions, told a 1975 conference of the

California Association of Airport Executives that liquid hydrogen was highly unlikely to become a viable commercial airline fuel in the next few decades. "We should not discount the possibility that liquid hydrogen-fueled airplanes may be built in the next few decades, but the probability is overwhelming that they will be built for special missions," he said. "For normal aircraft missions kerosene will probably be the fuel for many decades to come."

Bringing fuel logistics and investment problems into perspective, Schott pointed out that the amount of liquid hydrogen produced in the United States from the two most common commercial methods (steam reforming of natural gas and partial oxidation of petroleum products) was just enough to fuel only one Boeing 747 jumbo per day with liquid hydrogen. "Even at the peak of the Apollo program, the production rate of LH_2 was only twice the current rate," Schott said.

If, for example, Chicago's O'Hare, the world's busiest airport, were to be converted entirely to hydrogen operation, it would require something like 3,000 tons of LH_2 every day. The biggest LH_2 plants operating now produce about 60 tons a day.

If hydrogen were to be made via electrolysis, the investment required would be almost $4.9 billion (1973 dollars). For LH_2 made from coal, the outlay would still be $1.3 billion. To hydrolyze that amount of hydrogen, equal in energy content to the 8,300 tons of kerosene tanked at O'Hare every day, Schott calculated that the output of three of the world's biggest nuclear power plants (2000 megawatts each) would be required.

The late A. V. (Val) Cleaver, before his death in 1977 energy adviser to Rolls-Royce, the British maker of expensive cars and of jet engines, was even blunter in his assessment. In a letter to a German chemical-rocket-propulsion expert, Cleaver, after restating the obvious, that liquid hydrogen is often the "best available choice" for "certain very difficult rocket missions" and possibly for very high-altitude, high-speed planes, said that hydrogen simply didn't have a chance elsewhere:

It is . . . an *absolute nonsense* to suggest that liquid hydrogen would ever be an acceptable fuel for ordinary sub- or supersonic aircraft for operation from airfields all over the world. It is even more stupid to suggest it as a possible fuel for ordinary automobiles or road vehicles of any kind.

In the latter case storage as a gas or in a hydrided form has also been suggested but is similarly unacceptable on grounds of weight and volume for the whole system.

I would not go so far as to assert that these things could not be done, if mankind had no possible alternative. However, in practice, there are many preferable alternatives—most obviously, when natural oil sources are depleted, the manufacture of synthetic hydrocarbon fuels. This being so, all the considerations of infra-structure costs . . . become very significant together with the vast existing investment in infra-structure related to oil fuels. Most damning of all, however, is the sheer inconvenience which the use of liquid hydrogen would introduce, when handled by relatively unskilled people.

Cleaver makes it clear he is talking only about airplanes, not about a general hydrogen economy: "I don't often make such dogmatic and unqualified statements as the above, but have no hesitation in doing so in the present context." A general hydrogen economy, he says, may be expensive, but development "on a fairly large scale" is "very possible," although he cannot foresee hydrogen replacing electricity as "the major system of this sort."

Perhaps Cleaver was too dogmatic after all, too prudent, or both. In 1978, only a year after his death, Lockheed began cautiously floating the idea of a small liquid-hydrogen–fueled, four-plane, experimental cargo airline linking the United States, Europe, and the Middle East. Lockheed wanted to convert four Tri-Star wide-body jets to liquid-hydrogen operation. Even without the optimum design changes possible with liquid hydrogen, Lockheed felt that the modified air cargo planes would provide an aerial showcase that would convincingly demonstrate the technical, environmental, and potential economic advantages of liquid hydrogen as jet fuel.

Specifically, the four planes would be deployed on a continuous round trip linking Pittsburgh, Pennsylvania, Frankfurt, West Germany, and Riyadh, Saudi Arabia, stopping in Birmingham, England, instead of Frankfurt, on the return leg. The rationale for these particular choices was twofold: First, these important industrial and commercial centers already generate enough international cargo traffic to provide a reasonably high load factor for the four Tri-Stars. Second, the four airports are close enough to existing primary energy deposits—coal in the cases of Pittsburgh, Frankfurt, and Birmingham, oil and natural gas near Riyadh—to permit setting up advanced-design hydrogen production and liquefaction plants at those airports using whatever methods fit in best with national energy plans. These would be relatively small-scale (20 tons [22 short tons] per day) demonstration programs to help speed up the development of promising hydrogen production processes as well as airport and aircraft hydrogen handling systems.

There is some cautious interest in the project, but so far the governments concerned have shied away from committing themselves to the $1.4 billion required for converting four planes to hydrogen and for building airport facilities. The U.S. Department of Energy and NASA are

Figure 7.10. A rendering of a Lockheed L-1011 Tri-Star converted to liquid-hydrogen operations under the "LEAP" concept.

willing to chip in relatively small amounts towards development of hardware items, such as better cryogenic fuel pumps and better insulation materials. A September 1979 conference on the subject in Stuttgart, Germany, failed to come up with a clear endorsement of LEAP (for Liquidhydrogen Experimental Airline Project), as the project had been called. The degree of support from governments and experts ranged "from negative to lukewarm," as *Business Week* said in a story on the conference. Most of the 125 conferees agreed that liquid hydrogen would fuel airplanes ultimately, but not yet, and the consensus was that it would be sufficient to modify a single plane for demonstration purposes instead of operating a four-plane fleet.

In early 1980 it appeared, though, that interest was widening again. Representatives from seven governments met in Montreal in April to discuss the project again, and another meeting was held by a working group in Germany. However, not much was accomplished at these sessions, according to one participant, and the feeling was that no definitive decisions would be forthcoming from the U.S. government whether or not to support LEAP until after the inauguration of Ronald Reagan in January 1981. The German government was skeptical and was unlikely to support the project. Indicative of the attitude of the German Ministry for Research and Technology was the comment of one official who sniffed that Lockheed's proposal consisted of "an airplane full of hydrogen and one emergency seat"—not true, patently, but revealing. Nevertheless, Lockheed was still promoting the idea in 1980, supported by a group of Canadian businessmen who see potential for selling Canadian electrolysis equipment and related hardware. The overall plans called for a four-year R&D phase to last from 1981 until 1984, followed by construction of the four planes and the needed airport facilities. If the project gets underway it would indeed be a long leap from those early B-57 contrails over Lake Erie.

The Invisible Flame:
Hydrogen as Utility Gas

Hydrogen in the Home

In the late 1960s the American Institute of Gas Technology exhibited a Home for Tomorrow, powered by a fuel called "reformed natural gas," which was described as the "new super active form of natural gas." A four-page illustrated color brochure, with girls in costumes that looked like something out of an early Star Trek pilot, described new types of illumination based on gas only, portable gas appliances, wall-panel flameless heaters, gas-fueled cool luminescent lamps, gas-powered total climate control, and electricity generated in the house via fuel cells from this reformed natural gas.

Today, with natural gas supplies beginning to dwindle and prices going out of sight, when the more adventurous energy-saving souls are returning to wood-burning stoves, statements like "natural gas will still be in the future as it is today," or "Our Home for Tomorrow will demand a far higher level of indoor comfort than we know today" seem nostalgically silly.

Yet, there was significance in the enthusiastic prose. That "super active" form of natural gas IGT was talking about was nothing other than a hydrogen-rich gas mixture, similar but not identical to the manufactured town gas or coal gas produced in the late nineteenth and early twentieth centuries: While town gas typically had up to 50 percent hydrogen, "reformed natural" would contain around 80 percent hydrogen, 20 percent carbon dioxide, and less than one-half percent carbon monoxide.

Under the Home for Tomorrow concept developed by IGT together with the Pratt & Whitney Division of what was then United Aircraft (now United Technologies Corp.), the idea was to pipe straight natural gas to a home. Except for the portions burned directly—in space heating, for instance—the gas would be piped into a compact "reformer" that, using heat and steam, would convert natural gas in a three-step reaction with the help of catalysts into "reformed natural gas," i.e., mostly hydrogen.

The concept was described in a 1970 article in the industry magazine *Appliance Engineer* by Robert B. Rosenberg and Esher R. Kweller of IGT. Using hydrogen would open the way for what are known as catalytic burners for kitchen stoves, for example. Unlike conventional burners that burn with a blue flame, these burners produce an invisible flame. They transfer more usable heat to whatever food is being heated, broiled, or grilled. Temperature ranges are much wider and can be adjusted much more finely, and the heat is distributed much more evenly over the entire burner surface. A catalytic burner, said Rosenberg and Kweller, "is self-starting, requiring no pilot, glow coil or spark ignition." Ignition takes place when the hydrogen gas contacts the catalyst—in prototype burner models, typically a very thin coating of platinum—and the burner begins to give off heat. The by-product is water vapor, which is desirable if the room is to be humidified.

Using these general principles, IGT then developed a number of prototype appliances with some rather unusual features. For example, there was a smooth-top range that looked more like an ordinary sideboard surface with a couple of built-in dials. Because of the fine-tuning capability and wide range of heat available, "water can be boiled very rapidly or the most delicate sauce kept barely warm," Rosenberg and Kweller said. A warming tray can be made of wood because the temperature can be limited to a maximum 250°F. (121°C.), below wood's burning or scorching temperature. Room heaters could operate at low temperatures and could be hung on the wall, covered with formica or other panel materials.

"Reformed natural" was also the power source for a novel illumination process developed called candoluminescence. It involved a low-temperature combustion process in which light emission is stimulated by molecules, ions, and atoms excited by the flame. "The physical causes of candoluminescence are still unknown, but we do know that this phenomenon provides new product possibilities," Rosenberg and Kweller said.

The early optimism has cooled a great deal since then. The idea of installing a home-sized, "black box" natural gas converter in private suburban homes, fueled by normal natural gas, has faded. Natural gas is on the decline in terms of availability and on the increase in terms of price. Incentives for constructing natural gas reformers for the home on an assembly-line basis have disappeared, although work on commercial fuel cells, both for private homes and for central stations, is going on.

Instead, the realization has grown that if hydrogen is to play a large-scale role at all, it has to be produced at some central plant and be piped directly to individual customers—private homes, industry, airports—instead of "manufacturing" a hydrogen-rich gas near the end user. The Home for Tomorrow program was a commercially inspired public relations effort to promote natural gas in direct head-to-head (Or should it be heat-to-heat?) competition with electricity.

Fortunately, IGT's program had the salubrious effect of helping to initiate a research program into the mechanics of using hydrogen in the home that might not otherwise have happened before the oil crisis. As it was, IGT, under contract to the Southern California Gas Company, began developing high-temperature catalytic gas burners from scratch. Three IGT researchers presented a paper on the technical problems of burning hydrogen, both in modified conventional burners and advanced catalytic burners, at the 1976 Miami Beach hydrogen conference (no further mention of candoluminescence, though). The trio, Jon B. Pangborn, Maurice I. Scott, and John C. Sharer, said that hydrogen cannot be directly substituted for natural gas in domestic and commercial appliances but that burners would have to be modified, a prospect they did not regard as prohibitive. "Similar equipment modifications were necessary when natural gas was substituted for manufactured gas several decades ago in the United States," they pointed out.

Conventional atmospheric premix burners suffer from flashback when burning hydrogen. The flame will not travel back into the pipe beyond the metering orifice because beyond that point there is no air or oxygen to sustain the flame. Nevertheless, a flame traveling back to the orifice past the burner ports may "severely" damage the burner head, the three researchers said. The problem can be tackled either by increasing gas pressure and smaller burner port sizes or by reducing or eliminating the amount of so-called primary air (air that is mixed into the gas stream near the metering gas orifice, a couple of inches or so before reaching the burner ports where the flame is).

A second, minor, problem is that conventional burners make a relatively loud noise at startup and shutdown of the hydrogen flame. During startup, the flame made a popping sound, and a "muffled sound of higher intensity," according to Pangborn, Scott, and Sharer, was typically heard when the hydrogen gas was shut off. The three said no easy solution of this problem was apparent, but suggested that a decrease in the burner's internal volume, the area between the metering orifice and the ports through which the gas travels, might do the trick.

Hydrogen does not produce any deadly carbon monoxide or unburned hydrocarbons, but the three noted that tests showed that an open-flame hydrogen burner would produce around 30 percent more nitrogen oxide

(NOX) emissions than burning natural gas, caused by the flame's reaction with the air's nitrogen. Pangborn, Scott, and Sharer felt that most problems could be overcome with increased pressure drop and flow rate at the user's end, coupled with a redesigned burner along the lines mentioned, to make most current gas appliances compatible with hydrogen as fuel gas.

A much greater problem is whether hydrogen can be carried in existing natural gas pipeline networks, something that some researchers took pretty much for granted in the early seventies. This is not so, said the three: Before converting large stretches of pipeline to hydrogen operation, a great deal of research is required. "Any statement that hydrogen or hydrogen-rich gases can be adequately and safely delivered to the customer by using the in-place natural gas distribution system is a presumption," they said. What exists nowadays actually is not a single natural gas system but "a tremendous diversity of pipes and fittings." Early low-pressure manufactured-gas systems were made predominantly of gray cast iron. Since then ductile and wrought iron mains have been added, followed by steel mains and services lines (from the mains to the customer) with the advent of higher-pressure natural gas. Utilities now overwhelmingly lay plastic pipes for new and replacement mains and services lines. Then there are materials like brass (in valves), natural and synthetic rubber (in mechanical joint seals and meter diaphragms), lead and jute (sealer materials), cast aluminum (meter housings and regulator parts), and others. Verification that these materials can be used safely with hydrogen is needed.

Leakage, which some researchers consider serious, is not that problematic, according to Pangborn, Scott, and Sharer. In terms of volume hydrogen loss is about two and a half times the rate of natural gas, but the energy loss is about the same. At normal temperatures, they say, cast iron and steel are almost impermeable to both gases, but tests are still called for. Plastic pipes are probably more permeable, but still the three researchers felt that the hydrogen lost seeping through the plastic is still low enough to appear "insignificant." An earlier IGT study said that while hydrogen leaks a lot more through plastic pipes than natural gas—the ratios are roughly 7 times more for hydrogen through polyethylene pipes and as high as 88 times through ABS-type pipes—the absolute leakage rates may still be low enough to at least justify a closer look.

Metallurgical embrittlement, a problem considered serious by others, is not exactly dismissed but is not regarded as prohibitive either: "These modes of hydrogen attack have been observed to occur under pressure and temperature conditions far more extreme than those of a gas distribution system," they said. "These metallurgical effects would not be expected to occur in distribution equipment used for hydrogen service because of the operating pressures and ambient temperatures." The three make no reference to high pressures in future hydrogen supply systems, deemed essential by other researchers; Pangborn, Scott, and Sharer assume that hydrogen gas would merely flow faster and at somewhat higher pressures.

If existing pipeline materials are found to be safe for hydrogen, the three suggest that by simply speeding up the flow rate to about 2.8 times the rate of natural gas, but using currently used pipeline pressures to play it safe, existing lines could deliver as much as 85 percent of the energy transported nowadays by natural gas to the end user. In other words, by accepting an energy penalty of 15 percent at the burner end, which could be largely compensated for by using more efficient catalytic burners, Pangborn, Scott, and Sharer thought that the existing pipeline network could in fact be used, always assuming that materials compatibility and safety were established to all-around satisfaction.

This is not to say that hydrogen is simple and easy to use in every respect. Hydrogen does create greater problems than normal when new lines have to be installed or when old lines have to be repaired—during welding, for instance. Also, because hydrogen burns in such a wide range of air mixture ratios, from 4 to 74 percent hydrogen, lines going on stream have to be carefully purged with an inert gas or the hydrogen-air ratio would have to be safely above 75 percent. (With natural gas, utilities in the United States commonly weld pipelines when the gas content in the pipeline is well above 15 percent.) Pangborn, Scott, and Sharer call this "an area of serious concern."

In a follow-up study aimed at identifying problem areas in hydrogen distribution and using largely state-of-the-art gas distribution equipment, Pangborn, together with IGT colleagues D. G. Johnson and W. J. Jasionowski, reported some preliminary findings at the 1978 Zurich hydrogen conference. Among other things, the IGT team verified that under pressure conditions normally applying to natural gas delivery, hydrogen's volumetric flow rate in a test loop that simulated commercial and residential operations was about 300 percent that of natural gas. This meant that actual energy delivered was about 97 percent that of natural gas. A second loop simulating industrial delivery produced a volumetric flow rate of only 245 percent, translating into only 80 percent energy delivered at the user end.

As to leakage, the team presented preliminary findings only for the industrial loop test at Zurich. Not unexpectedly, hydrogen showed a volumetric leakage rate more than three times as large as for natural gas.

Figure 8.1. Roger Billings's "Hydrogen Homestead," a residence fueled entirely by hydrogen. The automobile in front and the garden tractor in the background are also fueled by hydrogen. (Photo courtesy of Billings Energy Corp.)

Compressor leakage increased with time, while with natural gas, the compressor leaked less with time, apparently as seals and rings "wore in." In general, the three found "leakage rates for most of the components are not unproportionately large for hydrogen versus natural gas." The commercial-residential test, completed after the conference, produced generally favorable results for hydrogen.

At the same conference, Roger Billings presented a report on the world's first hydrogen-powered home, his Hydrogen Homestead residence in Provo, Utah, where all natural gas appliances—oven, range, barbecue, fireplace log, and a booster heater in the heat pump system—have been converted to hydrogen. In addition, Billings's car, a 1977 Cadillac, has been equipped with an auxiliary hydride-hydrogen system for short shopping trips (for long-distance driving, the car uses a conventional fuel tank). Billings also converted a garden tractor to hydrogen operation by adding a small hydride storage tank. Cadillac and tractor are recharged with hydrogen from a commercial electrolyzer housed together with an experimental hydride storage vessel, hot-water storage tanks and a computer monitoring system, topped by 10 roof-mounted sun collectors, in a separate building.

The burners of the various appliances were converted essentially by eliminating primary air and by adding a spoke-shaped spreader nozzle to distribute hydrogen within a stainless-steel wire mesh around the burner ports. The mesh facilitates the gradual mixing of air and hydrogen. Stainless steel, an excellent catalyst, helps maintain combustion in parts of the flame zone where air-hydrogen mixtures are such that they would not burn by themselves. The stainless steel mesh helps also to control combustion temperatures in such a way that NOX emissions, which can go as high as 250 parts per million (ppm) in normal hydrogen burning, stay as low as 5 ppm (25 to 35 ppm is typical for natural gas).

This hydrogen home is a test facility "for the evaluation of hydrogen systems and the interface with electric and solar systems. . . . Test operations of available hardware will serve to promote interest in hydrogen application and speed development of hydrogen related technology," Billings concluded in his Zurich presentation. He hopes to expand his single home into an entire subdivision with 38 homes, to be called—what else?—Hydrogen Village.

Hydrogen Gas Storage

Underground Storage

Some 20 miles west of Paris, just northwest of Versailles, lies the small town of Beynes. In the hydrogen community the location carries a certain amount of fame because it is one of the few places so far where hydrogen, or rather hydrogen-rich town gas, has been successfully stored in a so-called aquifer underground formation. It has been suggested that large quantities of hydrogen could be stored underground, in exhausted natural gas fields, in natural or man-made caverns (leached salt caverns or caverns made by explosive blasts) fairly close to the surface, or in these aquifers—porous rock formations that contain water. The concept again stems from practices in the natural gas industry, which has long been using depleted gas and oil fields to store huge amounts of natural gas. With modifications, hydrogen may be storable in similar fashion, many researchers believe. In fact, one Dutch study group postulates that hydrogen may play a large role in that country's long-term energy future precisely because of the existence of large, depleted natural gas fields in the Netherlands.

Storage is an essential feature of any gas transmission system to maintain a "buffer" for seasonal, daily, and hourly swings in demand. In any type of gas production grid it is uneconomical to lay out the producing plant for maximum demand, because then the plant would have to operate at less than capacity, hence uneconomically, for long periods of time. Storage facilities even out the ups and downs of demand, including temporary interruptions and breakdowns, and still permit steady, maximum-efficiency production.

Although hydrogen is more "leaky" than natural gas, most experts feel that this has no bearing on storage, although the materials involved in injection and withdrawal equipment may pose some (not insuperable) problems. Also, because of gaseous hydrogen's low heating value compared to natural gas, hydrogen storage facilities of whatever shape will have to be bigger and more expensive than those for natural gas. Stored under pressure, hydrogen will require proportionately more volume than natural gas compressed to similar densities.

Aquifers are similar to natural gas and oil fields in that they are porous geological formations, but without the fossil fuel or natural gas content. Many of them feature a "caprock" formation, a layer on top of the formation that is usually saturated with water. This layer acts as a seal against the gas leaking out; it works for both natural gas and the lighter hydrogen.

Indirect proof that very light "leaky" gases can be successfully stored in underground formations has come from several years of work with helium by the U.S. Department of the Interior. Helium has been injected into depleted natural gas fields near Amarillo, Texas. Hydrogen advocates feel that the data obtained in these trials indicate that hydrogen can be stored in much the same way.

One problem is that a fairly large amount of gas, be it natural gas or hydrogen, has to be "invested" initially and written off as a loss in these storage formations in order to build up the underground pressure to squeeze out the recoverable gas later on. This "cushion gas" cannot be recovered, at least not easily. The Beynes field, for instance, has a storage capacity of 7 billion cubic feet (200 million cubic meters), but also needs an additional 6 billion cubic feet (170 million cubic meters) of cushion gas. (Ironically, this field came to the attention of the hydrogen community only after French authorities were making plans to phase out the hydrogen-rich town gas and convert the field to storage of natural gas in the middle and late 1960s.)

Given the higher cost of hydrogen production and storage, many hydrogen advocates feel it may be well worth while to investigate new, unconventional storage techniques that have been proposed in connection with natural gas storage. One such suggestion, first reported in a University of Michigan monograph for the American Gas Association in 1966, is the hydrostatically balanced, underwater storage vessel, a dome-shaped structure anchored to the bottom of the sea. These vessels resemble an old-fashioned diver's bell, with a gas duct for injection and withdrawal of hydrogen gas at the top of the dome. The vessel would be open at the bottom, and hydrogen pressure would be pushing the water level down inside the dome. The hydrogen gas would be in direct contact with the water below. A variant of this would be the addition of a floppy bottom to prevent direct contact between water and hydrogen gas and possible hydrogen loss through dissolution into the water. The idea has been revived recently by researchers at City University, London, and Middlesex Polytechnic, Enfield, in Britain. H. C. Chan, A.C.C. Tseung, and K. B. Cheng outlined their concept at the 1980 3rd World Hydrogen Conference in Tokyo. They envision storing gaseous hydrogen in flexible, balloon-like underwater containers made of fiber-reinforced butyl rubber and anchored to the sea bottom by gravel-ballasted concrete structures. They argue that such storage would be especially useful to store hydrogen generated by off-peak power from nuclear power plants, often sited near the sea to insure a plentiful supply of cooling water.

Cryogenic Storage

Cryogenic storage of large amounts of hydrogen is the space-age method. Most everybody has seen the white plumes billowing from the Apollo ships before blast-off, fumes of supercold liquid hydrogen boiling from the tanks and vented into the air. Cryogenic storage at below $-423°F.$ ($-252.7°C.$) is efficient, and liquefied hydrogen is a high-energy fuel. However, cooling the gaseous hydrogen down to its liquid stage is expensive. Apart from possible future aviation use and, perhaps, use as a car and truck fuel, cryogenic storage and widespread usage for utility customers seem remote, although some scientists have proposed combining liquid hydrogen pipelines with ultraconducting cryogenic cables in a frostily symbiotic distribution relationship. (More on this later in the chapter.) Some researchers, like Larry Williams at Marietta and workers at the German aerospace research agency, Deutsche Forschungs und Versuchsanstalt für Luft und Raumfahrt (German Aerospace Research and Experimental Institute [DFVLR]) in Stuttgart think that liquid hydrogen, despite all its handling complications, is the best future fuel for automotive applications.

Derek Gregory, in the 1972 report by the American Gas Association, "A Hydrogen Energy System," points out that at normal pressure liquid hydrogen takes only one eight-hundred-and-fiftieth the volume of hydrogen as a gas. (For liquid natural gas the factor is more than 600; hence the attraction of transporting LNG from Algeria to the United States in LNG tankers with their characteristic spherical LNG containers, a transport method that in principle could be used for liquid hydrogen as well.)[1]

Liquefying hydrogen is an expensive proposition, though. The HEST study concluded that the energy requirements for making one pound of liquid hydrogen—including the work of compressors, turbines, heat exchangers, converters, and precoolers, plus plant lighting, heating, and air-conditioning—amount to around 5.7 kilowatt hours with present commercial technology,[2] although there is promise for more efficient, less expensive refrigeration techniques with "adiabatic demagnetization," a line of research pursued in recent years in connection with work on superconducting magnets. Other sources give higher energy requirements, as much as 10 kilowatt hours.

Liquid hydrogen has been used and stored in fairly large quantities—typically between 15,000 and 26,000 gallons (57,000 and 98,500 liters)—for industrial use, but not as a fuel. The storage tanks at Kennedy Space Center were considerably larger, up to 900,000 gallons (3.4 million liters). Because of liquid hydrogen's peculiar characteristics, the containers are expensive, costing between $2 and $4 per gallon of storage capacity, according to the 1975 IGT survey. They are complicated double-walled structures, so-called dewars, similar to a thermos bottle in concept but with a stainless steel or aluminum inner liner, a vacuum between the two shells, and steel for the outer liner. They are spherical because with that shape the total surface is smallest in comparison to the volume of liquid stored, meaning that evaporation losses are kept to a minimum. Figures as low as one-half percent and even less (for big tanks) per day have been achieved. With a vacuum inside, curved steel sections withstand atmospheric pressure better than straight walls.

As with aquifer storage, some liquid hydrogen is always left in these tanks, not to build up pressure but to keep them permanently chilled. Once they are allowed to "heat up" to ambient temperature it takes sizable quantities of the expensive liquid hydrogen to get the temperature down to storage levels again. The tanks are slightly pressurized to keep outside air from coming in—it would freeze immediately, clogging up valves and other passages. Frozen solid oxygen from the air would present a hazard if it came into contact with hydrogen.

Aside from space applications, liquid hydrogen has not been widely used as a fuel. The type of double-walled piping, gauges, and instrumentation used in aerospace applications are far too expensive for down-to-earth energy usage, and cheaper, rugged equipment is needed. Nevertheless, the IGT study indicates that the notion of using liquid hydrogen as a large-scale commercial fuel is not being totally discounted.

Cryo-adsorption

A third new and untried storage idea that to some extent minimizes the drawbacks of both cryogenic and hydride storage is adsorption of hydrogen. Adsorption is a means of storing a gas or a liquid next to the surface of the adsorptive material, such as activated carbon or nickel silicate, rather than drawing it inside the storage medium itself, as in hydride storage.

The concept of cryogenic adsorption of hydrogen was first presented in a study at the 1976 Miami Beach hydrogen conference by Constantin Carpetis and Walter Peschka from the Institute for Energy Conversion of DFVLR in Stuttgart, the same scientists who are working on LH_2-fueled cars. It created considerable attention, in part because it was the first really new idea in hydrogen storage in several years.

As the name implies, cryogenic storage also means refrigeration of the gas, but the temperatures required are nowhere as extreme as those in pure cryogenic storage, which means a considerable energy saving. For cryo-adsorption, temperatures are in the minus 196°C. (minus 320°F.) range, already in fairly wide industrial use in the liquefaction of nitrogen. Unlike cryogenic storage, which proceeds at ambient pressure, cryo-adsorption requires pressure of about 60 bars (870 psi), which is low compared to the 1,500- to 2,000-bar pressure that hydrogen advocates suggest is necessary for efficient pipelining of hydrogen.

Compared to hydride storage, with its weight problem, cryo-adsorption looks better, on paper at least. Carpetis and Peschka claimed that weight could be cut by as much as one-third compared to the titanium-iron hydride, the material most frequently used in tests so far.

On the other hand, volume requirements are higher, as in pure cryogenic storage, by a factor of three compared to a hydride tank. Other scientists at the conference, impressed by the concept, figured that cryo-adsorption might require one-third less energy for cooling-down purposes than pure cryogenic storage—a considerable saving. Thus, cryo-adsorption represents a potential middle ground between hydride and cryogenic storage, and, in the words of the Peschka-Carpetis paper, is "a very attractive alternative for technical storage of large hydrogen quantities."

In a followup report presented two years later at the 1978 Zurich conference, Peschka and Carpetis said that hydrogen storage with cryogenically cooled adsorbent materials—activated carbon showed the best performance—is feasible and economical under certain conditions. They added that competitiveness of a cryo-adsorbent storage system as a least-cost storage method depends on utilization and capacity factors. At low capacity, such a system performs best with high utilization. As a hypothetical case in which cryo-adsorption storage might compete, Peschka cited energy storage in power plants for meeting daily or weekly peak demands, up to perhaps several hundred megawatts per hour, where storage costs might be "quite acceptable."

Hydride storage

Hydride storage of hydrogen, in which hydrogen is stored inside the metallic lattice structure of certain alloys such as titanium-iron, has received most attention in automotive applications (see Chapter 6).

Hydride storage is a simple, elegant method of storing hydrogen as a gas. About a dozen metals and metal combinations, including niobium, vanadium, lanthanium, and others, are considered suitable for this storage method. The concept is intriguingly simple: Under certain pressure and temperature conditions hydrides soak up hydrogen, giving off heat at the same time. When heat is applied and pressure reduced— e.g., by opening a valve at the reservoir's outlet pipe—hydrogen is released. These temperatures and pressures are different for different types of hydrides—important, for instance, in air-conditioning or heating cars and buses without their engines running, but also for future domestic heating and cooling systems.

While Daimler-Benz and Billings are the principal investigators of automotive applications, a number of other laboratories, among them Allied Chemical Corp., the International Nickel Co., Phillips Research, Sandia Laboratories, Battelle Laboratories, Brookhaven National Laboratory, and Public Service Electric & Gas Co. (PSE&G), of Newark, New Jersey, have been investigating the mechanics of hydride technology. In 1973 Brookhaven built the first engineering-scale titanium-iron hydride hydrogen reservoir for PSE&G in Maplewood, New Jersey, as part of an electric off-peak energy storage experiment conducted by the utility. This hydrogen reservoir was small; it held almost 900 pounds (408 kilograms) of titanium-iron but could store only 14 pounds (6.3 kilograms) of hydrogen gas. Hydrogen was generated from off-peak electricity by a Teledyne electrolyzer, stored in the reservoir, and reconverted to electricity in a small (12 kw/alternating current) fuel cell made by Pratt & Whitney. The experimenters, G. Strickland, J. J. Reilly, and R. H. Wiswall of Brookhaven, reported at the 1974 THEME conference that the design requirements were exceeded, that the flow rate of the discharging gas into the fuel cells was one and a half times higher than envisioned, and that thermal performance was nearly twice as good as asked for.

Next, Brookhaven teams, supported by ERDA, developed fairly detailed engineering concepts for a 26 Mwe peak-power electric plant driven by hydrogen stored in titanium-iron hydride storage beds. The plant would utilize a Lurgi water-alkaline-electrolyte pressure electrolyzer, 10 iron-titanium storage beds, and a 24-module hydrogen-air fuel cell. The heat given off during the hydriding phase, i.e., when the hydrogen gas is soaked up by the storage beds, is discharged into the atmosphere. The same amount of heat is needed again for liberating the gas and is supplied by the heat generated by the fuel cells when hydrogen combines with oxygen in the air to regenerate electric power. For the complete plant cycle, including hydriding, dehydriding, and power generation, overall efficiency (ratio of net plant output to total input) is calculated as 36 percent. Capital cost for the first such plant was estimated at $170 kwe-hr. The Brookhaven team forecast that a reduction of capital costs by more than 50 percent could be achieved by using future higher-temperature electrolyzers that would give greater overall efficiency.

The Brookhaven team pointed out the plant could achieve even better efficiency and higher utilization by what was dubbed the "dual mode" approach: The plant would produce hydrogen not only for storage for eventual reconversion to electricity but for injection into the existing natural gas system to "stretch" supplies.

In the meantime, further research into hydrides and hydride combinations with different pressure and temperature characteristics has spawned a host of applications going far beyond what was envisioned when research started in the late sixties. In addition to the initial investigation of hydrides as a hydrogen storage medium (mainly for cars), stationary hydride tanks or hydride systems are being proposed or investigated for hydrogen purification, compression without normal compressors, separation of hydrogen isotopes to produce deuterium for heavy water, heating and chemical heat pumps, air-conditioning and refrigeration, heat storage, and waste heat recovery.

Some of these applications were described in Zurich in 1978 in a paper by Frank E. Lynch, formerly with the Billings Energy Corporation and also with the Denver Research Institute of the University of Denver, and Ed Snape, of the Ergenics Division of MPD Technology Corp., Waldwick, New Jersey, a company in the vanguard of hydride metal production and research. These include for example, small portable containers to replace heavy, big compressed-gas cylinders for welding and research; they will accept and dispense only high-purity hydrogen (impurities quickly destroy or impair a hydride metal's hydrogen-absorbing capacity).

Also proposed are hydrogen compressors that do away with conventional compression equipment by simply heating a saturated hydride tank. This increases the pressure at which gas is released from the hydride, permitting the release of higher-pressure hydrogen. Lynch and Snape say that by using different hydride combinations and multi-stage operations, pressures of up to 100 atmospheres (atm) are possible, using only low-grade heat as energy source.

Isotope separation is based on a phenomenon being studied at Daimler-Benz, Brookhaven, and General Electric: Certain hydrides preferentially absorb light hydrogen (deuterium). Helmut Buchner at Daimler-Benz, for instance, has found that titanium-nickel hydrides display such selectivity. Buchner envisions large-scale separation processes in which deuterium would be extracted before the normal, lighter hydrogen is sold to motorists as car fuel. Deuterium's sale price creates a credit that could be applied to the hydrogen motor fuel. Lynch and Snape cite Buchner's calculation that a separation plant producing 40 metric tons (44 short tons) of deuterium annually (the amount needed for a heavy-water moderated nuclear plant) would also produce 300,000 metric tons (331,000 short tons) of hydrogen, sufficient to meet the annual fuel requirements of one million vehicles, at reduced costs.

Finally, the heat effects of hydrides—heat release during hydrogen absorption and heat takeup during hydrogen release, but at different levels and pressures for different metals—open up new possibilities of heat storage, pumping, air-conditioning, refrigeration, and power generation, Lynch and Snape said. An integrated system called HYCSOS (Hydrogen Conversion and Storage System), which does all this and employs two hydride materials, lanthanium-nickel ($LaNi_5$) and calcium-nickel ($CaNi_5$), has been developed experimentally by Argonne National Laboratory. By the selective shuttling back and forth of hydrogen among four hydride tanks, which exploits the different temperature and pressure gradients of the hydride materials and the input of solar heat, the desired effects of cooling or heating a room, of producing electricity via a fuel cell, and of refrigeration were achieved. At least one economic study says the system will be cost competitive with conventional absorption refrigeration systems, according to Lynch and Snape.

German car maker Daimler-Benz has also come up with a heating and cooling concept for houses that was developed as a sophisticated adjunct of the idea of refueling a car with hydrogen. But there are some crucial differences. Unlike HYCSOS, which is essentially a closed system with no hydrogen burn-up as such, the Daimler-Benz car fuel is produced at

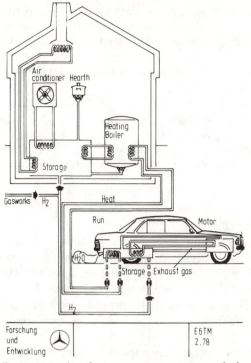

Figure 8.2. A schematic representation of the hydrogen-based house-heating and -cooling concept, adjunct of the idea of a hydrogen-operated car. (Drawing courtesy of Daimler-Benz)

home using hydrogen derived from electricity or natural gas networks. Essentially, Daimler-Benz proposes to derive hydrogen by splitting normal tap water with an electrolyzer in the home. Alternatively, there are certain hydrides that selectively absorb hydrogen from hydrogen-natural gas mixtures. This permits refueling of a car equipped with such hydride tanks from existing gas mains. In both energy-conversion methods heat that would otherwise be lost is produced as a by-product of hydride storage.

If either an electrolyzer or a gas reformer were installed in a home, the resulting heat could be used to heat the house with that waste heat. Daimler-Benz's Buchner says

Both systems utilize the heat streams that occur with the use of hydride storage equipment. HYCSOS essentially pumps hydrogen from one storage system to the other, employing relatively large storage units. We produce hydrogen as a car fuel at home. With the help of a relatively small intermediate storage tank in the house we use the heat streams that occur during hydrogen production and storage for cooling or heating a house.

The emphasis is on producing a car fuel—hydrogen—right at home, a revolutionary idea:

> We think it important not to have to wait until the time when hydrogen will be delivered by new systems to the home. We can use existing energy infrastructures—electric current or natural gas—to produce hydrogen at home and in the process recover and utilize energy that otherwise would be lost.

Hydrogen Distribution—Pipelines

West Germany's Ruhr area is synonymous with the country's industrial might, with steel foundries, coal mines, and production of big machinery. Generally less known is that up and down the banks of the Rhine and spread through the intermittently green-flecked urban sprawl are a number of large chemical plants producing basic chemicals that go into everything from aspirin to food additives, dyes, fertilizers, plastics, and fibers.

A dozen of these plants have the distinction of being linked to the world's oldest and most extensive hydrogen pipeline network, a 208-kilometer (130-mile) system of buried, bitumen-and-plastic-wrapped steel pipeline that traverses cities, crosses the Rhine in two places, and transports more than 300 million cubic meters (10.6 billion cubic feet) of hydrogen per year (almost one-third of the total industrial hydrogen production of the entire grid) between plants.

The system had its beginning in the late thirties with a humble 23-kilometer (14.3-mile) three-point system in which the then newly formed chemical firm of Chemische Werke Hüls began feeding hydrogen to two plants near Gelsenkirchen. Since then, the grid has expanded, linking four producers of the gas and nine users—two plants both produce and use hydrogen—shuttling the gas back and forth according to demand of the various locations.

Remarkably, in the more than three decades since the pipelines began operating, there has been no major damage, no major accident from escaping hydrogen or potentially explosive hydrogen-air mixtures, a record even more admirable in view of the fact that the line crosses mining areas where ground settlements occur. Expansion joints placed into the line have successfully coped with stresses caused by soil shifts in subsiding, worked-out coal mines.

Suggestions to expand the pipeline network were made in the mid-seventies to take care of the expected demand for more hydrogen, needed for new hydrocrackers in the petrochemical industry (plants that convert surplus heavy heating oil, an at times unsaleable by-product of conventional crude distillation, into products like gasoline). In 1976 the German Ruhrkohle company suggested a tenfold expansion of the existing network, meaning that such a grid would handle some three billion cubic meters (106 billion cubic feet) of hydrogen gas annually. Dr. Gerd Nashan, a Ruhrkohle executive, says that the wide availability of coke-oven gas as a raw material for hydrogen production in the Ruhr is an asset for the chemical industry and could ultimately serve as an energy base. Nashan points out that the Ruhr has a coking capacity of 29 million metric tons (32 million short tons) annually. At full-capacity utilization, the area could produce 11.5 billion cubic meters (406 billion cubic feet) of coke-oven gas, which, with a hydrogen content of around 60 percent, represents a hydrogen potential of about 6 billion cubic meters (212 billion cubic feet) per year.

In a thumbnail sketch of German hydrogen demands, Nashan says that Germany is using about 4 billion cubic meters (14 billion cubic feet) for ammonia synthesis, much of it for fertilizer production. While fertilizer needs are expected to stagnate, needs for plastics production may increase hydrogen demand by 50 percent by the year 2000. Refineries may also need more hydrogen if hydrogenation of heavy fuels to make light fuels like gasoline becomes a high priority. Hydrogen demand may also increase for future iron production if present coke-based iron reduction is increasingly replaced by direct reduction—so far this is an open question. But, Nashan says, even cautious projections indicate a "considerable growth in [hydrogen] demand."

Nashan believes the existing Hüls network could be doubled in capacity without major problems. "The whole aim basically is to make more hydrogen available as [chemical] raw material," he said. "But also, hydrogen is the real nonpolluting fuel of the future, and the aim is to lay the foundation for the year 2000."

The German grid thus has celebrity status among hydrogen economy advocates. From the early seventies, when hydrogen first began making news as the eco-fuel of the future, writers and scientists have pointed to the Hüls pipeline as proof that hydrogen can be transported safely and economically like natural gas, delivering clean energy over large distances at a fraction of the cost of delivering energy via electricity and with less "visual pollution"—unsightly high-voltage lines—because the pipes would be buried in the ground.

The fact that gases, including hydrogen, can be pipelined cheaply over large distances has important environmental implications beyond aesthetics. Some energy strategists, such as Marchetti, argue that the kind of massive nuclear plants that are likely to be built in the future may have to be located far away from population centers, perhaps on offshore islands or on remote atolls in the Pacific Ocean (see Chapter 11). Geographical isolation may be necessary because of fears of nuclear accidents, but also to meet huge cooling-water requirements. However, with increasing distance, beyond 1,000 miles (1,600 kilometers) or so, energy transportation via electricity would become disproportionately costly, whereas energy transportation costs via hydrogen would go up less severely.

Though the basic facts about hydrogen pipelines are not really in dispute, the details are, because of the myriad of variables that come into play, such as pipeline diameters and pressures, spacing of compression stations, materials, embrittlement problems, fuel costs for pumping stations, types of compressors available, and the geographical location of sources of hydrogen, for instance.

The Texas Gas Transmission Corporation early on funded research into hydrogen production by laser dissociation of water because, it said in various papers and announcements, it wanted to preserve its huge investment in natural gas transmission pipelines by converting them to the transport of synthetic methane made with "laser" hydrogen. One ballpark estimate for the total value of all existing pipelines in the United States put the total at around $40 billion.

However, as the Stanford Research Institute study notes, there are problems with that because of geography:

> The trunk natural gas pipeline network fans out from the major natural gas producing areas largely concentrated in the Gulf Coast region. These either terminate or taper in capacity with increasing distance from the gas fields as consumption lowers the quantity left to transmit. There is no natural reason to concentrate major hydrogen producing facilities in the Gulf Coast region—least of all hydrogen from coal gasification, a likely first source of hydrogen. Thus, because the existing trunk pipelines generally do not link the correct places and taper in the inappropriate direction, the argument that conversion to hydrogen would protect those investments seems to be overstated. At best, it appears that only some trunk pipelines would remain useful.

Two key studies that examined hydrogen distribution via pipelines were made by the Institute of Gas Technology and by EURATOM's research center in Ispra in the early and middle seventies. The studies agreed that energy is cheaper to transport as a gas (hydrogen or natural gas) than via high-voltage electricity lines, although they differed in their assessments of how much cheaper each would be. Many studies make the point that in addition to the cost of the fuel gas itself, a broad range of factors such as the cost of compressors to propel the gas through the lines, cost of the fuel to power the compressors, land costs for pipelines and compressor stations, and other factors make it very hard, if not impossible, to predict with any certainty what the actual numbers might be. Nevertheless, there seems to be a consensus that (1) hydrogen can carry energy at costs that IGT in 1975 estimated would be between 1/18th and 1/30th of the transport costs via standard 230-kilovolt power lines, but (2) energy transport via hydrogen would still be more expensive than transport via natural gas.

The reasons why hydrogen is more expensive to transport than natural gas lie not so much in any inherently physical problems but rather in the extra investment costs for bigger pipe for hydrogen for optimum efficiencies of transportation. Derek Gregory, the IGT's key researcher and advocate of hydrogen, says that at atmospheric pressure a given pipe indeed has the same energy capacity for natural gas and hydrogen gas. But gas has to be compressed for efficient pipeline transport. Because of differences in compressibility, and pressure requirements of around 750 to 1,000 psi (52 to 70 bars) for long-distance transmission—the longest distance so far is about 2,000 miles (3,600 kilometers)—these physical dissimilarities result in different energy-carrying capabilities in favor of natural gas; Gregory says the difference is "slight." Compressors, which are needed at regular intervals, also change the transport costs for hydrogen rather sharply. According to Gregory's calculations, if hydrogen were to be pumped through an existing 750-psi (52-bar) pipeline without any mechanical modifications to compressors, only one-fourth as much energy would be pushed through compared to natural gas. In order to achieve the same *energy* throughput, Gregory estimates that the compressor's capacity would have to be increased 3.8 times and its horsepower, 5.5 times.

The picture is further complicated by pressure efficiencies. The IGT study, for example, which examined a wide range of variables (pipe diameter from 24 to 28 inches [61 to 71 centimeters], pressures from 750 to 2000 psi [52 to 138 bars], hydrogen production costs ranging from $2 to $4 per million Btus) found that the maximum cost efficiency of current 24-inch and 30-inch pipes would be achieved with pressures of roughly double the current average pipeline pressures—somewhere between 1,500 and 2,000 psi (103 to 138 bars). Thus, hydrogen transmission at today's typical pipeline pressure of 750 psi (52 bars) would cost about two and a half times as much as natural gas, assuming an energy price of $3 per million Btus, IGT said. But at the future higher operating pressures of 1800 psi (124 bars) optimized for hydrogen transmission, the cost would be only 50 percent more than for natural gas, the study estimated.

So far, the availability of suitable compressors is in doubt. Hydrogen has a strong tendency to leak and also to attack materials like steel, especially at high pressures. This may present sealing problems. The IGT study points out that turbocompressors have been designed for high hydrogen gas throughput, but at relatively low pressures. Various manufacturers like Ingersoll-Rand, Worthington, and others have done work that promises a solution (via advanced turbocompressors, or reciprocating or screw compressors).

Much more serious are the metal embrittlement problems encountered with higher operating pressures, but also with high-purity hydrogen at normal room temperatures. Normally malleable, ductile metals like steel and iron become brittle under these conditions. High-strength steels are more susceptible than other metals. The effect disappears when the two materials are separated again, although the cracks remain. While the basic mechanism is not well understood—experts distinguish between three different types of embrittlement, and in one type the process actually can be reversed—the phenomenon has been experienced for a long time in the petrochemical industry as well as in NASA's space program in the sixties. At the time NASA had ordered up storage tanks for gaseous hydrogen to fuel its rockets. These tanks were designed for very high pressures, ranging from 5,000 to 10,000 psi (345 to 690 bars). Three such tanks suffered cracks and one experienced leaks, causing NASA to embark on an extensive research program. To date the problem appears still far from solved although some progress in understanding the basic mechanism has been made.

Two scientists, M. R. Louthran, Jr., and G. R. Caskey, Jr., reported in a paper in late 1976 that a decade's research at du Pont and elsewhere showed that all alloys are susceptible in different degrees to hydrogen embrittlement, but that aluminum and copper alloys are least affected. They also concluded that hydrogen absorption and permeation into metals cannot be accurately forecast with the usual analytical tools because the surface conditions of the metal—impurities, microstructural defects, oxide surface films—strongly influence the interaction between hydrogen and metal. They concluded that top performance and service life of materials exposed to hydrogen "demand careful analysis of service conditions, proper selection of materials and effective quality control during all stages of processing and fabrication." Coatings of aluminum or copper alloys plus precision manufacturing techniques on a level not required for normal natural gas pipelines may be one, probably a very expensive, answer.[3]

Another method of preventing embrittlement cracks in future hydrogen pipelines is the addition of impurities—very small amounts of other chemicals such as oxygen, which just about eliminates the phenomenon. It has also been suggested that other additives should be mixed in as a safety measure that would either give a characteristic smell to normally odorless hydrogen or add a distinctive color to the normally invisible hydrogen flame, as a warning to the user that hydrogen is around. This is fine as long as hydrogen is used only as an energy carrier, because those impurities generally don't interfere with the burning process. However, one of the aims is also to link any future hydrogen energy pipelines to chemical plants to supply them with "merchant hydrogen" as chemical raw material. Many chemical processes are dependent on extremely pure hydrogen, and even small impurities would render the element useless. Here lies a problem, as the chemical industry is being counted on as one of the main "drivers" towards a future hydrogen economy because of its use of hydrogen as a raw material. The chemical industry presumably can pay more for hydrogen, creating a bigger market that would help to lower prices and promote the more rapid phasing-in of hydrogen generally.

The problem may not be insoluble, though. JPL's HEST study lists some pipelines that, though short and small in diameter, have operated successfully with very pure hydrogen and very high pressures. Air Products & Chemicals, Inc. of Allentown, Pennsylvania, for instance, at one point was operating a pipeline 4 inches (10 centimeters) in diameter and 5 miles (8 kilometers) in length, made of a "converted natural gas" type of steel, which carried pure hydrogen at pressures of 800 psi (55 bars). In six years of operation no problems were reported. The same company has a longer pipe, 8 inches (20 centimeters) in diameter and 12 miles (19 kilometers) long, also carrying pure hydrogen but at lower pressure—200 psi (14 bars)—which operated for at least three years without trouble. NASA has a 10-year-old pipeline at Cape Kennedy's space center carrying what is described as "ultrapure" hydrogen at the very high pressure of 6,000 psi (413 bars)—three to four times what Gregory says will be commercially required—without any problems, but only over one mile (1.6 kilometers) and with a very small diameter— only 2 inches (5 centimeters).

The view that existing natural gas pipelines can be easily converted to hydrogen transport was also severely challenged by the HEST study. The writers, most of them materials specialists from various NASA installations, noted the point of view that the present acceptance by the public of natural gas systems could easily be extended to hydrogen as well. But, say these experts, it is more probable to assume that the public will demand low failure rates for any future hydrogen systems and that there is still an undercurrent of fear exemplified by the Hindenburg syndrome, similar to the widespread worry that nuclear power plants will blow up or kill and maim with leaking radiation. As long as these Hindenburg syndrome fears persist, the public will most likely insist on a "fail-safe" type of hydrogen system.

Given the wide range of flammability of hydrogen, which burns in concentrations ranging from 4 to 74 percent mixed with air, and high flame speed—a hydrogen flame shoots upward with speeds of up to 9 feet (2.7 meters) per second—there is bound to be fear. By comparison, methane burns only in the narrow range of 8 to 15 percent in air, and its low constant flame speed of only 1 foot (0.3 meters) per second is much less hazardous in this context. (As pointed out in Chapter 10, there are situations, such as crashes of hydrogen-fueled airplanes, where the safety factor may be inherently greater.) The team urged high-priority research in this area before making any major policy decisions and concluded: "It appears most unwise to contemplate pumping hydrogen through our natural gas system without a full-scale field validation even if, someday, it does become economically feasible."

One futuristic energy transmission concept that has come up in connection with cryogenic hydrogen as energy carrier is the combination of a superconducting cable with a liquid hydrogen pipeline. Superconducting electric power cables using liquid helium for cooling are known to be much more efficient than conventional power cables because at extremely low temperatures the resistance of the metal in the cable just about disappears, cutting transmission losses dramatically. A number of researchers have suggested substituting liquid hydrogen for liquid helium or nitrogen as coolant. This concept is sometimes dubbed the "energy pipe," in which both electric and chemical energy would be delivered to the users. Despite potential safety hazards—burnable liquid hydrogen doesn't mix too well with high-voltage electricity—the idea has generated a number of papers.

In a 1972 paper, two scientists at Los Alamos, John R. Bartlit and Frederick J. Edeskuty, proposed such a double-duty line, with electricity and liquid hydrogen flowing in opposite directions, for the U.S. Southwest. At the time, as the two explained, there were proposals to build a port for the space shuttle in White Sands, New Mexico. Hydrogen fuel for the space shuttle would have to be brought from several large-capacity liquid-hydrogen plants around Los Angeles, a distance of about 600 miles (965 kilometers). To carry the required 220,000 liters (58,000 gallons) of liquid hydrogen propellant per day, 65 tank trucks would have to shuttle every day between White Sands and the Los Angeles region at considerable cost—according to the authors, about $25 million annually.

At the same time, both electric power and natural gas were being generated in the Four Corners region (at the junction of New Mexico, Colorado, Utah, and Arizona) from natural gas fields and electricity plants for shipment to the Phoenix, Arizona, and Los Angeles areas. Production of SNG from future coal gasification plants is also a possibility. Why not, the authors asked, combine all three into one cryogenic transmission line—liquid hydrogen going one way for the space shuttle and liquid methane (natural or synthetic) and electricity via low-resistance cryogenic cables going the other to California in icy symbiosis: "The LNG benefits from better insulation, LH_2 receives and gives thermal shielding, and the electricity bears lower losses because of decreased or zero resistance in the conductor," Bartlit and Edeskuty concluded their scenario. A single such line would be visually less unsightly than the ugly overhead electricity transmission lines that have generated many public hearings. The $25 million saved by switching from trucking liquid hydrogen to pipelining it represented a credit and an incentive for such a permafrost line, the authors said.

More recently, two scientists from the Cryogenics Division of the National Bureau of Standards, R. O. Voth and J. Hord, have reexamined the idea of combining liquid hydrogen and electricity transport in greater detail. The study, presented at the 1976 Miami hydrogen energy conference, compared hydrogen with liquid-helium–cooled alternating-current cable concepts. Both are so-called cryo-resistive cables that function at a temperature somewhat above the point at which the conducting material loses all resistance. They were then compared with true superconductive cable with zero resistance. Nitrogen- and helium-cooled cables were also considered, mainly because these two inert gases are thought to provide greater safety. Voth and Hord concluded that helium- and hydrogen-cooled alternating-current superconductive power transmission lines (SPTLs) have comparable capital and operating costs and "both can transmit power at lower costs than conventional underground power cables. The hybrid hydrogen-cooled SPTL transmits energy (liquid hydrogen plus electricity) at lower costs than any of the other energy cables considered."

They added, though, that

hydrogen-cooled power cables and hybrid hydrogen-electric energy cables appear to be technically and economically feasible and would surely warrant development efforts if compelling economic advantages existed. Such advantages are not apparent in current designs, and the increased hazard of operating a hydrogen-cooled line cannot currently be justified on economic grounds.

As to safety, the two pointed out that the electrical utility industry is already using hydrogen-cooled power generating equipment—most large generators are H_2-cooled. Commercially available equipment and instruments and existing industrial handling procedures should suffice for hydrogen cryo-cable applications. Voth and Hord concluded: "A hydrogen-cooled cable is certainly more hazardous than an inert-fluid-cooled or oil-cooled cable; however, the safety problems are not overwhelming and it is felt that a hydrogen cryo-cable is no more hazardous than existing underground natural gas pipelines."

Perhaps the most improbable idea for hydrogen transport, one that seems to fly in the face of the Hindenburg Syndrome fears (see Chapter 10), is the suggestion to use huge hydrogen-buoyed airships to transport large tonnages of liquid hydrogen by air. As outlined by T. Ishigohka of Tokyo's Seikei University at the 1980 3rd World Hydrogen Conference, the concept involves construction of airships of more than half a kilometer (1,640 feet) in length and powered partially by solar cells that would carry 1,400 tons of liquid hydrogen from remote hydrogen production sites to end-users at speeds of 80 kilometers (50 miles) an hour. Power would be provided both by hydrogen-fueled 6,300-hp gas turbines and auxiliary solar cells covering the hull's upper half. Ishigohka claimed that in clear weather the cells' electric power output would be enough to drive the airship via light (and so far experimental) superconducting generators and motors. Taking his cue, apparently, from the early German Zeppelin experiment (described in Chapter 3), Ishigohka said that in bad weather or during night flights when there is no sun power available, the simultaneous burning of both gaseous hydrogen from the gas bag and of liquid hydrogen from the LH_2 load would maintain correct buoyancy of the giant airship. Also, as hydrogen is both lift medium and cargo, evaporating liquid hydrogen would not have to be vented and could be captured in the gas bag. According to Ishigohka, as airships, regardless of size, can land just about anywhere, it would be possible to fly directly from a remote production plant—an atoll in the Pacific, for example—to a big inland city, with no need to transfer the fuel from one transport system (a big tanker ship) to another (onshore pipelines). Ishigohka acknowledged that inert helium would be preferable to volatile hydrogen from a safety point of view but said that there just may not be enough to go around. He conceded that solar cells must first come down in price to become practical and admitted, almost as an afterthought, that an "anti-lightning protection method must be established"—somewhat of an understatement given the flammability of hydrogen.

One sophisticated energy transport concept involving hydrogen that seems closer to reality is the so-called ADAM/EVA[4] system developed in Germany's Nuclear Research Center in Jülich. The system does employ hydrogen in one phase of the energy transport, but it is not a hydrogen transmission system in the sense that hydrogen gas is burned at the user end and vented as water vapor. Rather, it utilizes different chemical binding energies in the combination and breakup of hydrocarbon molecules to transport the energy in a closed loop. What happens is this:

A heat source (either a future high temperature reactor or solar power plant) heats a circulating gas or fluid to a high temperature. In the case of the HTR, the cooling medium is helium, which is heated to a temperature of around 1,000°C. (1800°F.). The heat is transferred to a gas mixture of methane and ordinary steam, which then undergoes a transformation to carbon monoxide and hydrogen, absorbing energy in the process—49 kilocalories per mol.[5]

The new gas mixture, carbon monoxide and hydrogen, has thus absorbed a portion of the reactor-produced heat as chemical binding energy. This is the EVA part. This gas mixture can be piped through conventional natural gas pipelines for large distances to the user point, with little or none of the transport losses incurred in long-distance electricity transmission.

At the user end, the ADAM reactor employs catalysts in a well-known industrial process called methanation. Here the formula is reversed to produce methane again and water, releasing the chemically bound energy to produce heat—hot water for space heating or steam for driving electric generators. The whole system is a closed-circuit affair with no loss of the circulating gases.

The two prototype component parts Adam I and Eva I were mated for the first time in a short closed circuit at the Jülich research center in September 1979. First results, reported at the 1980 Tokyo hydrogen conference, said it worked well and that only small amounts of gas had to be added to the total gas volume to make up for minor leakages in the compressors. A paper presented by two Jülich staffers, H. Fedders and B. Höhlein, concluded that "850 operating hours have shown that the process parameters . . . do not undergo significant changes"—the system functioned pretty much as predicted.

The Germans are sufficiently intrigued to pursue ADAM/EVA in considerable detail. Studies by the German Research and Technology Ministry predict that ADAM/EVA could save large amounts of primary energy, but at huge investment costs. The ministry's experts found that a hypothetical ADAM/EVA system supplying a region around Stuttgart, along the Neckar River, with space and process heat derived from a 1,000-Mwe nuclear reactor would reduce space-heating requirements by about two-thirds and would cut electric energy consumption by about one-quarter, resulting in savings of around 700,000 metric tons (772,000 short tons) of light and heavy fuel oil annually. Another 150,000 metric tons (165,000 short tons) would be saved by funneling some reactor heat and reactor-produced electric power for uses immediately near the reactor site. However, such a system, with piping and ADAM/EVA reactors supplied to customers in a radius of about 60 miles (96 kilometers) around the reactor, would cost DM 2 billion (1974 prices), about $1.1 billion! Dietrich Natus, managing director of Germany's Lurgi company, a maker of chemical process equipment and a leader in commercial coal gasification research work, nevertheless predicts that ADAM/EVA will be gradually phased into the German energy landscape: "We think the ADAM/EVA principle is not a desk-drawer type project but that it will be brought to commercial status step by step in the eighties," he said in an article in a Lurgi company magazine. "The first commercial high temperature reactor in Germany is under construction. In the eighties, all elements for a total energy system will be available, and the system will be utilized."

Thus, hydrogen as an alternative clean fuel for the home and industry appears to be a long way off, but its unique properties may begin to be exploited in the not-too-distant future for advanced hydride-based heating and cooling systems and for long-distance energy transmission in ADAM/EVA fashion.

9

Fertilizer, Steel, and Protein-Producing Microbes: Nonenergy Uses of Hydrogen

"Up to now nobody could convince me that hydrogen will actually be the fuel of the future to generate the heat we need when our organic fuels run out," observed a chemistry expert at a hydrogen meeting in Ispra, Italy, in May 1977. "I'm sure, however, that the importance of hydrogen as a chemical will increase." The response of the audience, almost all of them pro-hydrogen people, was not recorded but presumably they disagreed with the speaker's first statement. Few, however, would quarrel with the second part: As production of hydrogen grows, more and more chemical usage is certain to result.

Hydrogen is a very good chemical reducing agent. Chemical reduction is essentially the reverse of oxidation, the process in which compounds absorb oxygen from the atmosphere; rust, for instance, is the product of the interaction of iron and atmospheric oxygen. Iron oxide can easily be transformed into iron by hydrogen. (In iron production ores are reduced to metallic iron in a smelter.)

Present Industrial Uses

For decades hydrogen has been one of the most important chemical raw materials for the production of many organic materials. Hydrogen plays a role in making ammonia-based fertilizers, in petroleum refining, and in making methanol, which in addition to its potential as an automotive fuel is the basis for resins, varnishes, plastics, solvents, and antifreezes.

In the oil industry, most plants routinely produce and consume hydrogen. Hydrogen is needed in "Hydrotreating" processes in which sulfur and other impurities are removed during distillation of crude oil.

193

In "catalytic cracking" hydrogen is produced as a by-product. In "hydrocracking," big oil molecules are broken down with hydrogen into fuel distillates that are blended into gasoline. Often, methanol plants are integrated with ammonia plants; of 12 methanol plants operating in the United States, 6 are working in tandem with ammonia plants.

In the United States, these three major areas account for about 90 percent of total hydrogen consumption, which in 1974 stood at roughly 2,200 billion cubic feet (62 billion cubic meters), according to a paper by IGT staffers Kenneth G. Darrow, Nicholas Biederman, and A. Konopka, at a cost then of about 60 cents per 100 cubic feet. Ammonia production alone accounted for roughly half of total U.S. usage at that time.

The refinery industry consumed roughly 740 billion cubic feet (21 billion cubic meters) in 1974, at a cost of about $1 per 100 cubic feet. Methanol production required about 220 billion cubic feet (6.2 billion cubic meters), at costs comparable to those of ammonia production because of the frequent integration of the two processes. Small users of hydrogen pay much more: Again in 1974, firms consuming as little as 20,000 cubic feet (566 cubic meters) of hydrogen per month paid as much as $30 per 100 cubic feet (2.8 cubic meters). (They account for only 5 percent of the total U.S. hydrogen market.)

There are many current industrial uses of hydrogen. Hydrogenation of edible organic oils from soybeans, fish, cotton seed, peanuts, corn, and coconuts slows their propensity to oxidize and become rancid. Also, the addition of hydrogen turns a liquid oil into a solid fat such as margarine or shortening. Inedible tallow and grease treated with hydrogen can be used to produce soap and animal feed.

In metal working, hydrogen atmospheres are used for heat treating of ferrous metals to change some of their characteristics. Heat treating is used to improve a ferrous metal's ductility and machining quality, to relieve stress, to harden the metal, to increase its tensile strength, and to change its magnetic or electrical characteristics. A hydrogen-nitrogen atmosphere is used in annealing steel to make it more machine-workable, make it amenable to cold rolling, and reduce stresses while the metal is being shaped or welded. Bright annealing makes for a smooth, shiny surface, like stainless steel. For nonferrous metals, a hydrogen-nitrogen atmosphere is used to reduce or prevent oxidation and annealing. A reducing atmosphere of relatively pure hydrogen is used in processing tungsten, in producing molybdenum, and in producing magnesium via electrolysis from magnesium chloride. Hydrogen is used in glass cutting and in cutting and high-temperature melting of quartz. Hydrogen is burned with oxygen to obtain very high temperatures.

In the manufacture of electronics components such as vacuum tubes or light bulbs, brazing (a process in which material is heat-bonded) is carried out in either a hydrogen atmosphere or in nonreactive gases such as argon or nitrogen to prevent oxidization.

In the electric power industry, gaseous hydrogen is used to cool large generators, motors, and frequency changers. Hydrogen has a greater thermal conductivity than normal air and therefore provides better cooling. The hydrogen cooling system is a closed circuit, with the gas being routed via heat exchangers through the generator shell and through the stator windings, but there is some leakage. Indirectly, this speaks for hydrogen's safety, because despite leakage and chances of sparks no major accidents have been reported over many years.

In nuclear research, liquid hydrogen is used to fill bubble chambers to make the traces of subatomic particles visible and photographable. In the nuclear industry, hydrogen is required in some stages of nuclear fuel processing.

Future Applications

At a workshop on industrial uses of hydrogen in April 1975 at the University of Michigan, Ann Arbor, the assembled experts from the university and the Institute of Gas Technology discussed a number of future industrial uses once hydrogen becomes available in large amounts. Professor Donald L. Katz from the university's Department of Chemical Engineering pointed out that hydrogen has no real competition in removing sulfur as a pollutant from coal and heavy oils. That may translate into a continual buildup of hydrogen demand. Hydrogen would also play a major role in any future production of synthetic fuels from coal and in exploiting tar sands and oil shale. Rather than mining materials and processing them in a type of refinery, Katz thinks "in situ" hydrogenation would be a technically challenging but interesting approach to extracting fuels from these deposits. If a method could be devised of bringing hydrogen into these deposits and making it react with them, a kind of synthetic, man-made oil well might be the result.

Physicist Larry Jones (see Chapter 3), who has devoted much time and energy to promoting hydrogen, pointed out the great potential of direct reduction of iron and other metal ores with hydrogen. In electronics, he felt that the use of hydrogen as a reducing atmosphere in making solid-state devices, a relatively small market, could pick up markedly if mass production of solar cells becomes a reality—an instance of one sector of a future hydrogen economy reinforcing another.

Hydrogen as a means of directly reducing iron ores into the metallic state is especially attractive to industrialized countries such as Japan, which have few raw materials and energy resources. Marchetti alluded to hydrogen's iron-refining potential in his 1970 Cornell lecture, in which he mentioned direct reduction processes in Canada and Mexico that use hydrogen in the H_2-CO reduction gas to produce iron sponge. "One cubic meter of hydrogen is needed roughly per kilogram of iron," Marchetti told the Cornell students. "Iron ore reduction accounts for about 5 to 10 per cent of the energy input in an advanced society. Assuming that 20 years from now, 50 per cent of ironmaking in the world switches to hydrogen, this would account for power [requirements] in water splitters on the order of 500 gigawatt,"[1] he said.

A detailed review of hydrogen's potential in ore reduction, which created a considerable stir among metallurgists, was presented five years later by a Japanese specialist in nonferrous extractive metallurgy, Professor Tokiaki Tanaka of Hokkaido University. Together with two collaborators, Tanaka pointed out that the metals industry, like all others, is faced not only with energy problems but also with mounting environmental concerns. Tanaka prefaced his paper in the December 1975 issue of the *Journal of Metals* by saying, "We in Japan are well aware that the rapidly increasing amounts of industrial wastes, particularly those from fossil fuels, have reached the limits of the cleansing ability of nature. This has forced a change in the customary concept of values which in the past, always gave preference to economics."

Tanaka's message was twofold: One, hydrogen would be invaluable in the low-pollution treatment of ores; and two, that hydrogen could be the by-product of processing sulfur-containing ores known as sulfides. Taking his cue from the work on thermochemical cycles at the EURATOM research center in Ispra, Italy, and elsewhere, Tanaka said that the chemical reactions in these cycles dovetail nicely with hydrogen reactions that could be used for metals refining. Hydrogen would be produced and metal would be refined in tandem, although, says Tanaka, "the importance of hydrogen production from sulfide ores lies more in the development of new non-polluting methods of metal production rather than in the production of hydrogen *per se*."

Another approach would be to use plentiful, presumably inexpensive, pipeline hydrogen for the direct hydrogen treatment of sulfide ores, analogous to the sulfur-removal treatment of heavy oils widely used in the petroleum industry. Copper smelting with hydrogen, for example, which now takes three or four energy-intensive steps, is regarded as potentially especially rewarding. Tanaka mentioned other materials obtainable from sulfide ores via hydrogen reduction: silver fibers, porous iron, and cobalt. Concluded Tanaka: "It would be safe to say, future developments in the field of hydrogen technology may possibly bring about a revolution in the field of metal extraction as we now know it."

Other States: Solid and Metallic Hydrogen

Perhaps the strangest, almost other-worldly aspect of hydrogen has to do with the creation and possible future use of atomic and of metallic hydrogen. Atomic, solid, and metallic hydrogen, researched in earnest since the late sixties in the United States, the Soviet Union, Europe, and Japan have the same "laboratory curiosity" status that liquid hydrogen had in the thirties and forties. If this analogy is correct, it is reasonable to speculate that these three related, but not identical, states of hydrogen may find industrial applications in the decades ahead.

Atomic hydrogen (H) exists only in infinitesimally small percentages in normal gaseous hydrogen, which is almost always molecular because the bonds between hydrogen atoms are so strong—stronger than any other chemical bond—that they immediately recombine into molecules (H_2). If the two hydrogen atoms are separated into atomic hydrogen their tendency is to immediately recombine.

This strong attraction of the hydrogen atoms for each other and the energy implied by this bond has persuaded the U.S. Air Force to try to break up the hydrogen molecule as a means of storing energy. When recombining into molecular hydrogen, atomic hydrogen would yield about four times more energy than the best currently available rocket fuel, a combination of liquid hydrogen and liquid oxygen.

NASA's Lewis Research Center in Cleveland has been working since the early seventies on methods to turn a percentage of gaseous molecular hydrogen into atomic hydrogen. Its work was based initially on the research of a German scientist, Dr. Rudiger Hess. Hess, whose doctoral dissertation, published in 1971, detailed his efforts, ran the gas through a pair of electrodes, splitting the hydrogen molecule into two atoms. Lewis researchers, according to a 1974 report in *Aviation Week and Space Technology*, cooled a mixture of molecular and atomic hydrogen down to a temperature barely above absolute zero, 4°K., and the mixture then condensed out on the walls of the experimental apparatus. The entire setup functions inside a superconducting magnet field that, theoretically at least, aligns the electrons in the hydrogen atoms in such a way that they cannot recombine into molecules. NASA's researchers believe that eventually a method might evolve by which the atomic-molecular hydrogen mixture could be stable, though very low temperatures would be necessary.

Professor Walter Peschka, of the German Aerospace Research and Experimental Institute (DFVLR) in Stuttgart, who is one of the pioneers investigating these phenomena (Hess was one of his students), in December 1978 managed to store 2 grams (0.071 ounces) of atomic hydrogen "for several hours," during which spin alignment of the electrons was observed. Peschka estimated the energy that could be stored in spin-aligned atomic hydrogen and released by reverting to the molecular state to be 10 to 20 times the amount available from current chemical fuels.

The second line of research has to do with creation of solid, "metallic" hydrogen, also a form of atomic hydrogen, which occurs under extremely high pressures of a million atmospheres or more. Metallic hydrogen packs the same energy content as spin-aligned atomic hydrogen, about 50,000 calories per gram (1,400,000 calories per ounce), but because the material is 14 to 15 times denser it would pack an even bigger wallop in the same small space.

Peschka says metallic hydrogen would be really a "rather wild explosive," 10 times as powerful as trinitrotoluene (TNT). Any future use as a rocket fuel would hinge on whether the rate of energy release could be controlled. Astrophysicists are fairly certain that the core of the planet Jupiter consists of metallic hydrogen. Peschka, who in recent years has turned his attention to developing viable liquid hydrogen fuel systems for cars (see Chapter 6), says there are clues that, once produced under pressures found in nature only deep inside a planet or a star,[2] metallic hydrogen would be "metastable": It would remain solid and metallic, below relatively low pressures of about 20K bar (29,000 psi). (Diamonds exhibit similar characteristics; they are a variant state of carbon, formed under extreme pressure, but remain stable and retain their sparkle as cutting tools and engagement rings under room temperatures and normal pressure.)

Metallic hydrogen is believed to be a "better" superconductor than any other metal. Superconductivity, the phenomenon in which a current pulses through a material without any resistance and hence without any electric losses, occurs at temperatures of up to 23.3°K.—23.2 degrees above nature's absolute zero point. Metallic hydrogen, on the other hand, should remain superconducting at room temperatures—in theory at least.

Peschka explains the relationship of solid, metallic, and atomic hydrogen by saying that there is a continuous transfer from one state into the other as pressures increase. Metallic hydrogen is a special phase of solid hydrogen created by pressures higher than those required for "mere" solid, crystalline hydrogen. When molecular solid hydrogen is subjected to pressure, the hydrogen molecules, normally spaced about 10 times as far apart as the two hydrogen atoms from each other, move closer together. When pressure reaches levels of 500,000 or 1 million bars (7.25 to 14.5 million psi)—500,000 to one million times the pressure of the earth's atmosphere—the molecules are so close together that the distances are about equal to the atoms' distance from each other. At that point, the atoms of different molecules begin to interact and, if the pressure goes still higher, eventually form a metal.

Atomic hydrogen, on the other hand, can be created without pressure but via a glow discharge in conjunction with a strong magnetic field at extremely low temperatures—the method Peschka used in his December 1978 experiment. Here, no solid is formed. But neither does the gaseous, spin-aligned atomic hydrogen recombine into molecules because of opposing electrical forces. This hydrogen state also displays characteristics, such as certain magnetic effects, expected to occur in metallic hydrogen.

To date, nobody has seen metallic hydrogen, but efforts to reach extremely high pressures have been going on in the United States, mainly at Cornell and the University of Maryland; in Japan, at the University of Osaka; and in the Soviet Union, at the Institute of High Pressure Physics in Moscow. The Soviet team, headed by Academician L. F. Vereshchagin, published a brief account of its work on February 5, 1975, in which Vereshchagin and his coworkers, E. N. Yakovlev and Y. A. Timofeev, said they had created what they thought was metallic hydrogen at temperatures of $4.2°K$. and pressures of about one million atmospheres. The indication that metallic hydrogen had been created was the change in electric resistivity: Hydrogen normally is a dielectric—an electric insulator—but the pressurized material "jumped" by some six orders of magnitude in terms of resistivity, an indication that the material acted like a true metal. "We note in conclusion that the return of the hydrogen to the dielectric state after the removal of the pressure cannot be regarded as a demonstration that metallic hydrogen cannot exist at normal pressures," Vereshchagin said in a double negative. In other words, the fact that in his experiment the hydrogen reverted to its normal insulating properties was in no way proof that metallic hydrogen cannot stay metallic after going back to atmospheric pressure.

While the Soviet work is the subject of some debate in the West—some observers have expressed doubt whether the Soviets actually achieved metallic hydrogen—two scientists at the Carnegie Institution's Geophysical Laboratory in Washington, D.C., reported in March 1979 that they had produced solid crystalline hydrogen for the first time at room temperatures and at pressures of "only" 650,000 bars (9.4 million psi). The two scientists, David Ho-kwang Mao and Peter M. Bell, pumped relatively dense liquid hydrogen at $-429.1°$ F. $(-256°$ C.) into a

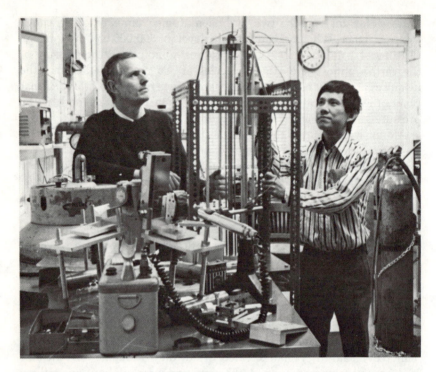

Figure 9.1. Peter M. Bell and David Ho-kwang Mao, scientists at the Carnegie Institution's Geophysical Laboratory, Washington, D.C., with their experimental high-pressure cell setup with which they produced solid, crystalline hydrogen for the first time in early 1979. (Photo courtesy of Carnegie Institution)

high-pressure cell between the flattened points of two diamonds, permitting the liquid's temperature to rise to room levels. At the same time, the pressure cell squeezed the liquid hydrogen until the scientists saw through an attached microscope the liquid hydrogen form "almost instantaneously" into crystals that "rapidly merged into a single, clear, transparent solid with no visible grain boundaries." At 360,000 bars (5.2 million psi), the measured density was 0.6 to 0.7 grams per cubic centimeter (0.34 to 0.39 oz per cubic inch), somewhat less than the density of 1.0 gram per cubic centimeter (0.58 oz per cubic inch) (the density of water) predicted for hydrogen's metallic state. The solid created by Mao and Bell looks like salt or sugar and turned yellowish at the highest pressures, the significance of which, if any, has not yet been determined (liquid hydrogen is colorless). The material created in the Carnegie Institution experiment is still molecular; only at around 1.0 megabar (14.5 million psi), according to current theory, will the molecules break apart into individual atoms, Bell said. "If they do, we will have metallic hydrogen."

Medical Uses

Mention should be made of a possible medical use of hydrogen in the treatment of a disease that causes more worry, anxiety, and public concern today than any other—cancer. In the September 22, 1975, issue of *Medical World News* a small item headlined "Hydrogen Kills Tumors" appeared. The story read in its entirety as follows:

> An experimental treatment using hyperbaric hydrogen has caused regression of squamous[3] cell carcinomas in mice. Baylor College investigators Malcolm Dole and F. Ray Wilson and Dr. William P. Fife of Texas A&M University put three mice into a hyperbaric chamber (along with food and water) which was then flushed with a mixture of 97.5 hydrogen and 2.5 percent oxygen at a pressure of 8.28 atmospheres. After an initial ten-day exposure, the tumors turned black, some dropped off, some appeared shrunk at their base and to be in the process of being "pinched off." None of the tumor effects were noted in control mice kept at normal room temperatures. Continual remission of multiple carcinomas were shown in mice returned to the chamber for another six days. Further research will study the permanency of these results.

Dole, Wilson, and Fife, who subsequently published their basic findings in *Science*, were not quite sure what happens in this treatment involving pressurized hydrogen. In a March 1976 letter Fife said "this work is very preliminary and we do not yet understand the mechanism, or, indeed, the full scope of its potential."

One possibility, Fife reasoned, was that molecular hydrogen under pressure scavenges, i.e., somehow binds, "free radicals which are well known to cause some forms of cancer." Free radicals are atoms or multiatom molecules that "possess at least one unpaired electron"—the atom or molecule is not internally balanced in terms of its electron-proton ratio but has excess electrical binding energy. Fife said, "one hypothesis is that destruction of these free radicals makes it possible for natural but weak immune systems of the body to cause the malignancy to regress." He added that the effect of hydrogen on substances used in current chemotherapeutic treatment of cancer is not known, but "we suspect that even if effective, hydrogen will not be used by itself for cancer treatment. If used, it probably will be in conjunction with chemotherapy or radiation." Fife, a professor of biology, adds that "we wonder if the use of hydrogen might be beneficial in preventing cancer," again based on the idea that hydrogen is known to destroy these free radicals.

Two and a half years later, Fife said the earlier work may have been "somewhat inconclusive." He suggests that what his team saw disappearing may actually have been "papaloma [a precancerous wart-like cell condition] and maybe not the carcinoma." Nevertheless, work is continuing, though at a fairly slow rate, due to other commitments and a lack of funding. Says Fife, "there are some indications that the hyperbaric hydrogen does have some stimulating effect on the immune system although we have not quantified this at all."

In another tack, Fife and his colleagues have done some research on the use of hyperbaric hydrogen in conjunction with other chemotherapy agents used in cancer research, such as Negromycin, a new and very powerful agent. Fife obtained about 4 grams (0.14 oz) of the material in 1978 from the National Cancer Institute; he was told this represented about half the world's supply at the time. He explained:

> There seems to be some kind of synergistic effect in that the use of both of these together does extend the life of rats which have leukemia. . . . Normally, Negromycin causes the animal to die. It may cure the malignancy but it causes them to die with some of the symptoms similar to radiation damage, such as destruction of the bone marrow, over a period of thirty days. The few animals which were looked at histologically and that had the hyperbaric hydrogen did not show the bone marrow destruction, although the animals died from other causes. This has just not been worked out.

In yet another preliminary study, Fife and his team found that if hyperbaric hydrogen does not cure those squamous-cell carcinomas, hyperbaric hydrogen may, "and I emphasize the may," have some use in preventing them. In one experiment, the backs of mice were painted with methyl colanthrene, a compound that induces such carcinoma. Those animals subsequently placed into a hyperbaric hydrogen atmosphere did not develop precancerous lesions within the first three weeks, although the other animals left outside did develop them. The reason for this, Fife guesses, is that hyperbaric hydrogen may be scavenging the hydroxy radicals known to cause cancer. He now plans research to see whether hyperbaric hydrogen would tend to prevent or suppress the development of squamous-cell carcinoma induced by ultraviolet radiation.[4]

Hydrogen as a Food Source

Finally, perhaps the most exciting aspect of a future hydrogen economy is the possibility of producing food—protein—on a large industrial scale from hydrogen with the help of certain bacteria. The thought of producing protein refinery-style may be abhorrent to gourmets, natural food advocates, and a lot of common folk in general. But it does offer at least the prospect of eliminating the worry about how to supply the world with staple primary proteins. Nor is the idea completely revolutionary: British Petroleum has already set up entire plants for producing protein from crude oil, and other companies are working on processes using natural gas as a basis for protein. Certain strains of yeast-like microorganisms grow rapidly on an oil base, a discovery that goes back to the early 1950s. The method is used industrially to make single-cell protein for animal feed.

Using hydrogen takes the idea one step further. Producing protein from oil or natural gas essentially involves the transformation of one organic material into another. Here, the idea is to use inorganic substances like hydrogen and carbon dioxide to synthesize organic materials—proteins in the end. The organisms capable of doing that are a type of bacteria first discovered more than a century ago. The bacterial strain most widely studied is known as *Hydrogenomonas* (recently renamed *Alcaligenes eutrophus*). These organisms use hydrogen as energy source, carbon dioxide as carbon source, and simple minerals from fertilizers to produce protein-rich cellular material—a spongy, whitish substance in appearance.

Marchetti had already explained in his 1970 Cornell lecture how both hydrogen and these bacteria can be the link between primary energy—nuclear, solar, or whatever—and the mechanism of food synthesis:

Chlorophyll is the keystone of the process. Energy from light's photons is accumulated by this phosphor and transferred into ATP, adenosin-triphosphate, the universal energy carrier in biological systems. But when an organism oxidizes an energetic substrate, be it sugar *or hydrogen*, the result is the same. With ATP, the function of chlorophyll is taken up by . . . enzymes. The privileged position of chlorophyll is given by the fact that it is coupled to primary-primary source of energy, the sun.

Marchetti went on to say that nuclear fission, the "revolutionary discovery of the century," could substitute for the sun. (Today, Marchetti would include solar power as primary source.)

If we find a link between the biosphere and this new source, chlorophyll *and agriculture* are going to lose their privileged position and the corresponding limitations are likely to fall. Hydrogen can be the link. A certain number of microorganisms are able to use hydrogen oxidation as a source of energy and thrive on a completely inorganic substrate. . . . the energy is used in a quite efficient way to synthesize all sorts of things necessary to build and run the biological machinery—proteins, vitamins, carbohydrates, and so on. The energy conversion efficiency . . . is quite high, 60 to 70 percent in the best cases, 50 percent in an easy routine.

An added bonus is the high multiplication rate of these microorganisms. Marchetti pointed out: "A cattle herd has a weight doubling of two, three years, and a *Hydrogenomonas* 'herd' has a doubling time of two, three hours." Elsewhere he noted, "Here then is a prospect of being able to create a food source independent of agriculture (and of oil deposits) linked only to nuclear reactors by a process rather similar to the beer-brewing process."

Research got a boost in the early sixties in the United States when NASA began to study prospects of producing proteins on board of spacecraft for long space missions, utilizing carbon dioxide and mineral salts produced by the astronauts. The idea was to employ electricity from solar cells to produce hydrogen and oxygen from water supplies on board in a permanent cycle. Two researchers from the Battelle Memorial Institute, John F. Foster and John H. Litchfield, presented their concept of a continuous-culture machine using hydrogen for protein production aboard a spaceship in 1964 at the national meeting of the American Institute of Chemical Engineers in Pittsburgh. They said in their summary that the "harvested bacterial substance is high in protein which contains all the essential amino acids."

In Germany, a team headed by Professors Hans Günter Schlegel at the Institute for Microbiology of Göttingen University has been investigating properties of *Hydrogenomonas* bacteria, initially for more academic purposes, since the 1950s. Independently of the NASA efforts, Schlegel and his team also looked into the idea of a closed-loop life support system for future long-term space missions, involving the use of protein-producing bacteria. But when the global food-supply implications of these bacteria became apparent, Schlegel began to investigate these aspects more intensively as well.

Starting with small culture dishes, the Göttingen team produced protein in so-called fermenter tanks of up to 200 liters (52 gallons) in size, testing different growth solutions and examining nutritional value and digestibility of different types of bacteria. Some researchers in the Schlegel team were concerned mostly with protein production, while others looked more at genetic manipulation of the hydrogen-devouring strains in an effort to come up with more efficient mutants.

"Basically, molecular hydrogen is not an unusual source of energy for living beings," Schlegel explained in a 1971 article.

All aerobic organisms derive the energy necessary for the construction of their cell substance and to maintain their life functions from the reaction between hydrogen and oxygen. Man as well derives his metabolic energy through the slow combustion of hydrogen, in other words, from the so-called "Knallgas" reaction[5] although he is not being offered hydrogen in its gaseous state as nourishment, but rather as part of his foodstuffs [in which] it is weakly bonded to carbon. Metabolic energy is not released through the combustion of the carbon but primarily through the oxidation of the hydrogen contained in foodstuffs. The product of burning hydrogen is water.

Hydrogen bacteria are capable of utilizing gaseous hydrogen (H_2) via a special enzyme, hydrogenase, which activates hydrogen and channels it into the metabolic process. These bacteria, just like green plants, use atmospheric CO_2 as carbon source and assimilate it via the same metabolic pathway, producing carbohydrates, proteins, and other cell substances in the process. They are capable of growth in a simple solution containing only inorganic salts into which gaseous hydrogen, oxygen (i.e., air), and carbon dioxide are fed.

Schlegel "harvests" the bacterial cells as a thick suspension—a broth really. The "soup" is heated for 10 minutes to a temperature of 65°C. (149°F.), activating certain enzymes that break down the nucleic acids. The "soup" is then run through a separator, something "like a milk centrifuge" that strains out the broken-down indigestible nucleic acids, reducing the concentration of these acids from a high 20–23 percent to a low, acceptable 5 percent.

After removing the nucleic acids, the remaining protein-rich cells can be handled pretty much conventionally; the paste can be dried in a spray-dryer into a powder. Like milk powder, it can be freeze-dried or it can be pressed into a moist cube like the baking yeast of yesteryear, Schlegel says. "From the point of view of biology, we are at the stage that we could do it." The disincentives are the economics, the worldwide oversupply of proteins in industrialized countries, and the explosion hazard: "We are working with fermenters with an explosive gas mixture of up to ten liters volume, but I don't dare to go beyond that," says Schlegel. "I'm a biologist, not an engineer."

Schlegel says that industrial-scale batch operations (he is also working on methods to make protein in a continuous process) would involve fermenters of up to 400,000 liters (105,000 gallons); the volume of the explosive hydrogen-oxygen mixture would be very large and a possible bang could be very big indeed. Schlegel has developed several methods to eliminate that risk, including one "which aims at the production of the gas mixture directly in the nutrient solution"—gases dissolved in a liquid can't burn or explode.

A more important explanation for industry's hesitancy is the glut of protein, at least in industrial countries. "There is a protein surplus everywhere," says Schlegel. "Even some types of green animal fodder [silage] now are just being cut up and plowed back under as green fertilizer."

What about the very idea of eating what are, after all, bacteria—"synthetic" food? "Until a few years ago bacteria were regarded as harmful and as enemies of human beings," observes Schlegel. The fact that bacteria were used to prepare many foodstuffs and medicines and that they are being ingested regularly in the form of cheese or yogurt was ignored. Schlegel says that after removal of components that are indigestible or even toxic for human beings, such as certain storage fats accumulated in the cell and RNA,[6] protein quality is high and the nutritive value is similar to that of the casein found in milk. The storage-fat problem has been solved in the laboratory by selectively breeding mutants incapable of producing the fat at all, a selection process that involves picking one mutant out of around one million cells. Schlegel's team in fact has found 50 such mutants. "Nowhere have we used the strains as nature offered them to us," observes Schlegel. "We have bred more suitable strains of rice, of wheat, and of pigs. In the same way we have to select the right bacteria. I don't see any problem in this." Schlegel adds that the protein can be extracted from the bacterial cell mass and processed the same way soybean protein is turned into synthetic meat, the fiber tissue sold commercially as "textured vegetable protein" (TVP).

As to the "synthetic" aspect, Marchetti has pointed out that the material is not synthetic at all but is in fact an animal product—admittedly an unusual one. Marchetti likens it to milk and its derivatives: "There is basically only one type of milk, but there are hundreds of types of cheese," he says.

Since food production via bacterial growth is linked to the availability of hydrogen, which in turn is largely determined by the availability of cheap power, the question arises, What amounts of energy does it take to provide basic staple protein? At Cornell, Marchetti performed the intellectual leap of relating the energy output of a nuclear reactor (or future solar plant) to the food requirements of man.

Now, a man needs a caloric input of 2,500–3,000 Kcal per day, corresponding to a rounded mean power of 150 watts. Taking into account all the losses from nuclear energy to hydrogen, and from hydrogen to food synthesized by microorganisms, to have 150 watts "at the mouth" one should count on roughly 500 watts at the reactor level. This means that a reactor designed to run a power station of current commercial size, say, 1000 Megawatt (electric) . . . and assuming a conversion efficiency in the plant of 40 percent, [this] could be the primary energy source to feed about five million people.

As such a food plant can presumably be packed over a few acres of barren land, one can easily see the consequences of this crude arithmetic.

Marchetti, permitting his *persona* to break through the sober scientific shell, waxed poetic for a moment about the prospects:

This is not to say that agriculture is bound to disappear overnight. Orchards producing beautiful flowers and tasty fruit, or vineyards producing exquisite wines have a long life ahead. But the pressure to produce staple food will certainly be reduced and farmland released to live in and enjoying it in a golden post-agricultural era. I'm pretty sure that an evolution in this sense will occur, perhaps slowly, certainly it will begin before the end of this century.

10

The Hindenburg Syndrome: Is Hydrogen Safe?

March 27, 1977, will go down in history books as the "Bloody Sunday" of jet aviation. That day, the statistically near-impossible happened: Two huge B-747 jumbo jets crashed into each other on a foggy runway on the sunny vacation island of Santa Cruz de Tenerife. A Dutch KLM plane, apparently unaware of a Pan Am plane that was taxiing on the runway, struck the Pan Am craft just as it was lifting off. The result was the worst disaster in civil aviation history. A total of 583 persons perished.

Daniel G. Brewer, Lockheed's hydrogen programs manager and the most outspoken advocate of liquid hydrogen as airplane fuel in the U.S. aircraft industry, feels that many of the deaths in that Tenerife disaster were probably due to the kerosene-fueled fire that raged for about ten and one-half hours. "If both aircraft had been fueled with liquid hydrogen there is a reasonable possibility that many lives could have been saved," Brewer told an audience of experts six weeks after the tragedy at a hydrogen symposium at the Joint Research Center in Ispra, Italy.

Brewer says under identical circumstances (except for the fuel used), with the ascending KLM plane striking the Pan Am plane's upper lounge right behind the cockpit, some 25 or 30 persons would also have been killed by the direct impact. Fire presumably would have broken out as well, but because of different burn characteristics, Brewer asserts that many passengers could have been rescued had the fuel been hydrogen. His reasoning goes as follows:

1. The fuel-fed portion of the fire would have lasted only a few minutes. Hydrogen burns at about 10 times the rate of kerosene.
2. The fire would have been confined to a relatively small area. LH_2 would

vaporize and disperse before it could spread widely.[1] Also, a much
smaller portion of the total fuel would presumably have been spilled.

3. Radiation (*i.e., radiated heat*) from the fire would be significantly less, so
   that only those persons and that part of the structure directly above or
   immediately adjacent to the flames would have been burned.

4. The absence of smoke from the burning fuel may have saved some lives;
   however, smoke from other incendiary material in the aircraft would
   tend to negate this advantage for hydrogen.

Whatever the merits of Brewer's speculation, one cannot help comparing the Tenerife disaster, which faded fairly quickly from the public's
consciousness, with the *Hindenburg* dirigible accident of 1937. Although
only 35 people perished in that tragedy, it created enough interest and
morbid curiosity 40 years later to persuade Hollywood to make another
B-grade disaster epic. The *Hindenburg* film played to full houses in many
countries; its fascination can perhaps be explained by the notion that the
Hindenburg represented an archetypal disaster of high technology—the
Titanic was another—that received full media coverage.

To hydrogen-as-fuel advocates, both the *Hindenburg* disaster and the
hydrogen bomb are negatively charged trigger words, terms that sym-
bolize irrational fears of the public about the Faustian-pact aspects of
new technologies, stumbling blocks standing in the way of introducing
new, benign technologies—such as a hydrogen economy. In the United
States, the H₂indenburg Society combats what its members perceive to
be the *Hindenburg* syndrome, fear coupled with a large dose of public ig-
norance about the real or imagined lack of safety of hydrogen (see
Chapter 3).

H₂indenburg Society members like Brewer and others point out that in
calling up the image of that huge blazing cigar shape near its mooring
mast in Lakehurst, New Jersey, many tend to forget that while 35 people
were killed, another 65 survived. This is a much better survival rate than
in most contemporary air disasters. The *Hindenburg* did not explode, as
is often believed. Rather, it burned, sinking rapidly to the ground. Also,
it is usually forgotten that the *Hindenburg*'s sister ship, the *Graf Zeppelin*, made regular scheduled transatlantic crossings for nine years, from
1928 until its retirement in 1937, with no mishap. Prior to the *Hindenburg* disaster, in which more than seven million cubic feet (198,000 cubic
meters) of hydrogen were consumed within less than a minute, the airship had successfully completed 10 roundtrips between the United States
and Europe.

Although initially sabotage was suspected as the cause of the conflagration, it is thought more likely that electrostatic charges present in

the atmosphere after more than an hour of thunderstorm and rain ignited the hydrogen that was being vented as the big ship tried to tie up to the mooring tower. Finally, it should be pointed out that the *Hindenburg* and its sister dirigibles were designed to be filled with nonflammable helium gas for buoyancy, but had to be inflated with hydrogen after the United States refused to sell helium to the Germans.

In the case of the H-bomb, there is no technical connection between the bomb and hydrogen fuel other than the word itself, but as Brewer said in his Ispra paper, the link provided by that word "is apparently enough to stir the imagination of the public and excite fear and suspicion of the fuel."

Characteristics of Hydrogen

To understand more fully the safety implications of hydrogen, we need to examine hydrogen's physical properties, which are given here, based on the 1976 SRI study:

1. Liquid hydrogen is a very cold material, $-423°F.$ ($-252.8°C.$). Contact with human body tissue might result in severe burns, destroying tissue almost like the burn from a flame.

2. As a gas, hydrogen diffuses very quickly into other areas, such as air. It has a very low density, meaning it rises very quickly through the air.

3. Hydrogen burns mixed with air over a much wider range than methane or gasoline, for instance. A mixture of as low as 4 percent of hydrogen in air and as high as 74 percent will burn. The corresponding ranges for methane are 5.3 to 15 percent, and for gasoline it is a very narrow range from 1.0 to 7.6 percent. Jet fuel's flammability range is even narrower, from 0.8 to 5.6 percent.

4. When confined in a completely enclosed space—a room, or a tank—hydrogen can be detonated, i.e., exploded over a wide range of concentrations, ranging from 18 to 59 percent (by volume) in air. Methane explodes only in concentrations ranging from 6.3 to 14 percent, and gasoline and jet fuel detonate in a range from 1.1 to 3.3 percent.

5. It takes very little energy to ignite a hydrogen flame—about 20 micro-joules (MJ). Methane requires about 12 times as much energy, about 290 MJ, to set off a burn, and gasoline needs about 240 MJ.[2] However, out in the open without confinement, it is almost impossible to bring hydrogen to an explosion with a spark heat or flame. Hydrogen-air mixtures can be detonated only with a suitable initiator, such as a heavy blasting cap.

6. The hydrogen flame is almost invisible in daylight (unless some special colorant is added), and it travels much faster than a methane flame. A hydrogen flame shoots upward at a rate of 2.75 meters (9 feet) per second, while methane and gasoline burn much more slowly at 0.37 meters (1.2 feet) per second.

7. Unlike kerosene or gasoline flames, hydrogen flames radiate very little energy, meaning heat is not felt at a distance.[3]

The Stanford study clarifies some of the implications, saying:

> while the invisibility of the flame makes the fire difficult to locate and fight, firefighters can get very close to the flame (assuming they know where it is) without injury. Since it is also difficult to feel warmth from the flame, a person can easily move right into the flame and be burned; but surrounding objects do not heat up and ignite unless touched by the flame directly. . . . in normal fires, one of the major causes of fire spreading and injury is the large amount of energy radiated by oxidizing carbon atoms. Thus, the lack of flame luminosity in hydrogen fires can be both a help and a hindrance. The energy radiated from fires above pools of liquid hydrogen and liquid methane of the same area and volume would be nearly identical because the lower emissivity of hydrogen is offset by the more rapid rate of combustion. Of course this also means that the available fuel is more quickly exhausted in the hydrogen fire. However, owing to its rapid rate of evaporation, pools of liquid hydrogen are not likely to form except after a very large spill. A liquid-hydrogen fueled airplane that crashed on takeoff would probably result in such a spill.
>
> Hydrogen's wide range of flammability and low ignition energy is offset by its great tendency to disperse from the scene of a leak or a spill because of its buoyancy and high rate of diffusion. In one of the few hydrogen accidents so far that has become somewhat famous a tank truck full of liquid hydrogen rolled over with no resulting fire and no harm to the driver . . . the hydrogen evaporated and dispersed quickly upwards from the crashed truck. When gasoline is spilled, vapors heavier than air spread in a wide layer near the ground. This greatly increases the hazardous area. Thus, the tendency of hydrogen to disperse much more rapidly than other fuels, even gaseous methane, is a large point in its favor.

Studies of Hydrogen Safety

Brewer and the SRI team were not the first to point out the safety differences between hydrogen and conventional carbon-based fuels. In 1956 Arthur D. Little, as well as Lockheed, ran tests to get an idea of what hazards existed in handling the large quantities of hydrogen expected to be used in the U.S. space program and what type of procedures would be required. Among other things, the Little researchers spilled and ignited as much as 5,000 gallons (19,000 liters) of liquid hydrogen in an open space, but there were no explosions.

Judging partially on the Little data, A. A. Du Pont, a researcher for the Garrett Corporation of Los Angeles, California, said in a 1967 paper that the "use of hydrogen in normal aircraft operation can be as safe or safer than the use of fuel. Questions arise as to the relative hazard of hydrogen fuel in case of serious accident where the airplane is partially destroyed and the fuel is spilled." Du Pont said it is "very difficult" to obtain an explosive air-hydrogen mixture even in a confined space—a claim disputed by others—and Du Pont asserted that a hydrogen fire is "very much better from a safety standpoint. A spill of cryogenic hydrogen boils furiously on contact with the relatively warm ground, so the area of spilled fuel is therefore confined whereas the spill of hydrocarbon fuel spreads along the ground and covers a considerable area." In an accident in which fuel is spilled and ignited, a kerosene fire covers a much larger area than a hydrogen blaze, Du Pont claimed.

Du Pont concluded that "it appears, after objectively evaluating the properties of the two fuels and the probable size of the fuel loads involved, that a passenger's chances of walking away from a crash of a hydrogen-fueled airplane are as good or better than they would be with a kerosene-fueled airplane."

Possibly Du Pont went a bit overboard in accentuating the positive. The SRI study, compiled nine years later, points out that hydrogen is simply different in its safety aspects. Comparison in safety with conventional fuels yields "no clear cut answers." Rather, the study maintains, "it can be said . . . that since the physical and chemical properties of hydrogen are quite different from commonly encountered substances, the hazards associated with hydrogen appear to be far more influenced by *circumstances than for other fuels*. . . . blanket statements about the safety of hydrogen relative to other substances are generally misleading" (italics added).

Thus, hydrogen safety so far is an "on one hand, but on the other" type of proposition, a situation that remains unchanged due to the lack of any significant amount of hard data.

The SRI study points out that acceptance or rejection of a future hydrogen economy depends not so much on the facts involved; rather, "public *perceptions* of the safety of hydrogen may be one of the major obstacles to a transition to a hydrogen economy." Policymakers should be aware of the difference between two types of perceptions and their implications: familiarity with "real" hazards as opposed to "nonreal," imagined hazards. Most fears about hydrogen safety belong in the second category so far, the study says.

> Certainly, many 'real' hazards exist in the utilization of hydrogen but these hazards are not absolute; instead, they are relative to the specific conditions of use. . . . Perceptions of 'nonreal' hazards are based on incomplete knowledge and can be further influenced by many factors. . . . Since the actual safety of hydrogen is so variable and so dependent on the specific conditions of its use, the factor of education seems to be especially important. A fairly high level of knowledge about the technology would be required to understand all the relevant qualifying conditions.

The SRI team lists three factors as

> especially relevant in the conditioning of the public's perception about the safety of hydrogen:
> 1. The newness of many aspects of the technology.
> 2. The usual lack of understandable technical information for the general public.
> 3. The apparently contradictory experience and statements about hydrogen safety.

Blanket judgments of how safe or unsafe hydrogen is depend to a large extent on the actual circumstances of a spill, the study says, on "the nature of the rupture, the degree of confinement, the nature of the actual nearby objects, and whether combustion is initiated."

The SRI study suggests that these three factors could easily create an atmosphere of opposition to hydrogen, especially since the hazardous aspects are likely to be emphasized. It wouldn't make much difference whether possible negative attitudes had their roots in "real" or "nonreal" factors, since "both could have the same impact on ultimate acceptance or rejection of the hydrogen economy." Especially in view of much increased general interest in environmental and consumer affairs over the last dozen years, influencing legislation as well as corporate policies, "it will be crucial to obtain general acceptance prior to implementation of major hydrogen facilities. If acceptance fails to develop, attempts to block or modify implementation should be expected," the study concludes.

There is some evidence that liquid hydrogen may be less of a danger element than kerosene under combat conditions. Recent U.S. Air Force experiments indicate that liquid hydrogen is "more forgiving" when a plane is being shot at and when fuel tanks are penetrated by explosive devices or fragments—perhaps making commercial airplanes less vulnerable in instances of on-board shoot-outs during highjack attempts.

Researchers at the air force Flight Dynamics Laboratory at Wright-Patterson Air Base fired armor-piercing incendiary and fragment-simulator bullets into styrofoam-lined aluminum containers, some filled with liquid hydrogen, others with JP-4 jet fuel. In another series of tests, the researchers simulated lightning strikes into the containers. The results, described by Jack R. Lippert at the 1976 Miami Beach conference, indicated that the incendiary weapons ignited but did not detonate the liquid hydrogen samples. The resulting hydrogen fire was "less severe and expired more quickly" than a comparable JP-4 fire, even if the total heat content of the hydrogen sample was twice as large as that of the JP-4 sample.

Shooting at the sample containers with the nonexplosive fragmentation bullets indicated that the liquid hydrogen volume experienced little so-called hydraulic ram effect, an internal pressure wave in the liquid that could rip open the container or tank and cause damage to surrounding sheet metal. The nonexplosive bullets also did not ignite the liquid hydrogen, which simply poured out through the bullets' entry and exit holes. A similar styrofoam-covered container filled with JP-4 was also shot at. The bullet caused overpressure that forced the kerosene through the lid and ripped a good-sized exit hole. Lippert explains the difference in hydraulic behavior by the fact that liquid hydrogen is only about one-tenth as dense as the petroleum-based fuel. A bullet racing through a fluid creates much more impact and shock wave in a dense than a thin one.

Similarly, in the lightning strikes—the researcher used a 6 million-volt generator, 65 feet (20 meters) high—big arcs were shot into the liquid hydrogen containers. Again, fire resulted but no explosion. Concluded Lippert:

> The data indicates that the hazards associated with LH_2 utilization in combat aircraft may be less severe than those with JP-4 and therefore it is recommended that LH_2 should not be disregarded as future alternate fuel for military as well as commercial aircraft.

NASA's Experience with Hydrogen Safety

The National Aeronautics and Space Administration is probably the preeminent organization in the West with large hydrogen-handling experience—nobody knows what kind of a fuel-handling safety record the Soviets have with their rocket program—but given the complexity of rocketry in general, the NASA experience by and large is not very relevant to safety problems posed by a future civilian hydrogen economy.

Still, NASA has used and handled stupendous amounts of liquid hydrogen, most of it hauled by barge and tanker trailers over hundreds of miles to Cape Kennedy. In 1974, a paper reviewing 96 hydrogen accidents and incidents was presented by NASA researcher Paul M. Ordin at the Ninth Intersociety Energy Conversion Engineering Conference in San Francisco. Ordin reported that NASA tanker trailers had hauled more than 16 million gallons (60.5 million liters) of liquid hydrogen for the Apollo-Saturn program alone. His study found that most mishaps occurred "when the guidelines and prescribed procedures in the safety program were neglected." Most of the mishaps were of such a specialized nature that they shed little light on safety aspects of future wide use of hydrogen. Still, his review included descriptions of 17 mishaps involving tanker-trailers carrying between 3,000 and 16,000 gallons (11,000 and 60,500 liters) of LH_2, 12 of them during off-loading operations at the test site and 5 involving highway accidents. In 3 accidents the tractor was heavily damaged, but the load-carrying trailer remained intact. In the other 2, the trucks were not damaged, but in 1 case liquid hydrogen spilled onto the ground, with no ignition of the hydrogen-air mixture.

The over-the-road accidents were such that they might have caused a real conflagration and spectacular blaze had the load been gasoline or kerosene. In one case the truck and trailer were going too fast into a curve on a bad road with the truck and trailer first weaving and then rolling over an embankment 40 feet (12 meters) downhill. The trailer rolled over one and a half times and the truck once, winding up upright. The tractor "was a complete loss" but the trailer was little damaged, with the shell in still satisfactory shape and venting normally.

In another accident, the hydrogen carrier jackknifed on a wet road with strong wind after braking, swinging around 180 degrees and sliding into a shoulder. The trailer unhitched, turned over into a ditch, and slid some 80 feet (24 meters) down the ditch on its side. The safety disks ruptured, as designed, and about one hour later the liquid hydrogen had safely vented into the air.

In a third accident, a tractor-trailer returning from fuel delivery but still containing gaseous hydrogen and traveling at about 50–55 miles per hour (80–88 kilometers per hour) was hit in rainy weather by a truck that spun in front of the hydrogen carrier. The hydrogen tractor was demolished, but the LH_2 trailer did not suffer any leaks and the vacuum was not broken.

In general, most of the NASA accidents were brought about by (in descending order of frequency): valve malfunctions, including valve leaks; leaking connections; safety disk failures; unsatisfactory materials and embrittlement; high venting rates; air in the system; and other causes. Highway traffic accidents, vacuum loss, and line rupture accounted for the least frequent accidents. In 80 of the 96 incidents, hydrogen was released, and 61 involved the outbreak of a fire. While this may sound like a high percentage, researchers think that the fact that in 25 cases there was no fire is more significant.

Although the NASA experience "offers encouragement about the safe use of liquid hydrogen" and should serve as a point of departure for developing future safety procedures, the SRI study says NASA's record is "simply inadequate to serve as a basis for decision-making" for a more general hydrogen economy. NASA personnel who handled hydrogen were specially chosen and trained; use of hydrogen in the space effort was restricted to "rigorously controlled" outdoor environments to limit explosion hazards; "extreme concern about the reliability of systems" was dominant in the entire space program, cutting the chances for disaster to the bone; and hydrogen safety procedures involved "expensive, often unique" hardware.

Another departure point for hydrogen safety as it relates to future hydrogen pipelines is provided by the experience of the world's first long-distance pipeline, operated by Chemische Werke Hüls (CWH) in Germany, but again it is no more than a departure point. It is important to remember that the German chemical hydrogen pipelines (1) are very small in diameter, nowhere near the diameter sizes postulated for future hydrogen energy pipelines; (2) operate at pressures that are very low in comparison to the thousands of pounds per square inch demanded for efficient energy transport. Also, the hydrogen gas is not very pure (only about 95 percent) and this has a bearing on leakage, embrittlement, and flammability, reducing hazards somewhat.

Christian Isting, a Hüls executive, who has written much about the CWH experience, said in a paper during a 1974 European energy symposium that "compressed hydrogen frequently ignites on expansion" for reasons that are not clearly understood yet but most likely have to do with electrostatic charges caused by dust particles in the air. Isting says that pressurized hydrogen will almost always ignite if it is vented through a seldom-used line. However, ignition can be generally avoided if initially only small amounts are sent through the venting line, increasing amounts and flow speed only gradually. Big amounts can be vented to the atmosphere in large quantities without ignition except during thunderstorms. He concludes:

> During the many years of operation of the integrated pipeline network of CWH, explosions have not occurred. Either the hydrogen will ignite immediately on escape or, if no ignition takes place an explosive mixture can-

not form near the ground because of its low density. Explosions or even detonations in the pipeline need not be feared as explosive gas-air mixtures cannot build up because of the pressure prevailing in the line.

It seems, then, that whatever fears exist in the public's mind about hydrogen are mainly fears of the unknown. Like any fuel, hydrogen has some dangerous properties, but it also possesses quite forgiving characteristics. On balance, the dangers of hydrogen do not seem to be any worse than those of gasoline, natural gas, or any other fuel; they are merely different.

Scenarios for the Future

"TOMORROW'S HYDROGEN ECONOMY: STILL NEEDING
ITS BIG PUSH"

"HYDROGEN ECONOMY IS POSSIBLE BY 1990S"

The first of these two headlines appeared in an April 1976 article in the industry magazine *Chemical Engineering*; it summed up the prevailing hard-nosed school of corporate and governmental skepticism. "Work on using hydrogen at utilities and in vehicles offers some hope for its widespread role as a fuel. But hydrogen lacks solid government or industry backing," said the subhead.

The article quoted Albert Landgrebe, then ERDA's chief hydrogen program administrator: "The idea of using hydrogen as a universal fuel . . . has great appeal to the frontier instincts of all technologists," but "one must weigh this alternative carefully and take a practical and rational view in considering where, how, why, and at what cost hydrogen may be produced and used in the energy system, as well as the timing." The story also cited a staff member of Representative Mike McCormack (D-Wash.), the chairman of the House Energy Research, Development, and Demonstration Subcommittee, as saying, "In the past four years, most of us have come to realize the expense of extracting hydrogen. . . . it has dropped down on our list of energy priorities."

ERDA's budget figures were eloquent: According to *Chemical Engineering*, ERDA's hydrogen-related spending that year amounted to only $7.5 million compared to $27.3 million for the probably more esoteric, far-future field of magnetohydrodynamics, $80 million for coal liquefaction, and a staggering $575.4 million for the liquid-metal fast breeder. Two years later, funding for hydrogen research had grown to around $24 million, a considerable gain, but still a drop in the bucket compared to the $200 million the U.S. Department of Energy was spending on coal gasification research.

The second headline introduced an interview with John O'M. Bockris in an October 1977 article in a competing magazine, *Chemical & Engineering News (C&EN)*. Bockris acknowledged that hydrogen technology will face rough sledding for a number of reasons, including a poor image and the required huge investments. But, he added, a society faced with the prospect of fossil fuels in critically short supply will have to do a lot of converting to other energy sources and carriers in any event, so why not hydrogen, which does have a lot of advantages? With proper government planning and organization—"another resource in short supply," *C&EN* paraphrased Bockris as saying—"the hydrogen economy could be well on its way by 1990."

Bockris fully recognized the problem: Aside from general inertia, there is the question of hydrogen's price, which in 1978 was roughly twice that of gasoline, based on production via electrolysis. Derived from coal, it would cost the end user somewhat more than methane extracted from that same coal.

"But everything has to be related to some date," Bockris said in *C&EN*. "In 20 years the price of fossil fuels will more than double, but the price of hydrogen, because of technological advances, will not." Bockris claimed that if the United States were to begin laying the groundwork for a hydrogen economy infrastructure right now, electrolytic hydrogen could be the cheaper fuel by 1985. With sufficient government planning a hydrogen economy could be phased in smoothly within a few years.

In his scenario, this phasing-in process might involve a pilot project with a small group of houses and buildings using hydrogen as a heating and appliance fuel by the early 1980s. Then, parts of smog-troubled cities like Los Angeles could be converted to hydrogen. From the mid-1980s, the automotive population of such a city could be "weaned" from gasoline. Further on, entire regions—Hawaii for example, which needs to import fuel anyway—could be converted (using perhaps hot-rock or geothermal power, potentially abundant in volcanic areas like Hawaii as primary source) to hydrogen. By 1990 then, a national hydrogen economy would be well on its way.

The two major difficulties in the way of a hydrogen economy are cost and political will, Bockris thought. "The price of any new energy system is going to be roughly $1,000 per kilowatt, and we are going to need about 10 kw per person. Multiply by the U.S. population and you have about three times the 1977 gross national product"—in numerals, $2,200,000,000,000, or if you spell it out, two trillion two hundred billion dollars.

Nor is there any political will, he believed. "Congress is loath to risk making its constituents uncomfortable. President Carter's energy plan offers only 'vague bleeps' in the appropriate direction, and even that is running into trouble," *C&EN* summed up Bockris' thinking. "It's like we were going down the turnpike in a car," he says; "it's warm in the car, it's snowing outside, so don't let's stop to get some gas. Let's wait until the needle is on zero—well, that's fine unless you run out of gas between stations."

Who is right? Nobody knows. How and when to mesh hydrogen in all of its manifestations into the total energy usage pattern has been the truly knotty problem ever since energy researchers began thinking earnestly about hydrogen as a fuel.

Early Illusions, Broadening Interest

In the early seventies it was somehow assumed that hydrogen would blend painlessly into the energy market almost overnight, in genie-from-the-pipeline fashion. It was believed, for instance, that hydrogen could be mixed in ever larger proportions into gas pipelines until it would almost entirely replace natural gas. However, it was found that even if problems like pipeline embrittlement or availability of high-pressure compressors were solved, simple things would present huge difficulties. For example, metering the gas flow would be a problem, because at different concentrations the meters would give different and therefore misleading readings that would not reflect the true energy content of the various mixture ratios.

Similarly, hydrogen enthusiasts believed early on that hydrogen from water would find a ready market in ammonia production, one of the entering wedges via the chemical industry. So far it hasn't happened; hydrogen produced via steam reforming from natural gas is still cheaper, despite the steep increases in natural gas prices in recent years.

Aviation, which was also thought to be a natural entry point, especially in view of hydrogen's potential as a fuel for environmentally clean transports, has so far failed to live up to those early hopes, Lockheed's NASA contracts notwithstanding. Aside from a few diehard SST enthusiasts, there doesn't seem to be any sentiment in Washington for a U.S. SST, especially in view of the Concorde's less than stellar performance—although once hydrogen enters the picture as a fuel, both economic and environmental aspects assume totally different coloring.

Today, we have the somewhat paradoxical situation that, on the one hand, the go-go enthusiasm of the hydrogen avant garde of zero hour, the people who wrote the early pieces in *Science, Chemical & Engineering News*, and *Scientific American*, the members of the H₂indenburg Society, has become muted. The early belief that hitching lots of readily available nuclear reactors to large, economical water splitters that were just around the corner would enable the United States to thumb its energetic nose at Yamani et al. within a few years turned out to be false.

On the other hand, interest in hydrogen has steadily percolated upward and outward, at least among scientists and scientific institutions, some governments, and some industrial firms. It's been a diffusing process that has made up by its breadth—notably also among Third World nations—for what it has lost in intensity among the early hydrogen elite: a technological democratization process, if there is such a thing, that is actually rather welcome. Among governments and industry, by and large the interest is not red hot, certainly not in the United States. On the other hand, countries like Japan and organizations such as the European Economic Community seem to be committed to significant steady growth over the long haul in this area.

Professor Karl-Friedrich Knoche, a leading European authority in thermodynamics, who has spent at least half a decade analyzing many potential thermochemical water-splitting cycles at the University of Aachen and who has worked with leading experts in the United States, illustrates the forecasting problem succinctly. Knoche explains that one of the key goals of hydrogen researchers everywhere is to make thermochemical cycles more energy- and cost-effective: "Overall efficiencies of below 20 percent are pointless and 30 percent is still prohibitive," he says.

So when does he think a final yea or nay judgment about the worth of any thermochemical process might be forthcoming? "Well," he smiled somewhat ruefully during a 1978 interview, "four years ago we would have said in four years. In fact we were careless enough to say just that." Today, despite the additional knowledge gained, neither he nor anybody else working on thermochemical cycles would dare to make any hard and fast forecast. Nevertheless, Knoche, going out on a limb once more but with a great deal more confidence, feels that by 1982 or thereabouts a final verdict as to whether thermochemical cycles are feasible on a large scale should be in.

Knoche essentially agrees with the prognosis made by other energy experts who foresee a change in the entire energy use pattern, including the adoption of hydrogen, in three long stages. According to this scenario, in the first stage coal in all its forms—as a mineral, liquid, or gas—will gradually replace oil usage in the next 15 years, between now and, say, the middle 1990s, coupled to a larger use of light-water nuclear reactors and first trials for the breeder and high-temperature reactors. Work on hydrogen would continue, but it would not make any significant inroads.

In the second stage, a 50-year period after the 1990s, a hydrogen economy "in the widest sense" would be phased in. Oil and natural gas would have been largely eliminated as primary sources, having been replaced by solar and nuclear energy (HTR and breeder reactors) as main primary sources. For cars, methanol rather than hydrogen is most likely the best-suited fuel.

After that period, beginning around 2040, the third stage, the golden age of the environmentally clean, planet-wide energy systems would come into being. Ocean mining would flourish, and primary energy would come from solar sources of all types—solar power plants in deserts and oceans and solar satellites—and perhaps clean nuclear-fusion power, producing helium as its main by-product. Power would be generated at a handful of super power-sites, far removed from population centers, with the generated energy transported either as electricity through long-distance, low-resistance cryogenic cables, or as hydrogen—as gas via pipelines or as cryogenic liquid in huge cryo-tankers—to population centers.

Gearing Up for the Long Haul

The belief that widespread hydrogen usage is not around the corner but is an inherently long-term proposition is supported by work Marchetti has done in recent years. He has investigated the rate at which new energy systems—new technologies of any type—have arrived. (Marchetti has been investigating the substitutability of "primary energy sources" rather than secondary energy carriers such as hydrogen or electricity, but these studies are still strongly suggestive of things to come for hydrogen as well. At any rate, he believes that the increased use of solar and/or nuclear primary energy goes hand in hand with hydrogen.)

Marchetti started from the "somehow iconoclastic hypotheses that the different primary energy sources are commodities competing for a market, like different brands of soap, or different processes to make steel, and that the rules of the game may, after all be the same," as he put it in a November 1974 lecture in Moscow. Marchetti drew largely on the work of two American scientists, J. C. Fisher and R. H. Fry, who have analyzed the substitution rates of new technologies and who attempted to forecast the rate of diffusion of new technologies for General Electric. Using certain basic data and formulas, Marchetti found he could predict market shares decades in the future.

In a paper based on his Moscow lecture, Marchetti included some amazing graphs that show the market penetration curves for various competing pairs of products or technological processes over periods ranging from 60 to 80 years, such as the replacement of the open-hearth method of making steel by the Bessemer method, substitution of sulfate turpentine for natural turpentine, and replacement of water-based paint by oil-based paint. The astounding part of these graphs was that the equations describing market penetration worked so well as a decades-spanning forecasting tool: The curve derived from these formulas matched the historical data with "extraordinary precision," according to Marchetti.[1] The implication was that if market penetration proceeded according to some law, some force independent of legislation, short-term economics or price, it should be possible to predict with reasonable certainty to what extent a new product or technology—or new energy—would replace its precursors.

Marchetti decided to put the theory to the test by trying to predict what percentage of the U.S. energy market would be covered by oil in our time period by using data from four decades earlier. As he told his Moscow audience, the results were astonishing:

> I took the data for the U.S. from 1930 to 1935 and tried to forecast oil coverage of the U.S. market up to 1970. The predicted values, even for the saturation period, fit the statistical data better than 1 percent which, after all, is the minimum error that can be expected from this kind of statistics. This means that the contribution of oil to the U.S. energy budget, e.g., in 1965, was completely predetermined 30 years before, with the only assumption that a new primary source of energy, e.g., nuclear, was not going to play a *major* (italics added) role in the meantime.
>
> As the history of substitutions shows, however, the time a new source takes to make some inroads in the market is very long indeed, about a hundred years to become dominant starting from scratch, so that also this assumption appears really unimportant for predictions up to 50 years ahead.

Two years later, Marchetti elaborated on the theme at a seminar on Microbial Energy Conversion in Göttingen. Pointing out the truly long periods of time it takes for a new technology to percolate into society, he observed that the "takeover time," the time it takes this technology to go from 1 percent of the market to 99 percent, is in the range of 50 years, for the United States at least—an observation that presumably will be valid for hydrogen as well. "The extreme stability of the functions over very long periods of time, including wars, depressions, economic miracles, and a perceived acceleration of knowledge and 'progress'" do not detract from the validity of this phenomenon, Marchetti said. "My feeling is that all this is linked to learning processes at the societal and individual level which evolve very slowly and perhaps were the same 1,000 years ago."

Flashing some slides on the screen that showed charts depicting various energy-mix scenarios through the twenty-first century, Marchetti observed,

> as you can see, the takeover times are of the order of a century, so there is not much purpose in darting ahead, but meaningful influences on the system can be obtained only through really long-term thinking and planning. . . . In fact, the spreading of a new technology always follows the rule of penetrating first small favorable eco-niches, acquiring force and momentum for the next step.

He illustrated that thesis with a brilliant thumbnail description of how crude oil wormed its way into the energy capillaries of the world:

> The oil industry was not born as a competitor to coal, too big an industry and too well entrenched to fight against, but as a welcome substitute for dwindling resources of whale oil for illumination. Being small and aggressive, through the development of a superb chemistry it was able to conquer the new, very specialized markets such as the one of "motor spirits" and finally, after almost hundred years, fight back coal in the last trenches, electricity production, and steel making.

The moral, Marchetti told the Göttingen assembly, was to forget for the time being heroic concerns like "the world energy market and world salvation. . . . Concentrate on the special case, the special product, the favorable eco-niche. A new technology needs very special conditions to root."

Discussing the historical oil phenomenon elsewhere, he noted that in the United States, oil's share of total energy consumption peaked in the fifties; in the world, it peaked in the seventies. He acknowledged that it is pretty hard *not* to blame the closure of the Suez Canal for the former and the fourfold oil price rise for the latter. But, as he wrote in a German popular science magazine in 1977,

> the facts indicate, one should look for the real and qualitative causes of these phenomena in the activities of some obscure oil bosses looking for their profits in the wilds of Texas around the turn of the century. Certainly, this does not fit into the normal range of our imagination and is hard to believe—but the facts speak for it. The activities of those oil magnates at that time determined the starting point and the slope of the oil consumption curve.

The inference from Marchetti's analyses is clear: Regardless of legislative activities, subsidies, or other stimuli, there is a "natural rhythm" learning curve for the introduction of new technologies that stretches over decades—up to a century—determined by the peculiar qualities of that product or technology at earliest infancy. And what has been true for basic commodities like oil (or steel, or paint, or ammonia) is likely to be true for hydrogen as well.

Planning for a Hydrogen Economy

Somewhat similar considerations in the massive Stanford Research Institute study of 1976, *The Hydrogen Economy, A Preliminary Technology Assessment*, led the authors to argue that long-range changes affecting entire nations should not be left to private corporations with their inherent short-term outlook. Corporations formally discount the value of future earnings because their philosophy is essentially piecemeal, pushing the needed ultimate transformation further into the future, which in turn requires additional and essentially unnecessary changes at high cost. According to the study:

> Decisions in both the private and public sector are generally made with a planning horizon of 5 to 10 years. Corporations formally discount the value of future earnings anticipated from an investment according to the profit or interest the same investment could earn elsewhere.
>
> As a result, a dollar that could be earned this year is considered more valuable than a dollar that could be earned next year. Discounting of the future tends to justify a preoccupation with short- rather than long-term goals in decision making.

Because of the massive investments and long lead times required for phasing into a hydrogen economy, "corporations (and governments as well) tend to dismiss hydrogen in favor of concentrating on those activities that continue the viability of the existing order." Thus, for example, instead of hydrogen, the natural gas industry is concentrating on making synthetic fuels from oil shale and coal.

> This concentration derives from the fact that those materials can be blended with traditional supplies without much perturbation of either the distribution or end-use aspects of the energy system. Although coal gasification and liquefaction and oil shale development require large amounts of capital investment, they offer the advantage of being carried out on an incremental basis without the fundamental alteration of the entire fuel supply system. Because the transition to hydrogen is genuinely only a long-term option and would take more time to implement than the

private sector is normally concerned about, the role of hydrogen in the future U.S. energy economy is rightfully a matter of public policy.

The study tried to assess the likely effects of neutral, pro-hydrogen, and anti-hydrogen policies on the part of the U.S. government. It concluded that in the event of a neutral stance, "hydrogen would not be likely to gain favor until fuel options more compatible with existing corporate, societal and governmental institutions have been exploited and perhaps nearly exhausted. This would make the ultimate transition period needlessly rushed and, hence, disruptive."

In the event of an anti-hydrogen position, "manifested by failure to support significant hydrogen R&D efforts while giving support to R&D on other synthetic fuels," which is the case today, the study asserts that

> the emergence of the hydrogen economy in the United States would probably be delayed until fossil-fuel reserves of all kinds become truly scarce globally. Countries with fewer domestic energy sources than the United States, however, would probably take the R&D lead and begin actual implementation of some aspects of the hydrogen economy concept before 2000. The United States could then find itself a buyer of foreign hydrogen economy technology.

The study lists a number of technological developments that would tend to either enhance or diminish the prospects of a transition to hydrogen. The push toward a hydrogen economy would be stimulated by "economical solar energy collection" plus advances in chemical catalysis (helpful in developing electrolyzers and fuel cells) and development of practical superconductors (helpful toward wide use of liquid hydrogen). Any move towards a hydrogen economy would be reduced by the "technical and economic success of nuclear fusion" because it would tend to stimulate an "all-electric economy," lessening the role of hydrogen.[2] Also, the development of better, more efficient electric storage batteries would be counterproductive because it would reduce hydrogen's potential in mobile applications, according to the SRI analysis.

The study concludes:

> It has been said that nations and individuals inevitably do the right thing but only after they have exhausted all the other possibilities. Viewed in the abstract, ultimate conversion to a hydrogen/electric economy may very well be the "right" thing for the United States. However, the hydrogen economy concept cannot be viewed solely in the abstract. If the concept is ever to be implemented, a feasible pathway linking the present—with its

various established institutions, investments, interests, biases, and preferences—to the future must be found. It is not enough that hydrogen might be the best final solution, it would also have to be found the best transitional solution. An institutionally feasible pathway would be characterized by a series of small incremental changes (each of which may, nevertheless, be painful to some established interests) rather than a series of drastic changes.

If adequate research and development is not performed to remove the uncertainties about hydrogen use and to improve the viability of the hydrogen economy concept, society may well find that it has, figuratively, painted itself into a dark corner because it has continued to make massive investments in expedient short-term solutions while neglecting to set, and make progress towards, long-term goals.

To illustrate, the SRI study says that with a basically neutral government attitude towards hydrogen, which seemed to be the case in the late seventies, the series of individual corporate decisions will take the energy mix in a direction that will make a later, perhaps inevitable transition to a hydrogen or hydrogen-electric economy that much more difficult. Development and use of coal liquefaction plants to make synthetic crude to maintain the current petroleum-based liquid-fuel system, the study argues, will add to the complexity and to the "entrenched investment of the hydrocarbon system." In contrast, investment in solar energy technologies, requiring energy storage systems to tide over nighttime and bad-weather conditions, would tend to advance the use of hydrogen storage systems and would help to spur the delivery of energy in the form of hydrogen. If this is true, the 1978 calls for solar action by the White House Council on Environmental Quality and, even more significantly, the push by the Sunsat Energy Council for solar-power satellites with all the muscle of major multinationals behind it—the council includes Boeing, McDonnell Douglas, Lockheed, Grumman, General Electric, and Westinghouse—point in the right direction.

The SRI study concludes:

> Importantly, a transition to hydrogen as a means to deliver energy to end users could be *permanent* because *any primary energy resource developed in the future could be used to produce hydrogen* (italics added). Thus, in the future, a sequence of basic energy resources could be utilized without ever again affecting consumers. In this respect hydrogen offers a clear advantage to implementations of synthetic gasoline, diesel, methane, etc., because ultimately the concentrated carbonaceous resources on which these synthetics are based will be in short supply. Thus, while synthetic fuels from fossil resources would be easier to implement in the structural

framework set by today's culture, they can only be a temporary solution and yet another transition will be required later.

It is worth noting that not only hydrogen advocates but also others are becoming increasingly impatient with the financial preoccupations of energy planners, the kind of economic defensiveness that says we can't afford to push hydrogen research because (1) it's too expensive and (2) we have to explore all other options first. There is a feeling that these arguments essentially reflect the short-term-profit dogma of the corporate world, which, some feel, is simply becoming irrelevant in the face of the wrenching changes that are in store for the world, a feeling that the "dismal science" representatives, the economists, are just having too much say at a time when issues of the real, physical world are at stake.

"When I hear people . . . make these terribly pragmatic projections, predictions how hydrogen will enter into the market place because of this, that, or the other, because of cost-effective, objective criteria, I suspect that a lot of the determinants may in fact be subjective, emotional," observed the University of Michigan's Larry Jones at one point during the March 1976 Miami Beach hydrogen energy conference. Jones, referring to the then upcoming California nuclear referendum (actually won by the pro-nuclear forces) said that a

> prime example of that is the turmoil in the nuclear industry because of a subjective, popular reaction, apprehension, fear of the unknown. They [the public] know that radioactivity is scary because they don't understand it, and they are able to perceive that we don't know enough about the problems of nuclear reactors, or that's at least what's transmitted to the public.
>
> For example, if one were to have in this California referendum an alternative, "would you vote for nuclear power or solar power?" I'm sure solar power would win hands down although economically, from the standpoint of capital investment, [and] cost effectiveness it can't compete with nuclear power for the next 20 years or so. Here is a terribly subjective aspect to nuclear power which is now, if you will, the tail that's wagging the dog of where we're going in our nuclear energy budget.

Jones added: "It's not inconceivable to me that that sort of a factor may enter into such things as the hydrogen economy. My prejudice, based on my own emotional experience with this, is that a perhaps less objective, popular reaction would work in favor of the hydrogen economy."

NASA's Bob Witcofski agrees, saying that cost estimates are becoming increasingly irrelevant: "The money numbers change every year," he observed over drinks at the bar of the Konover Hotel in Miami Beach, where the 1976 conference was held. "Look, for example, at the cost comparisons we've heard of 1972 and 1971 when I really started getting into it. I have the stuff packed in volumes I never look at because it's absolutely useless now. The more you know about money and the cost aspect, the less it does for me."

Grinning, he added: "I give you an example, a beautiful one I heard today. There were three men stranded on an island, and a can of beans washed up. The scientist said, 'Why don't we get a committee together and study the possibility of designing a can opener to get this thing open?' And the engineer said, 'Why don't we get to work together on building the can opener?' And they also had a financial wizard, an economist, who said, 'Why don't we just assume that we have a can opener?'"

More somberly, he added: "You know, it seems that people have a tendency now to stick their heads out of the ground every day to see which way the wind is blowing, and then you change your tack and go accordingly. You never get anything done if you do that. You're all wrong. You've got to start all over again if you do that."

Pretty much the same points, although they were not specifically related to hydrogen, were made in a May 12, 1975, interview in *Business Week* by Dennis L. Meadows, principal author of the controversial first Club of Rome report, *The Limits of Growth* (1972), a worldwide best seller. That report was "a profound and sober message" to environmentalists, *Business Week* said, but "to economists, it was an intellectual fraud, a computerized update of the discredited theories of Malthus." Meadows, an associate professor of engineering and business at Dartmouth College, had not been impressed by the rampant criticism: "Nothing has happened to alter any of the basic ideas in *Limits of Growth*," he told the magazine then, and he specifically endorsed his earlier views in a conversation with me five years later. Asked by *Business Week* why the price mechanism doesn't warn of impending scarcity of oil and adjust accordingly, Meadows observed,

> price just doesn't provide information on long-term issues. To have evolved our energy system in orderly fashion, we should have begun in the early 1950s to develop a coordinated program of conservation and alternative power sources. Yet the price signals that would have triggered that response didn't show up for another 20 years. . . .
>
> If you want to understand where we are going, don't pay attention to price. Pay attention to the underlying physical realities. The U.S. will be plagued by an energy crisis in one form or another for the next 20 years at serious cost to our material standard of living and political stability.

We're moving into a period where price will play less of a role anyway. That's because price rations supply disproportionately to the rich. As the unrich grow in political power, they'll be less willing to see things allocated by price. They'll put pressure on the government to keep prices down. You're seeing that in energy now. Everybody is in favor of higher prices as long as they don't have to pay them—the poor, the truckers, the consumers in New England. The adaptive mechanism that economists always talk about as a way of solving problems of scarcity tends to break down under scarcity.

Meadows had this to say about long-term planning, social and institutional limits, and the free enterprise system:

Our current institutions are terribly shortsighted. In politics, we have a short electoral cycle, a one-year budget, and so forth. In economics, corporations are concerned with a rapid payback period for their investments. In every case we're capturing the benefits now and deferring the costs. These are institutional limits to growth not subject to technological release. We have to tend our preoccupation with the short term.

There was a time when the notion of the invisible hand had a dominant influence. If you subscribe to this idea, then you believe solving a series of short-run problems will lead to the optimal path. But it's becoming increasingly clear that they lead to long-term deterioration. Until we create a clientele for the long term, until we give the future a voice in our economic and political system, we're going to be in trouble. Our problems are not 5- or 10-year problems. They can be resolved only by a consistent program over 50 and 70 years.

We have to go to planning. There has to be a long-term image of where we want to go and a plan to get there. It remains to be seen whether that means a bureaucracy in Washington or whether we can develop a more subtle decentralized process. I haven't any reverence for the vast bureaucracies of the Socialist countries.

In 1980, Meadows believed his predictions of eight years earlier had been pretty much borne out by actual experience since then: "It seems now that growth will come to a stop even earlier than we believed at the time. By 1990, energy consumption will be below what we have now, and it won't go up again, ever."

Meadows believes an approximation of a subtle decentralized process is provided by "really outstanding companies" like IBM or Polaroid, which tend to have a small leadership, "maybe one guy, able to diffuse throughout the organization a concept of goals and values. He pushes those down, not decisions. It guides people in a fashion much more coordinated than you'd have with central planning. We have the capability to achieve that. It takes an image."

Meadows compares the situation to

> moving through a fog on a fast ship that takes a long time to turn. And
> we're being guided by a guy on the bow who is using an 8-foot stick to
> probe for obstacles ahead. We need an idea where we're going and some
> radar as a forecasting technique. If you don't like where you're going, you
> change directions.

Marchetti's Energy Island:
The Ultimate, Safe Nuclear Plant

Cesare Marchetti has been trying to do just that—gauge the future and chart a new course. Marchetti, who has evolved from a hydrogen advocate to a global energy thinker, has been considering ways of insuring energy supplies for the entire world while reducing possible dangers to a minimum. One concept he has developed is the Energy Island, derived from the suggestion of nuclear power parks. These parks could group large nuclear reactors and their auxiliary facilities—waste and fuel reprocessing, storage facilities—inside an enclave, perhaps fenced in and guarded, to minimize risk to the population and to reduce road or rail travel of nuclear materials and the attendant risk of hijacking for political or criminal purposes. Marchetti's nuclear-powered Energy Island is an extension of that idea. Hydrogen's potential as an efficient long-distance energy carrier, much better than short-range electricity, is pivotal in this concept. Essentially, Marchetti proposes to convert a few selected atolls or islands into what would amount to planetary power stations for the era beginning in the next century. Criteria for these sites would include geographic isolation, availability of deep, cold water for cooling, existence of ocean and air currents to disperse waste heat over wide ocean areas, and the availability of a basalt sea bottom through which encapsulated hot, radioactive wastes could melt their way irretrievably into the earth's crust.

The nuclear plants would produce hydrogen from seawater on a gigantic scale. The hydrogen would be transported in liquid form, analogous to the technology of transporting liquid natural gas (LNG) in huge cryogenic tankers to distribution centers on the various continents. Marchetti says a 1-terawatt island would produce about 10 billion cubic meters (350 billion cubic feet) of *liquid* hydrogen (LH_2) a year, requiring a fleet of LH_2 tankers with a carrying capacity of about 2 million cubic meters (70 million cubic feet) each. For comparison, the biggest LNG tankers now under construction are designed to carry about 150,000 cubic meters (5.3 million cubic feet). These behemoth catamarans or barges, 500 meters (1,640 feet) in length and 250 meters (820 feet) in width, would all but dwarf current supertankers. However, because of the low density of liquid hydrogen, these vessels would have drafts much shallower than today's supertankers, enabling them to put into terminals where supertankers would not dare to venture.

The dimensions of Marchetti's ideas are truly staggering. He proposes to install about one terawatt (thermal) worth of nuclear power on five floating concrete barges in Canton Island, a 6-by-9 mile (9.6-by-14.4-kilometer) atoll in the equatorial boondocks of Micronesia some 1,300 miles (2,000 kilometers) west of New Guinea and almost 1,000 miles (1,600 kilometers) southeast of Eniwetok Atoll.

To get an idea of the amounts of energy involved: The largest commercial nuclear power plant today, Biblis in Germany, is rated at 1,300 megawatts electrical output, or about 3,500 Mwth. In other words, a Canton Island hydrogen-making plant would produce about 286 times the primary energy going into Biblis! It would represent roughly one-seventh of today's total energy production *on this planet*, maybe one-tenth of what may be needed by the end of the decade.

Marchetti's sense of history and of proportions is not fazed by the prospect: "The size of such a reactor is certainly mindboggling to nuclear engineers, as would be the sight of a 1,000-Mw generator to Thomas Edison for whom a giant generator was in the range of hundreds of kilowatt," he observed in a paper outlining the plan. He envisions around nine such energy islands, to be run by a hybrid utility-cum-multinational-organization, with all the implications of serving many clients and many nations, but also subject to many controls like a utility.

Undoubtedly such technological gigantism will put off the "small is beautiful" fraternity. It has already turned off Robert Jungk, a prominent German doomsday futurologist who in 1977 published an angry antinuclear book, *The Atomic State—Progress Towards Inhumanity*, that held top positions on the German bestseller lists for weeks on end. In his book, Jungk implies that Marchetti is some sort of Dr. Strangelove of the nuclear industry. For those who know him personally, that assessment is hard to swallow. An Italian scientist-intellectual with a broad perspective of history, Marchetti strikes others as a man with faith in the future, even if some of his proposals seem outlandish, bizarre, or both; humankind will prevail not by retrogressing into a magical-primitivist lifestyle but by using benign technology intelligently and humanely to cope with upcoming scarcity and at the same time making life more livable rather than less so. "Doomtellers tend to wrap their bad moods in sophisticated technological arguments," Marchetti says. "The rejection of technology perceived as a Faustian deal, after two thousand years of passionate technological endeavor . . . is a curious phenomenon, to say the least."

Marchetti is very much aware that energy, especially nuclear energy, is perceived as "necessary" but also as "evil" by many. Radioactive wastes are indeed "very toxic, almost impossible to degrade, very long-lived, difficult to dispose of and potentially very powerful explosives," he agrees. But there is a solution that goes back through the ages and Marchetti thinks this remedy would work for nuclear power as well: Isolate the problem. "The old way to deal with plagues is the lazaret [isolation ward] and it is still valid today," he says.

Building nuclear reactors in humanity's backyard and transporting evil nuclear materials through the Ruhr or Pennsylvania over freeways and by rail provokes terror: "It is this intricate meshing between the socio-sphere and the nuclear energy system [that is] at the very root of the 'evil' of nuclear energy," Marchetti observes. Putting his nine planetary nuclear-power plants in the global boondocks, far away from concentrated humanity, would do a lot for people's sense of security, he believes, especially if the security blanket of large distances were backed up by the type of advanced safety features and ultimate nuclear waste disposal methods Marchetti has incorporated in his energy island concept.

For Canton Island Marchetti envisions five moored, barge-mounted high-temperature reactors of the pebble-bed type rated at 200 gigawatts (thermal) supplemented by a number of fast breeders to "stretch" the required uranium and thorium fuel. The fuel—Marchetti estimates a 1-terawatt island would require about 500 tons (550 short tons) per year—would be extracted from the cooling water pumped up from deep layers to cool the nuclear plants. Seawater carries highly diluted uranium; in the sixties, British scientists had already begun experiments to capture this uranium with a type of titanium sponge. More recently, Japanese scientists also began research into uranium-from-seawater extraction along similar lines, and German researchers have found and bred algae capable of fixing uranium in their cell structure with fairly high efficiency.

The reactor-carrying barges would be of a size not yet seen in ships—Marchetti talks in terms of millions of tons of displacement. The barges would be fabricated of prestressed concrete, a shipbuilding technology that dates back at least to World War II. The method is already being employed in the construction of large yachts, and it is being developed further for large LNG tankers and for offshore oil drilling stations. The primary reason for barge-mounting the reactors would be that they can be produced on an assembly-line basis in shipyard-like plants on the shores of, say, California, but also in shipping centers like Singapore or Hong Kong, making deployment and transport of these seagoing powerplants relatively easy.

Hydrogen would be produced either by electrolysis or by a thermochemical cycle. Specifically, Marchetti proposes a sulfur-based thermochemical cycle, under development by Westinghouse, that was unveiled at the 1976 Miami Beach hydrogen conference (see Chapter 4).

The proposed waste disposal methods, both for heat pollution and for nuclear wastes, are ingenious. Normally, cooling water from a river or lake is taken in at surface-water temperatures, and the rejected waste heat from the plant is absorbed by the coolant and transferred back to the body of water at higher temperatures than normal. In an atoll of the Canton Island type, which essentially sits on top of an underwater mountain made of basalt, very cold water, as much as 20 degrees centigrade (36 degrees Fahrenheit) colder than the ocean's surface water, is available close to the atoll from deep ocean layers on the flanks of that subsea mountain. If sufficiently large amounts of this cold water can be pumped up for plant cooling via large "penstock" pipes—and there seems to be no technical reason why this can't be done—then the plant's waste heat can be diluted to the level where the cooling water cycles back into the ocean either *at* or even *below* surface temperatures—meaning no change at the surface. At the same time the deep water is nutrient-rich; brought to the warm surface it is expected to produce a richer marine life full of algae and fish growth. If the cooling water is rejected below surface temperatures, it will seek its own level in the ocean and will be safely carried away over thousands of miles by the ocean currents.

If the rejected waste heat were higher than the surface temperature, the meteorological peculiarities of Canton Island's location still would make waste heat removal even on a large scale a harmless proposition, Marchetti says. This has to do with "Walker circulation" along the equator in the Pacific. The Walker circulation is the term used for the phenomenon of a more or less constant air circulation from east to west along equatorial latitudes that corresponds to similar east-west currents in the Pacific waters below. During this parallel travel of ocean and air currents, the air soaks up heat and humidity from the water, resulting in clouds at the western end of the system. In Djakarta, Indonesia, therefore, cloudiness is much more frequent than at the eastern branch of the system in Lima, Peru, for instance, where clear skies are the rule. The prevalent white cloud cover over Djakarta reflects part of the solar radiation back into space, lowering the temperatures beneath it. The extent of that cloud cover is determined by the temperature of the oceanic current—and therefore also by any extra artificial, nuclear-generated waste heat rejected into the water.

Marchetti's argument is, that if the surface temperature of the waters west of Canton Island were to become higher due to excess nuclear heat, more clouds would tend to form. These clouds would reflect a bigger share of the solar input back into the atmosphere and ultimately into space. Naturally, Marchetti is not totally certain that this would be so, but on the basis of satellite studies of cloud patterns and other meteorological data, he believes "the system appears to have a built-in negative feedback, tending to compensate waste heat rejection with reduced solar input." The hoped-for result: Total temperature patterns in the ocean remain essentially the same, regardless of whether waste heat from the nuclear power plant on Canton Island is fed into the ocean or not; the net difference would be only greater cloudiness in the western portion of the Walker circulation.

Equally sophisicated are the plans for the final disposal of the island's nuclear wastes, putting them out of reach of terrorists as well as future generations: Marchetti proposes to put the hot nuclear wastes in tennis ball–sized spheres, which would be placed into a bigger sphere of maybe a meter (about three feet) in diameter. Each reactor would have a vertical disposal shaft drilled through the atoll's coral bottom and down to the basalt core that forms the ocean bottom proper. The hot spheres, developing temperatures of around 800°C. (1,470°F.) would melt through the basalt and would "drop" toward the earth's core at speeds of several meters a day initially, gradually slowing and coming to a halt, still totally encapsulated, 80 to 100 years later at depths varying between 8 and 16 kilometers (5 and 10 miles) below the surface. The molten rock would harden again after the passage of the sphere. The starting shafts would be instrumented and filled with salt, enabling the island's operators to monitor the initial descent and permit retrieval of the sphere for a year or so should that be necessary. However, in the end the deadly wastes would be gone forever: "We believe the system to be tamper-proof and consider its final non-retrievability as the best insurance against criminal use of fission products or inadvertent removal by future generations," said Marchetti in a paper.

Nor is his idea a Jules-Vernish brainstorm: When Marchetti was at the EURATOM Research Center in Ispra, other scientists there were experimenting with this concept, letting hot spheres sink through blocks of paraffin experimentally to get a fix on heat requirements and sinking rates. Obviously, paraffin isn't the same stuff as basalt rock, but these experiments provided enough data to convince Marchetti that it is a viable method for getting rid of hot dangerous nuclear wastes—forever. Marchetti's entire proposal is attracting attention, and some government planners have become sufficiently interested to double-check Marchetti's data with calculations of their own.

Changing Planetary Politics

Marchetti believes that hydrogen and a hydrogen economy have meaning going far beyond clean fuel and clean environments. He thinks that the physical changes in making and distributing hydrogen energy globally would also fundamentally affect global politics. He speculates that "energy vectors," such as a world-wide hydrogen system, would represent a watershed in the world's evolution, a process that began billions of years ago, involving interrelated physical, chemical, biological, social, and political changes that now may lead to a world government or something approximating it.

Marchetti outlined his ideas in the keynote address, an intellectual *tour de force*, at the banquet of the 1976 Miami Beach hydrogen conference. Appropriately titled "From the Primeval Soup to World Government—An Essay on Comparative Evolution," Marchetti's talk depicted his startling politico-economic guesses as a more or less logical outcome of the development of a hydrogen economy, analogous to the physical processes that have shaped the earth since its beginning. "The question I have leisurely been asking myself is whether all this circus of a Hydrogen Economy, Hydrogen for the Future, Hydrogen the Ecomate, is a transitory fad or has some meaning in a larger context." Clearly, Marchetti thinks the latter is true.

In 40 minutes of densely argued reasoning that left a not inconsiderable part of his sophisticated audience alternately stunned and bewildered, Marchetti interpreted the large-scale production of hydrogen and a move away from fossil fuels as a planetary liberating process. Such a development, Marchetti said, would be almost comparable to the move away from the primeval soup as energy and life carrier millions of years ago, which was made possible then by the release of tremendous amounts of oxygen through a series of complicated chemical and physical processes. Oxygen formed the ozone layer and, by filtering out lethal ultraviolet radiation, allowed living organisms to come out of the water and conquer the land, or, viewed another way, "life had grown to take control of the environment on a global scale," he asserted.

"Now, if humanity starts producing hydrogen from water using 'new' sources of free energy—fission, fusion, or perhaps directly tapping the old sun—the moves away from fossil fuels which in my analogy are the equivalent of the primeval soup, what kind of new control of the environment can occur as by-products of this operation?" Marchetti asked.

Before he provided his answer, Marchetti dwelt on factors that determine the structure of energy systems—any energy system. The existing electrical system provides a clue: Energy systems are defined by competition between two or three contradictory requirements. Economy of scale, which promotes construction of ever larger power plants, is countered by the diseconomy of transporting electricity over large distances, which demands small, widely dispersed power stations. The result nowadays is that electricity is transported at a mean distance of about 100 kilometers (60 miles), the characteristic dimension of what Marchetti called the electrical energy system's "unit cell."

This dimension is fairly small. Marchetti now says that if you increase the "transportability" of this energy by higher voltages, for instance, or by switching to pipelined hydrogen, this cell becomes much larger and power stations can be spaced apart much further and can be made bigger and correspondingly more efficient. "With hydrogen as an energy vector a unit cell of 1000 kilometers [600 miles] takes the dimensions of a continent, or a subcontinent," Marchetti told his audience. "The USA may have three or four cells, Western Europe one or two, and the optimal size of the generating plants would be two orders of magnitude larger than for electricity"—in other words, a power plant with a generating capacity of 100,000 megawatts would be optimum for production of pipelined hydrogen.

The story doesn't end there. Marchetti, drawing on the analogy to transporting liquefied natural gas by huge cryo-tankers, which is now beginning to emerge, says liquid hydrogen one day may become economically transportable by tanker from far-flung sources, such as his Energy Island, and the economical transport distance may be 10,000 kilometers (6,000 miles). "Then, the unit cell is the world, and the optimal configuration would be to generate all the energy at ten sites," he said. The world at present uses about seven terawatts[3] of energy but ten terawatts are required to include standby capacity. Investment for each of such global superpower plants would run to hundreds of billions of dollars, "an operation that will become technically and economically the most important in the world."

What would be the political implications? Marchetti views the emerging situation as a conflict between the "vertically integrated" power structure of national states and the "horizontal" power system covering many states typical of the multinational corporation. The conflict is inevitable but will not necessarily lead to the destruction of either, nor to a bleak Orwellian 1984-type situation, he implies.

"A state can be seen as a vertically integrated power system filling a geographical area," he argued. "A multinational is a horizontal power system organizing a thin layer of human activities without precise geographical boundaries. The horizontal power [the multinational] generates 'confusion' and loss of control by the vertical one [the state], and, with the layers thickening, will inevitably lock with it. The ostensible muck-raking against multinationals is a clear symptom of that. But what will be the outcome?"

Marchetti has an interesting and persuasive historical analogy, that of the relations between the one "multinational" corporation of medieval times, the Catholic church, and the states of the day. "A fight between geographically bound political powers and a pervasive horizontal power went on in the Middle Ages," he said. The multinational of the age, the Church, was "interfering and competing in many ways with the geographically fragmented political power of the time."

Both systems were necessary and could not be done without: "As the two power systems cannot be interchanged, nor either one eliminated, a compromise finally had to be worked out. The political power handed its thin top layer to a supernational power structure, producing a kind of political multinational: the Holy Roman Empire. The maneuvering space of the emperor was politically narrow, but territorially broad and at the proper hierarchical level of abstraction to deal with the Pope on an even basis."

Declared Marchetti: "My educated analogy says that the outcome will be a world government, or more flexibly defined, a world authority to make a dialogue possible."

He concluded:

Energy is the largest single business in the world. At 12 dollars per barrel of oil, the turnover is five hundred billion dollars a year. It will be 2,000 billion dollars at the beginning of the next century. This means that energy multinationals will be the strongest forces in the struggle with political power, and their field of activity a sensitive one. The system attraction of the ten-islands scheme will make this inevitable, and the issue exquisitely political.

Very large energy centers and energy generation as a world operation are direct consequences of the technological process of watersplitting, and they may modify the political atmosphere, just as oxygen did for the earth atmosphere, leading finally to a world government.

The grand design is deploying itself, and we have the privilege and the responsibility of living at a great turning point in history.

Notes

Chapter 1

1. *Utopia or Oblivion: The Prospects for Humanity* (New York: Bantam Books, 1969).
2. Reported by United Press International (summarizing a Saudi television broadcast 21 December 1976, following a Doha, Qatar, OPEC conference).
3. *International Herald Tribune*, 23 April 1979.
4. Comment by an international energy expert in Bonn, West Germany, February 1980.
5. *Encyclopedia of Chemistry*, 3rd ed. (New York: Van Nostrand Reinhold, 1973), p. 544.
6. "The Forever Fuel" was the title of a 1979 TV documentary about hydrogen produced by the BBC's "Horizon" program, shown in the United States under the title "The Invisible Flame." Permission by the BBC to use it as this book's title is gratefully acknowledged.

Chapter 2

1. Julius Ruska, in G. Bugge, ed., *Das Buch der grossen Chemiker* (Weinheim: Chemie Verlag, 1974), p. 2.
2. Pilgrim, E. *Entdeckung der Elemente* (Stuttgart: Mundus-Verlag, 1950), p. 144.
3. Ibid., p. 147.
4. Richard Koch, in Bugge, *Das Buch der grossen Chemiker*, p. 194.
5. Pilgrim, *Entdeckung der Elemente*, p. 151.
6. Ibid., p. 155.
7. Georg Lockemann, in Bugge, *Das Buch der grossen Chemiker*, p. 256.
8. Georges Cuvier, in E. Farber (ed.), *Great Chemists* (New York: Interscience, 1961).
9. Quoted in Bugge, *Das Buch der grossen Chemiker*, p. 304.

Chapter 3

1. The Bergius process breaks down coal into a kind of synthetic crude oil with

the help of hydrogen and a catalyst, a method that enabled Nazi Germany to produce large amounts of synthetic gasoline for its air force. The Fischer-Tropsch
process synthesizes various hydrocarbons from carbon monoxide and hydrogen.

2. VW's methanol efforts will be described in Chapter 6. Another methanol
detractor is Weil, Erren's former technical director. "I am probably the only one
who flew during the First World War with methanol," he told me at the 1976
Miami Beach conference. "If I have any grey hairs they come from that time
'[Weil's hair is completely white]. Methanol is the most miserable motor fuel you
can imagine."

3. J. O'M. Bockris, *Energy: The Solar-Hydrogen Alternative* (New York:
Halsted Press, 1975).

4. The forerunner of NASA.

5. Major international hydrogen conferences have been held every two years,
beginning with the 1974 THEME conference. The next one, held in 1976, also in
Miami Beach, was called the First World Hydrogen Energy Conference, followed
by the Second World Hydrogen Energy Conference (1978) in Zurich, and the
Third World Hydrogen Energy Conference (1980) in Tokyo. The Fourth World
Hydrogen Energy Conference is to be held in 1982 in Los Angeles. The numbering
is somewhat misleading because THEME was really the first such conference.

6. The Department of Energy, established in 1977, combined several other
agencies, including the Energy Research and Development Administration (ER-
DA), an administrative agency established in 1974.

Chapter 4

1. An idea of the truly widespread, international interest in the subject can be
seen in the variety of contributors, including industrial household names as well
as relatively unknown institutions. For example, U.S. papers on hydrogen pro-
duction came from Westinghouse, General Electric, General Atomic, Los Alamos
Scientific Laboratory, the University of Miami, Lockheed Missile and Space
Company, and Allied Chemical, among many others. Other papers were
presented by researchers from Japan, Germany, the Netherlands, France, Italy,
Britain, Belgium, Switzerland, Canada, South Africa, India, Israel, and
Romania. Three scientists from the Soviet Union presented papers, whereas the
Soviets had sent only observers to previous conferences.

2. SNG originally stood for "synthetic natural gas"—obviously too much of a
contradiction.

3. Also known as HEST (Hydrogen Energy Systems Technology) study, which
was sponsored by NASA.

4. The overall reaction is $CH_{0.8} + 2\ H_2O \longrightarrow CO_2 + 2.4\ H_2$. Included
are two main subreactions, the "reforming" and the "shift" reactions. Considerable energy input is needed to accomplish the reactions—85.267 joules per
gram of hydrogen. Today that energy is supplied by burning some of the coal
with oxygen from the air. In future processes, that energy would be supplied,
presumably less expensively, from high-temperature nuclear reactors. Most of the
hydrogen produced in coal gasification, about 83 percent, is actually derived

from the water molecules rather than from the coal itself, according to the JPL report.

The joule is defined as a unit of energy or work equal to the work done by a force of one newton when the point at which the force is applied is displaced one meter in the direction of the energy. One newton is a force that will impart an acceleration of one meter/second^2 to a mass of one kilogram.

5. A British thermal unit (Btu) is a unit quantity of energy equalling 251.996 calories, or 778.26 foot-pounds, or approximately 1/3 watt hour.

6. Dry residues, both say, contain about 40 percent carbon by weight, the same as low-grade lignite-type coal used to fuel electricity power plants. Total carbon content of these renewable wastes/resources exceeds the carbon content of all coal mined annually in the United States!

7. Very pure hydrogen is required in a variety of applications, such as the hardening of fats (hydrogenation) for human foodstuffs, annealing of metals, and in the manufacture of electronic components.

8. One point periodically made by hydrogen-from-electrolysis advocates is that inexpensive off-peak electricity—power produced at night during low consumption periods—could be used to produce hydrogen cheaply. The 1976 "Hydrogen Economy" report by the Stanford Research Institute doubted this, saying that "this would amount to forcing electricity consumers to subsidize hydrogen consumers. Lacking such a subsidy, hydrogen cannot become competitive with alternative energy forms for the rest of this century."

9. *Knallgas* is the German word for the highly explosive mixture of gaseous hydrogen and oxygen. A *Knall* is a bang, an explosion. The German term is occasionally used in the English literature.

Chapter 5

1. Except for such cumbersome methods as pumped storage in which excess electricity—generated at night, for instance—is used to pump hydropower water back up the mountain into a reservoir to cascade again through hydro turbines later to provide electrical energy when it is needed most during peak demand periods.

2. J. O'M. Bockris, *Energy: The Solar-Hydrogen Alternative* (New York: Halsted Press, 1975), pp. 12–13.

3. AVR stands for Arbeitsgemeinschaft Versuchsreaktor, a Düsseldorf-based consortium of German utilities that owns the reactor.

4. There will, however, also be some radioactive material problems, caused by high-energy neutrons.

5. "Troposkien" is a symmetrical shape, attached at both ends to the vertical turbine shaft. Troposkien is the term for the shape a perfectly flexible cable of uniform density would assume if it were spun around a vertical axis.

Chapter 6

1. Other researchers reported, though, that power and thermal efficiency were

compromised by the injector mechanism.

2. Western hydrogen researchers say these numbers are even beyond the theoretical capabilities of titanium-iron hydride. It may be a case of inaccurate journalism.

3. At the Zurich conference, Daimler-Benz's Buchner mentioned in his paper the possibility of refueling a hydride-equipped, hydrogen-fueled car from city gas mains. Basing its research on work originally done at Brookhaven National Laboratories, Daimler-Benz is trying to develop selective hydrides, materials that would sponge up hydrogen but none of the other gases found in natural gas or town gas—residual carbon monoxide, carbon dioxide, and oxygen. The implications of this concept are enormous: It would mean "that there is no need for a special hydrogen infrastructure for cars but the already existing gas networks could be used instead," Buchner said. (More on this concept in Chapter 8.)

4. Others, such as ammonia, hydrazine, or ethanol, have undesirable characteristics with respect to cost, safety hazards, and incompatibility with existing engines.

Chapter 7

1. The reasons for the different tank arrangements have to do with the characteristics of the fuels. JP-4 is stable at ambient temperatures; therefore, the shape of the tank doesn't make much difference. Also, carrying fuel in the wings helps to stabilize and strengthen the wing structure. LH_2 is supercold and boils off, creating pressure gas. To contain this pressure and to minimize the "chinks in the armor"—odd angles and curves where pressure might build up to the bursting point—a round, or nearly round (possibly elliptical), pressure tank is best. Such a shape is most easily carried in the fuselage.

2. At the 1973 Langley Conference, NASA scientist Linwood B. Callis, reporting on the Climatic Assessment Program sponsored by the U.S. Department of Transportation, said that the program tried to assess the impact of jet emissions, mainly kerosene-based exhaust, but also taking into account future hydrogen usage, through 1990. Callis said early indications were that LH_2 produced no problem in the troposphere because future SSTs would traverse this atmosphere segment only during climb and descent, but much increased combustion of LH_2 in the stratosphere from fleets of hydrogen-burning SSTs needs studying. Questions such as the possibility of cloud formation in water-rich low-temperature regions, perturbation of stratosphere dynamics, and a need to evaluate a so-called coupling mechanism that would explain a temperature-drop phenomenon that seems to occur with the injection of water vapor are unresolved. Callis summed up by saying that it would be premature to conclude that no environmental problems are associated with the use of LH_2 and that there may still be NOX problems that could affect ozone layers, which are very delicate and vital in shielding the earth from harmful ultraviolet radiation.

3. Witcofski made that prediction in the early seventies, but actual developments seem to be outpacing his forecast: In early 1980, the average daily number of transatlantic flights between Europe and the North American conti-

nent already stood at 278, many of them 747s and other wide-bodied planes that carry considerably more than 200 passengers each.

4. The Lockheed studies also concluded that short- and medium-range aircraft, such as the French-German airbus, would not benefit from hydrogen usage and would use more energy, making hydrogen less economical. This, of course, leaves out the important area of environmental concerns, where hydrogen still wins hands down.

5. A lighter LH$_2$ plane can take off from shorter runways, for example

6. G. D. Brewer, "Hydrogen Usage in Air Transportation," *International Journal of Hydrogen Energy*, Vol. 3, No. 2, 1978, p. 225.

7. The data cited by Brewer: In 1970, total energy consumption in the United States was 64.6 Q (quadrillion Btus). Total transportation required 16.3 Q and commercial aviation only 1.23 Q. For the year 2000, total energy consumption in the United States is forecast at between 140 and 160 Q, with transportation taking up 48 Q and commercial aviation between 13.4 and 15.3 Q.

8. The idea of hydrogen from Saudi Arabia might strike some as ludicrous, but the Saudis are watching hydrogen developments closely. Sheikh Yamani, the Saudi Arabian oil minister, told me in October 1975 that "we are very much concerned with alternative sources of energy. We do believe that the real answer to our problems is solar energy. We don't believe so much in atomic energy. We think that the hazards and problems surrounding this energy are great; therefore Saudi Arabia is trying to cooperate and help in solar energy research." Asked whether hydrogen is of interest as a chemical energy carrier, Yamani said "we are very much interested in this. I think this is the type of energy we should concentrate on." (See Chapter 5 for Saudi interest in hydrogen production by laser fusion.)

Another Saudi planner, Farouk M. Akhdar, adviser for petroleum and monetary affairs and chief of the Special Office for Technological Affairs of the Saudi Arabian Planning Ministry, told me that interest in solar energy is great: "Saudi Arabia now is a principal country in energy, and we would like to continue to be in that position even after the depletion of oil." Saudi Arabia hosted its first solar energy conference in Dhahran in November 1975.

Chapter 8

1. It is this possibility that interests Saudi Arabia, for instance. Very broadly, one can imagine a scenario in which Saudi Arabia would retain its current role as the world's major energy exporter even after its oil runs out. Barren desert with a high year-round solar input, not much good for anything else, could be converted to large solar-energy farms producing electricity, which would be used with advanced, more efficient electrolysis methods to convert seawater from the Persian Gulf and the Red Sea into hydrogen. The hydrogen then would be liquefied and sold to Europe, the United States, and Japan, much as the Algerians at present are selling LNG. The Saudis, through present oil sales, are accumulating a capital base large enough to be able to afford the huge outlays needed for such solar-hydrogen schemes.

2. Additional energy losses in cooling hydrogen to cryogenic levels are due to the existence of two types of hydrogen, so-called ortho and para hydrogen. Hydrogen usually exists in molecule form—two hydrogen atoms are linked to form H_2. In some molecules the electrons spin symmetrically, all in the same direction; these molecules are referred to as ortho hydrogen. Molecules whose electrons spin asymmetrically in opposite directions are called para hydrogen molecules. Para hydrogen contains less energy than ortho hydrogen. Normally, at room temperatures para hydrogen accounts for about 25 percent of a given volume of hydrogen gas. However, in liquefying the gas, more and more of the other 75 percent of ortho hydrogen converts to the para version. At the liquefaction point of —423°F. (—252.8°C.) almost all of the ortho version has been converted to para hydrogen.

3. Some people have suggested that steel pipelines be lined on the inside with plastic, an idea prompted perhaps by the switch of some utilities from steel to plastic pipelines for carrying natural gas. It won't work because, unlike natural gas, light hydrogen under pressure diffuses easily through the plastic, attacking the outer steel casing just the same.

4. EVA is the acronym for the German working name for the piece of equipment that the Jülich Center first built to demonstrate the conversion of nuclear heat via steam and methane into carbon monoxide and hydrogen, *Einzelspaltrohr-Versuchs-Anlage* (single splitting tube test apparatus). ADAM was the obvious counterpart for the reconversion device at the user end.

5. A mole or mol, is a measure used in chemistry. It denotes a quantity of particles of any type (atoms, electrons, molecules, etc.) equal to Avogadro's number. The term is often used instead of *gram-molecular weight*. In the case of water, scientists customarily refer to 18 grams of water as one mole of water (rather than as one gram-molecular weight of water).

Chapter 9

1. One gigawatt is 1,000 megawatts. The world's biggest current nuclear plants produce about 1,300 megawatts—1.3 gigawatts.

2. It is estimated that the pressure at the boundary between the earth's mantle and core, about 1,800 miles (2,900 kilometers) down, is about 1.5 million bars (21.7 million psi), 1.5 million times the pressure of the earth's atmosphere.

3. Medical synonym for "scaly."

4. Fife also mentioned that hydrogen appears to be benign to normal tissue at pressures of up to 22,000 mm mercury (29.3 bars). Fife says he himself has lived on a "non-explosive hydrogen-oxygen mixture at a simulated depth of 200 feet [60 meters] for a total of three hours and 300 feet [91 meters] for two hours. I cannot tell the difference between hydrogen and helium when breathing it, and I could notice no ill effects." It seemed possible to use hydrogen-oxygen breathing mixtures to depths of at least 3,000 feet (910 meters), deeper than with a standard oxygen-helium mixture, because of what he said was hydrogen's reduced

"breathing resistance." Fife used an interesting trick to get around the explosion hazard normally associated with a hydrogen-oxygen mixture:

> It has been found that a hydrox mixture containing five percent or less of oxygen cannot be exploded, even with a spark. We simply use a mixture of 3 percent oxygen and 97 percent hydrogen, giving ourselves a 2 percent safety factor.
>
> Since 3 percent oxygen is 1/7th of 21 percent which is the percentage of oxygen required for adequate oxygenation (i.e., breathing) at ground level we simply compress to seven atmospheres before we start to breathe the hydrox. At seven atmospheres the partial pressure of 3 percent oxygen is normal for the body but the mixture remains non-explosive.

The trick is to mix the two gases in the first place, taking care not to exceed the 3 percent oxygen limit, a technical problem that can be solved fairly conveniently in a hyperbaric chamber to obtain the required seven atmospheres, Fife noted.

5. Because *Hydrogenomonas* bacteria have to be fed with gaseous hydrogen, oxygen, and carbon dioxide, they are also known as "Knallgas" bacteria.

6. RNA is absorbed by some animals, though. To remove it for human consumption, the bacterial mass is heated up quickly to 60°C. (140°F.), activating certain enzymes that split the RNA. The resulting RNA components are excreted from the cell and can then be removed from the bacteria volume by centrifugation.

Chapter 10

1. Brewer bases this conclusion on the report by the Spanish Ministry of Transport and Communications, which said, among other things, that the KLM plane's fuselage was not particularly deformed and neither the impact against the Pan Am plane nor that against the ground was particularly violent. Brewer thinks that under these circumstances the liquid hydrogen tanks, which would be located inside the fuselage rather than in the wings (as in current kerosene-fueled planes), would probably not have ruptured; the only fire would have been due to the relatively small amounts of hydrogen in the feedlines running through the wings to the engines.

2. However, even a weak spark such as one due to the discharge of static electricity from a human body is enough to ignite any of these fuels. Such a spark produces about 10,000 megajoules.

3. Data taken from Jesse Hord, "Is Hydrogen Safe," National Bureau of Standards Technical Note 690, issued October 1976.

Chapter 11

1. Marchetti sums up these rules as "the fractional rate at which a new commodity penetrates a market is proportional to the fraction of the market not yet covered." It includes two constants as characteristics of the particular commodity and market.

2. Although that proposition is not clear cut: Some hydrogen people feel an abundance of electricity from fusion would stimulate hydrogen production as well from off-peak, nighttime surplus electricity.

3. A terawatt is one million megawatts. A terawatt-year corresponds roughly to a billion tons of coal.

For Further Reading

History

Association des Ingénieurs Electriciens (A.I.M.). 1976. Symposium proceedings, L'hydrogène et ses perspectives, Liège, Belgium.

Automobile Engineer. Submarine power plants. August 1942, pp. 297–304.

Billings, R. E., and Lynch, F. E. (n.d.). *History of hydrogen-fueled internal combustion engines.* Provo, Utah: Energy Research Corporation.

Bockris, J. O'M. 1975. *Energy: The solar-hydrogen alternative.* New York: Wiley.

Bugge, G. (ed.). 1974. *Das Buch der grossen Chemiker.* Rev. ed. Weinheim: Chemie Verlag.

Business Week. Groundwork for a hydrogen-fueled economy. Vol. 4., September 1978, pp. 36B–36F.

Cecil, W. 1822. On the application of hydrogen gas to produce a moving power in machinery; with a description of an engine which is moved by the pressure of the atmosphere upon a vacuum caused by explosions of hydrogen gas and atmospheric air. *Transactions of the Cambridge Philosophical Society* 1: 217–239.

Cosci, D. 1937. Impiego dell' idrogeno nei motori a combustione interna. *Rivista Aeronautica* 13 (2): 253–286.

Commission of the European Community. 1977. The hydrogen-energy concept—proceedings. Joint Research Center, Ispra, Italy.

———. 1977. The hydrogen-energy concept—Ispra courses. Joint Research Center, Ispra, Italy.

De Beni, G., and Marchetti, C. 1970. Wasserstoff—Energieträger der Zukunft. *euro-spectra* (German edition) 9: 46–50.

Dickson, E. M., Ryan, J. W., and Smulyan, M. H. 1976. *The hydrogen economy, a preliminary technology assessment.* Menlo Park, Calif.: Stanford Research Institute.

Erren, R. A., and Campbell, W. H. 1933. Hydrogen: a commercial fuel for internal combustion engines and other purposes. *Journal of the Institute of Fuel* 6(29): 277–290.

Weil, K. H. The hydrogen i.c. engine—its origins and future in the emerging energy-transportation-environment system. In proceedings, 7th Intersociety

Energy Conversion Engineering Conference, San Diego, Calif., pp. 1355–1363.
Weinberg, S., 1979. *The first three minutes.* New York. Bantam Books.

Production

Bauser, H., Behret, H., and Klöpffer, W. 1978. Photochemische Wasserstoff-erzeugung—ein Weg zur Umwandlung und Speicherung der Solarenergie? *Information 27, Battelle Institut,* pp. 2–8.
Bylinsky, G. Green plants might provide cheapest energy of all. *Fortune,* September 1976, pp. 152–157.
Chemical Week. A hydrogen economy by the year 2000? 9 June 1976, pp. 53–54.
De Beni, G., and Marchetti, C. 1972. Mark-1, a chemical process to decompose water using nuclear heat. Paper presented at American Chemical Society Annual Meeting, Boston.
Donat, G., Esteve, B., and Roncato, J. P. Thermochemical production of hydrogen, myth or reality? *Revue de L'Energie,* no. 293, April 1977, pp. 1–17.
Dönitz, W. Wasserstofferzeugung mit HOT ELLY. *Dornier Post,* no. 1, 1977, pp. 17–19.
Engineering and Mining Journal. Experiments to obtain uranium from sea water. June 1977, p. 9.
Engineering News Record. Water-magma mix: hot new fuel ideas. 1 December 1977, p. 16.
Funk, J. N., and Reinstrom, R. M. 1966. Energy requirements in the production of hydrogen from water. *I&EC Process Design and Development* 5: 336–342.
Farber, E. (ed.) 1961. *Great Chemists.* New York: Interscience.
Federal Council on Science and Technology. 1972. *Hydrogen and other synthetic fuels.* Oak Ridge, Tenn.: Oak Ridge National Laboratory.
German Federal Ministry for Research and Technology. 1974. *Neuen Kraftstoffen auf der Spur.* Bonn.
———. 1975. *Aug dem Weg zu neuen Energiesystemen.* Bonn.
Gregory, D. P. 1972. *A hydrogen-energy system.* Chicago: Institute of Gas Technology.
Institute of Gas Technology. 1975. *Survey of hydrogen production and utilization methods.* Chicago.
———. 1978. Proceedings, Hydrogen for Energy Distribution Symposium. Chicago.
International Herald Tribune. Presley Cos. Sues Inventor. 15 July 1977.
International Journal of Hydrogen Energy. Vols. 1–5 (1976–1980). T. Nejat Veziroglu (ed.). Oxford: Pergamon Press.
Jones, L. W. 1971. Liquid hydrogen as fuel for the future. *Science* 174: 367–370.
———. 1973. The hydrogen fuel economy: an early retrospective. *Journal of Environmental Planning and Pollution Control* 1(3): 12–22.
Kelley, J. H., and Lauman, E. A. 1975. *Hydrogen tomorrow.* Pasadena, Calif.: Jet Propulsion Laboratory, California Institute of Technology.
Kohn, P. M. Hopes fly high for new hydrogen processes. *Chemical Engineering,*

14 March 1977, p. 86.

Lessing, L. The master fuel of a new age. *Fortune*, May 1961, p. 152.

Lindsey, R. Cheap energy from water is reported. *International Herald Tribune*, 30 March 1976.

Marchetti, C. 1970. Proteus vs. Procrustes. Lecture at Cornell University, Ithaca, N.Y.

———. 1971. Hydrogen, master key to the energy market. *euro-spectra* (English edition) 10: 117–129.

———. 1973. Hydrogen and energy. *Chemical Economy & Engineering Review* 5 (1): 7–25.

Newsweek. Sam Leach's box. 19 April 1976, p. 52.

Shipbuilding and Shipping Record. The oxy-hydrogen cycle and submarine propulsion. 19 November 1942, p. 495.

Verne, J. *The Mysterious Island*. New York: Airmont Publishing Co., 1965.

Veziroglu, T. N. (ed.). 1974. *Conference proceedings, The Hydrogen Economy Miami Energy Conference*. Coral Gables, Fla.: University of Miami.

———. 1976. *Proceedings, 1st World Hydrogen Energy Conference*. 3 vols. Coral Gables, Fla.: University of Miami.

Veziroglu, T. N., and Seifritz, W. (eds.). 1978. *Hydrogen energy system, proceedings of the 2nd World Hydrogen Conference*. Oxford: Pergamon Press.

Veziroglu, T. N., Fueki, K., and Ohta, T. 1980. *Hydrogen energy progress, proceedings of the 3rd World Hydrogen Energy Conference*. Oxford: Pergamon Press.

Marchetti, C. 1977. The energy plantation revisited: milking the forest. Unpublished paper, International Institute for Applied Systems Analysis, Schloss Laxenburg, Austria.

O'Neal, R. D. 1976. The promise of laser fusion. Remarks made at a New York Society of Security Analysts seminar, Energy Options—Fuels of the Future, 17 February, New York.

Quade, R. N., and McMain, A. T. 1974. Hydrogen production with a high-temperature gas-cooled reactor (HTGR). Preprint of paper read at The Hydrogen Economy Miami Energy Conference, Miami, Fla.

Sprintschnik, G., Sprintschnik, H. W., Kirsch, P. P., and Whitten, D. G. 1976. Photochemical cleavage of water: a system for solar energy conversion using monolayer-bound transition metal complexes. *Journal of the American Chemical Society* 98: 2337–2338.

Primary Energy Sources

Nuclear

Barnert, H. 1975. The HTR as the nuclear energy source for the hydrogen economy. In Proceedings, 26th Annual Meeting of the Italian Chemical Society, Milan.

Burnett, S. C., and Davies, N. A. Fusion: the ultimate power source? *Electrical World*, 1 August 1974, pp. 41–43.

Business Week. The hopped-up pace of laser fusion technology. 15 May 1978.

Bylinsky, G. KMS Industries bets its life on laser fusion. *Fortune,* December 1974, p. 149.

Gomberg, H. J. 1977. Synthetic fuels from laser fusion. Preprint for Symposium on Engineering Aspects of Laser Fusion, New York.

Hosegood, S. B., and Lockett, G. E. 1971. Expanding horizons for the HTR. *Industries Atomiques* 4: 3–15.

Power. Laser fusion gets a fresh start. June 1978, pp. 11–12.

Solar

Frankfurter Rundschau. Wasserstoff als Speicher für die Sonnenenergie. 10 April 1978.

International Herald Tribune. U.S. could form solar society. 14 April 1978, p. 5.

Justi, E. W. 1974. Sonnenenergie—die dritte Energiemacht? In *Akademie der Wissenschaften und der Literatur in Mainz, 1949–1974,* pp. 41–53. Wiesbaden: Published for the Academy of Sciences and Literature by Franz Steiner Verlag.

Laupsien, H. Energie aus dem All mit der "Kraftsoletta." *Handelsblatt,* 6 September 1977.

Meinel, A. B., and Meinel, M. P. Physics looks at solar energy. *Physics Today,* Vol. 25, no. 2, February 1972, pp. 44–50.

Weyss, N. Sonnenkraftwerke und die Arbeitswelt. *arbeit & wirtschaft,* Vol. 32, February 1978, pp. 13–20.

Wind

Financial Times. Europe's largest aerogenerator. 16 January 1978.

Heronemus, W. E. 1972. Pollution-free energy from offshore winds. In preprints, 8th Annual Conference and Exposition, Marine Technology Society, Washington, D.C.

Newsweek. Power in the wind. 20 February 1978, p. 34.

Bréelle, Y. 1973. Using hydrogen fuel cells for urban traction. Paris: Institut Français du Pétrole.

Bernhardt, W. E. 1975. Engine performance and exhaust emission characteristics from a methanol-fueled automobile. Symposium, Future Automotive Fuels—Prospects, Performance and Perspective. Warren, Michigan.

Breshears, R., Cottrill, W., and Rupe, J. 1974. Partial hydrogen injection into internal combustion engines, effect on emission and fuel economy. Project briefing paper, Jet Propulsion Laboratory, California Institute of Technology, Pasadena, Calif.

Eastwest Markets. Soviet Union—pollution-free fuels. 6 March 1976, p. 12.

Ellis, M. Water makes the wheels go round. *New Era,* October 1972, pp. 6–8.

Finegold, J. G., Lynch, F. E., Baker, N. R., Takahashi, R., and Bush, A. F. 1973. The UCLA hydrogen car: design, construction and performance. Reprint, Society of Automotive Engineers, Automobile Engineering Meeting, Detroit.

General Motors Corporation. 1978. Statement of General Motors Corporation to

Senate Appropriations Committee on Alcohol Fuels. Washington, D.C. Mimeographed.

General Motors Technical Center. 1977. Background paper from Fuels & Lubricants Department. General Motors Research Laboratories, Warren, Michigan.

Henkel, H.-J., Koch, C., Kostka, H., and von Szabo, E. 1973. Compact gas generator for combustion with low levels of noxious products. *Siemens Forschungs und Entwicklungs-Berichte* 2 (1): 1–4.

Hoffman, K. C., Winsche, W. E., Wiswall, R. H., Reilly, J. J., Sheehan, T. V., and Waide, C. H. 1969. Metal hydrides as a source of fuel for vehicular propulsion. Proceedings, International Automotive Engineering Congress, Detroit.

Proceedings, International Symposium on Alcohol Fuel Technology. Wolfsburg. 1977.

Ocean-Thermal

Beck, E. J. 1975. Ocean thermal gradient hydraulic power plant. *Science* 189: 294–295.

Bockris, J. O'M. n.d. Is massive solar energy conversion a practical prospect? Unpublished paper made available by author.

Engineering News Record. Ocean energy plant proposal set. 4 August 1977, p. 4.

Kohn, P. M. Ocean thermal gradients beckon energy planners. *Chemical Engineering,* 2 February 1976.

Science News. Ocean thermal? It's all wet. Vol. 114, 1 July 1978, p. 8.

Geothermal

Engineering and Mining Journal. US geothermal resources—no panacea, but potential for additional energy. October 1975, pp. 29–30.

Science News. Generating hydrogen in magma deposits. Vol. 113, 7 January 1978, p. 5.

Automotive

Perris Smogless Automobile Association. 1971. An answer to the automotive air pollution problem. *First Annual Report.* Perris, Calif.

Sorensen, H. 1972. The Boston reformed fuel car—a low polluting gasoline fuel system for internal combustion engines. Proceedings, 7th Intersociety Energy Conversion Engineering Conference, San Diego, Calif.

Stewart, W. F., and Edeskuty, F. J. 1973. Logistics, economics and safety of a liquid hydrogen system for automotive transportation. Intersociety Conference on Transportation, Denver.

Swain, M. R., and Adt, R. A., Jr. 1972. The hydrogen-air fueled automobile. Proceedings, 7th Intersociety Energy Conversion Engineering Conference, San Diego, Calif.

Williams, L. O. Hydrogen powered automobiles must use liquid hydrogen. *Cryogenics*, December 1973, pp. 693–698.

Aviation

Brewer, G. D. 1973. The case for hydrogen fueled transport aircraft. Proceedings, American Institute of Aeronautics and Astronautics/Society of Automotive Engineers (AIAA/SAE) 9th Propulsion Conference. Las Vegas, Nev.

———. 1979. A plan for active development of LH_2 for use in aircraft. *International Journal of Hydrogen Energy* 4: 169–177.

Brewer, G. D., and Morris, R. E. 1976. Study of LH_2 fueled subsonic passenger transport aircraft. Contract report for NASA, Lockheed-California Company, Burbank, Calif.

Lockheed-California Company. Lockheed will study a hydrogen fueled, 4000 m.p.h. aircraft design. Press release, 26 October 1977.

Mikolowsky, A. T., and Noggle, L. W. 1976. The potential of liquid hydrogen as a military aircraft fuel. Rand Paper Series. Santa Monica, Calif.: Rand Corporation.

National Advisory Committee for Aeronautics. 1957. Hydrogen for turbojet and ramjet powered flight. Unclassified research memorandum, Lewis Flight Propulsion Laboratory, Cleveland, Ohio.

Silverstein, A., and Hall, H. W. 1955. *Liquid hydrogen as a jet fuel for high-altitude aircraft.* National Advisory Committee for Aeronautics, Lewis Flight Propulsion Laboratory, Cleveland, Ohio.

Witcofski, R. D. 1972a. Potential and problems of hydrogen fueled supersonic and hypersonic aircraft. Proceedings, 7th Intersociety Energy Conversion Engineering Conference, San Diego, Calif.

———. 1972b. Hydrogen fueled hypersonic transports. American Chemical Society, Symposium on Non-fossil Chemical Fuels, Boston.

———. 1976. The thermal efficiency and cost of producing hydrogen and other synthetic aircraft fuels from coal. In *Proceedings, 1st World Hydrogen Energy Conference*, vol. 3, pp. 5C-3–5C-29.

Utility Use

Europa-Chemie. 1976. Grösseres H_2-Verbundsystem fur das Ruhrgebiet? Vol. 20, p. 367.

Gregory, D. P. 1976. The status of the hydrogen-energy concept. Paper presented at 13th World Gas Conference, London.

Isting, C. 1976. The hydrogen pipeline network in the Rhine-Ruhr area. In symposium *L'hydrogène et ses perspectives*, Liège, Belgium.

Johnson, J. H. 1973. Energy transmission via hydrogen. Paper presented at Cornell Hydrogen Symposium, Ithaca, N.Y.

Lurgi Information. Technologie von morgen. No. 1, 1976, pp. 7–10.

Nashan, G. 1976. Koksofen gas—Energieträger—und wieder Rohstoff. Proceedings, Österreichische Gesellschaft fur Erdölwisenschaften/Deutsche Gesellschaft fur Mineralölwissenschaft und Kohlechemie e.V. (ÖGEW/DGMK) Symposium, Salzburg, pp. 406–417.

Rosenberg, R. B., and Kweller, E. R. 1970. Catalytic combustion of reformed natural gas. *Appliance Engineer Magazine* 4 (4): 2.

Sharer, J. C., and Pangborn, J. B. 1974. Utilization of hydrogen as an appliance fuel. Preprint for The Hydrogen Economy Miami Energy Conference.

Voth, R. O., and Hord, J. 1976. H₂-Energy cable. Preprint for First World Hydrogen Energy Conference.

Other Applications

Dole, M., Wilson, F. R., and Fife, W. P. 1975. Hyperbaric hydrogen therapy: a possible treatment for cancer. *Science* 190: 152–154.

Foster, J. F., and Litchfield, J. H. 1964. A continuous culture apparatus for the microbial utilization of hydrogen produced by electrolysis of water in closed-cycle space systems. *Biotechnology and Bioengineering* 6: 441–456.

Mao, H. K., and Bell, P. M. 1979. Observations of hydrogen at room temperature (25°C) and high pressure (to 500 kilobars). *Science* 203: 1004–1006.

Medical World News. Hydrogen kills tumors. 22 September 1975, p. 21.

Schlegel, H. G. 1976a. Protein aus unkonventionellen Rohstoffen. Unpublished paper, Institut für Mikrobiologie, Göttingen.

———. 1976b. Wasserstoffökonomie und Wasserstoffbiologie. Unpublished paper.

Schlegel, H. G., and Lafferty, R. M. 1971. The production of biomass from hydrogen and carbon dioxide. In *Advances in Biochemical Engineering.* Vol. 1. Heidelberg and New York: Springer, pp. 143–167.

Tanaka, T., Shibayama, R., and Kiuchi, H. Hydrogen economy from the viewpoint of nonferrous extractive metallurgy. *Journal of Metals.* December 1975, pp. 6–15.

Vereshchagin, L. F., Yakovlev, E. N., and Timofeev, Y. A. Possibility of transition of hydrogen into the metallic state. *Journal of Experimental and Theoretical Physics* (USSR) (*Soviet Physics—JETP*), Vol. 21, no. 3, 5 February 1975.

Yaffee, M. L. Atomic hydrogen rocket fuels studied. *Aviation Week and Space Technology.* 25 November 1974, p. 47.

Safety

Bowen, T. L. 1975. Investigation of hazards associated with using hydrogen as a military fuel. Unpublished paper, Naval Ship Research and Development Center, Bethesda, Md.

Du Pont, A. A. 1967. Liquid hydrogen as a supersonic transport fuel. *Advances in Cryogenic Engineering* 12: 1–10.

Ordin, P. M. 1974. Review of hydrogen accidents and incidents in NASA operations. Paper presented at Ninth Intersociety Energy Conversion Engineering Conference, San Francisco.

Outlook

Business Week. Meadows: curbing growth. 12 May 1975, pp. 58–60.

Chemical and Engineering News. Hydrogen economy is possible by 1990's. 3 October 1977, p. 27.

Chopey, N. P. Tomorrow's hydrogen economy: still needing its big push. *Chemical Engineering*, 26 April 1976, pp. 51–53.

Marchetti, C. 1975. Primary energy substitution models. Staff paper (based on a 1974 Moscow lecture), International Institute for Applied Systems Analysis, Schloss Laxenburg, Austria.

———. Sind die bisherigen Energie-Berechnungen falsch? *Bild der Wissenschaft*, July 1977, pp. 68–77.

Japanese Ministry of International Trade and Industry. 1977. *Japan's Sunshine Project*. Sunshine Project Promotion Headquarters, Agency of Industrial Science and Technology.

Index

Aachen Technical University
(Germany), 75
ADAC. *See* Allgemeiner Deutscher
Automobil Club
ADAM/EVA system, 191–192,
246(n4)
Adenosine triphosphate (ATP), 43,
203
"Adiabatic demagnetization," 176
Adt, Robert R., Jr., 115
Advanced Research Projects Agency
(ARPA), 27
Advanced Supersonic Transport
(AST), 152, 154–155
AEG-Telefunken (company)
(Germany), 68
Agnone, Anthony, 150
Aircraft, hydrogen-powered,
140–144, 145–150, 163–165.
See also Advanced Supersonic
Transport; B-57 bomber,
hydrogen-fueled; Hypersonic
transports; Supersonic
transports
AiResearch (company), 140
Air Products & Chemicals, Inc., 187
Alaskan North Slope, 160
Albedo, 103
Albuquerque project, 81, 84–85
Alcaligenes eutrophus, 203
Alcohol, 134–135
Aldehydes, 133
Algae. *See* Cyanobacteria
Algeria, 56
Allgemeiner Deutscher Automobil

Club (ADAC), 131
Allied Chemical Corp., 178
Allis-Chalmers (company), 66
Aluminum, 97, 98, 170, 176, 186
American Chemical Society, 40, 44,
51
American Gas Association, 175
American Institute of Chemical
Engineers, 94, 204
American Institute of Electrical
Engineers, 23
American Institute of Gas
Technology. *See* Institute of
Gas Technology
Ammonia, 38, 52, 58, 95, 96, 97,
102, 183, 193, 194
Analog, 40
Anaximenos, 9
"Anodic Oxydation of Sulfur
Dioxide in the Frame of the
Sulfuric Acid Hybrid Cycle,
The," 44
Appliance Engineer, 168
Aquifer underground formation,
173, 174
Arbeitsgemeinschaft Versuchsreaktor
(AVR), 89–91
Argon, 79
Argonne National Laboratory, 180
Arora, J. L., 59
ARPA. *See* Advanced Research
Projects Agency
Arthur D. Little (company), 212,
213
Associated Press, 85

AST. *See* Advanced Supersonic
    Transport
Aswan Dam (Egypt), 65
*Atomic State, The—Progress
    Towards Inhumanity* (Jungk),
    233
ATP. *See* Adenosine triphosphate
Australia, 33–35
*Aviation Week & Space
    Technology*, 152, 197
AVR. *See* Arbeitsgemeinschaft
    Versuchsreaktor

Backfiring, 109, 113, 121–122, 125,
    127, 130
Bacon, Francis T., 34
Bacterium, 78. *See also*
    Hydrogenomonas
Balloons. *See* Hot air balloons
Bamberger, C. E., 63
Barnert, Heiko, 44, 92
Bartlit, John R., 188, 189
Basalt, 232, 236
BASF (company) (Germany), 133
Battelle Laboratories, 178
Battelle Memorial Institute, 77, 204
Battelle-Pacific Northwest
    Laboratories, 61
Batteries, 123, 136
BBC. *See* British Broadcasting
    Corporation
Beardmore (company), 28
Beech Aircraft Corp., 118, 119, 120
Beghi, Giorgio, 72, 74
Beldimano, A., 23
Bell, Peter M., 199–200
Bench-scale apparatus. *See* Mark 13
    cycle
Bergius, Friedrich, 32
Bergius system, 27, 32
Beynes (France), 173, 174
B-57 bomber, hydrogen-fueled, 106,
    139–140
Biblis nuclear power plant
    (Germany), 233
Biederman, Nicholas P., 101, 194

Billings, Roger, 105, 110, 111–113,
    114(port.), 119, 120, 126, 127,
    138, 172–173, 178
Billings Energy Corporation, 112
Bipolar cell. *See* Filter-press
    electrolyzer
Blagden, Charles, 15
Bockris, John O'M., 34, 35, 37, 63,
    83, 96, 220
Boeing Aerospace Co., 88, 151, 153,
    161, 228
Boerhaave, Herman, 10
Boiling water reactor (BWR), 89
Bonner, Tom F., 145
Borman, Frank, 152
Boron, 117
Boston Reformed Fuel Car, 116
Bova, Ben, 40
Boyle, Robert, 10, 13
Brass, 170
Brazing, 195
Brewer, Daniel G., 146–147, 149,
    150, 152, 154, 157, 159, 160,
    161, 209–210, 211, 212
British Admiralty, 31
British Airways, 151
British Broadcasting Corporation
    (BBC), 7
British Petroleum, 203
British Railways, 123
Bromine, 53, 70, 71, 72
Brookhaven National Laboratories,
    52, 119, 121, 178, 179, 180
Brown coal. *See* Lignite
Buchner, Helmut, 121, 123, 125,
    127, 180, 181
Burnham, K. B., 59
Burstall, A. F., 23
Buses, hydrogen-powered, 109, 112,
    113(illus.), 120–122, 123, 124,
    125, 138
Business Week, 40, 44, 45, 48, 57,
    84, 94, 97, 116, 165, 230
Büssing (company) (Germany), 28
Butane, 133
BWR. *See* Boiling water reactor
Bylinski, Gene, 76, 78

Calcium, 53, 70
-nickel (CaNi₅), 180
California Air Resources Board, 107
California Association of Airport
Executives, 162
California Institute of Technology
(Caltech), 116
California Society of Professional
Engineers, 108
Caltech. *See* California Institute of
Technology
Campbell, W. Hastings, 21, 23, 39
Cancer, 201–202
*C&EN. See Chemical & Engineering
News*
Candoluminescence, 168, 169
Canton Island (Micronesia), 233,
234–237
Carbon, 117, 177, 198
dioxide (CO₂), 3, 6–7, 13, 60, 93,
151, 167, 203, 205
monoxide (CO), 3, 93, 113, 116,
124, 133, 150, 151, 154, 167,
169, 191, 196
Carburetor, 115, 116, 122, 133. *See
also* "Oxyburetor"
Carlisle, Sir Anthony, 20
Carnegie Institution Geophysical
Laboratory, 199–200
Carpetis, Constantin, 127–129,
177–178
Cars and trucks, hydrogen-powered,
37, 105, 106(illus.), 107, 110,
112, 115–117, 123, 124(illus.),
125–127, 129–130, 135, 138,
172, 180–181
Carter, Jimmy, 221
Carter-Paterson (company), 28
"Case for a Hydrogen-Fueled
Supersonic Transport, The"
(Brewer), 152
Caskey, G. R., Jr., 186
Catalytic
burners, 168, 169
converters, 135
cracking, 194
reforming, 55. *See also* Natural

gas, reformed
Cavendish, Henry, 13, 14–15, 17
Cecil, William, 19–20
CH. *See* Hydrocarbons, unburned
Chan, H. C., 175
Chao, R. E., 72
Charles, Jacques Alexandre César,
13
"Charlière" balloon, 13
*Chemical & Engineering News
(C&EN)*, 220, 221
*Chemical Economy & Engineering
Review* (Japan), 64
Chemical energy, 2. *See also*
Hydrogen, as chemical fuel
Chemical Engineering, 56, 78, 96,
219
"Chemical Process to Decompose
Water Using Nuclear Heat, A"
(Marchetti and De Beni), 51
Chemical Treatise on Air and Fire
(Scheele), 11
Chemische Werke Hüls (CWH)
(company) (Germany), 182,
183, 217
Chemonuclear processes, 52
Cheng, K. B., 175
"China Syndrome," 89
Chlorine, 72
Chlorophyll, 76, 78, 203
Chloroplasts, 79
Chrysler (company), 37
City gas, 58, 130, 167, 173, 174
City University (London), 175
Claude, Georges, 95
Clean Air Race (1970), 107–108
Clean Energy Research Institute
(University of Miami), 57
Cleaver, A. V. (Val), 162–163
CL-400 spy plane, 140, 141–144
Club of Rome, 230
Coal, 56–58, 74, 158, 161, 162, 222,
228
gasification, 4, 45, 57, 58–59, 92,
130, 158, 161, 220
"Cold Combustion—Fuel Cells"
(Justi and Winsel), 34

Collett, Emil, 69
Colucci, Joseph, 134
Combustion. *See* Phlogiston theory
Cominco (company), 65
Compressors, 185–186
Concorde, 151, 152, 221
Contrails, 139–140
Convair (company), 144
Cook, E., 160
Copper, 186
Crude oil, 56, 160, 193
    Arabian light, 59, 60
    Libyan Es Sider, 59
    protein from, 203
Cryo-adsorption, 177–178
Cuckoo clock, hydrogen-powered,
    40, 41(illus.)
CWH. *See* Chemische Werke Hüls
Cyanobacteria, 79

Dahlberg, Reinhard, 68
Daimler-Benz (company) (Germany),
    28, 32, 35, 109, 113, 119,
    120–123, 125, 126, 130, 131,
    136, 137, 178, 180–181
Dams, 103
Darrow, Kenneth G., 194
d'Arsonval, Jacques, 95
Deacon reaction, 72
De Beni, Gianfranco, 40, 44, 51, 53,
    54, 55
Decentralized process, 231–232
De Havilland airplane, 30
Demag (company) (Germany), 65
Denmark, 98
De Nora (company) (Italy), 65
"Dephlogisticated air," 11
Deuterium, 93, 180
Deutsche Erren Studien GmbH, 32
Deutsche Forschungs und
    Versuchsanstalt für Luft und
    Raumfahrt (DFVLR), 175, 298
    Institute for Energy Conversion,
    127, 177
Deutz (company) (Germany), 28
Devco International Inc., 97
Dewars, 107, 118, 119, 120, 176

DFVLR. *See* Deutsche Forschungs
    und Versuchsanstalt für Luft
    und Raumfahrt
Diamonds, 198
Dieges, Paul B., 107, 108
Direct operating cost (DOC), 154
Dirigibles. *See* Zeppelins
DOC. *See* Direct operating cost
DoE. *See* U.S. Department of
    Energy
Dole, Malcolm, 201
Donat, Georges, 75
Dönitz, Wolfgang, 67
Dornier (company) (Germany), 32,
    64, 67, 70
Douglas, James H., 143
Dragon (high-temperature reactor),
    91
Driver, Cornelius, 145
Dugger, Gordon L., 96
Du Pont, A. A., 213
Du Pont (company), 186

Eastwest Markets, 126
"Ecotopia," 5
Edeskuty, Frederick J., 188, 189
Effective Perceived Noise Level in
    terms of decibels (EPNdB),
    149–150, 154
Ehricke, Krafft A., 88
Electric cars, 110–111, 123, 135, 136
Electric cell, 20, 22
*Electrochemistry of Cleaner
    Environments, The* (Bockris),
    37
Electrolyser Corporation Ltd.
    (Canada), 65
Electrolysis
    steam, 67–68
    water, 3, 20, 32, 39, 44, 52, 53,
    54–55, 62–67, 89, 162. *See also*
    Water splitting
Electrolytes, 55, 62, 66, 68, 179
Electrolyzer, 24, 31, 34, 63–67, 99,
    103, 173, 178, 179, 181
Electrovair, 136
Electrovan, 136

Empedocles, 9
Empire State Electric Energy
    Research Corporation, 67
Encyclopedia of Chemistry, 3
Energy Conversion Conference
    (1972), 111
Energy efficiency, 131
Energy Island, 232–237
"Energy mining," 96
Energy Research and Development
    Administration (ERDA), 101,
    179, 219
Energy systems, 238
Engineering Mining Journal, 101
Engineering News Record (ENR),
    88, 98, 103
ENI. *See* Ente Nazionale Idrocarburi
ENR. *See Engineering News Record*
Ente Nazionale Idrocarburi (ENI), 43
Environmental Protection Agency
    (EPA), 114, 116
EPA. *See* Environmental Protection
    Agency
EPNdB. *See* Effective Perceived
    Noise Level in terms of decibels
ERDA. *See* Energy Research and
    Development Administration
Ergenics Division (MPD Technology
    Corp.), 179
Erren, Rudolf A., 23, 25–33, 39
Erren Engineering Co., Ltd.
    (England), 27
Erren Hydrogen Motobus, 29(illus.)
"Errenizing," 27, 28
Erren Motoren GmbH Spezial-
    versuchsanstalt, 25
Escher, William J. D. (Bill), 37,
    40–41, 42, 48, 49, 95, 113, 142,
    152
Esteve, Bernard, 75
Ethylene-glycol solution, 155
EURATOM (European Atomic
    Energy Community). *See* Ispra
    Research Center
European Economic Community,
    45, 81, 222. *See also* Ispra
    Research Center

Experimental Center for the
    Advancement of Invention &
    Innovation (University of
    Oregon), 48
Experiments on Air (Cavendish), 15

"Factitious air," 13
Faraday's law, 63
Farbman, Gerald H., 74
Fedders, H., 191
Feldwick, R. D., 66
Ferme-Générale, 15
Ferri, Antonio, 150
Fertilizer, 52, 56, 58, 65, 96, 183,
    193
Fiala, Ernst, 131, 134
Fife, William P., 201–202
Filter-press electrolyzer, 65–66
Finegold, Joe, 122
*First Annual Report of the Perris
    Smogless Automobile
    Association* (1971), 106, 108
First Three Minutes, The
    (Weinberg), 9
Fischer-Tropsch system, 27, 32, 58
Fisher, J. C., 223
Fishing industry, 100
Fletcher, James C., 152
Flight Dynamics Laboratory
    (Wright-Patterson Air Base),
    215
Ford Motor Co., 37, 123
Fortune, 44, 76, 78, 79, 93
Fossil fuels, 39, 55–62, 220
Foster, John F., 204
France, 56, 75
Francis, E. J., 96
Franklin, Benjamin, 13
Free radicals, 201–202
"From the Primeval Soup to World
    Government—An Essay on
    Comparative Evolution"
    (Marchetti), 237
Fry, R. H., 223
Fuel cell, 22, 34, 38, 136–137
Fuel injection, 27
Fujishima, Akira, 76, 79

Fuller, R. Buckminster, 2, 3, 4, 105
Funk, James E., 52–53, 74
Furuhama, S., 130
Fusion, 92. *See also* Laser fusion;
    Thermonuclear fusion
Futures Group (company), 71, 101

GA. *See* General Atomic
Garrett Corporation, 213
Gasmischer, 122
Gas mixer. *See Gasmischer*
Gasoline, 132, 133, 135, 194, 211,
    212
    -hydrogen car, 125–126
    -methanol mixture, 133, 134, 138
Gaz de France (company), 75
GE. *See* General Electric
General Atomic (GA) (company),
    53, 55, 60, 69, 72, 91
General Electric (GE) (company),
    64, 66–67, 89, 103, 180,
    223–225, 228
General Motors (GM) (company),
    34, 35, 37, 52, 107, 108, 116,
    134, 135, 136
Geothermal energy, 101–102, 220
German Aerospace and Experimental
    Institute. *See* Deutsche
    Forschungs und Versuchsanstalt
    für Luft und Raumfahrt
German Association of Plastics-
    based Manufacturers, 32
German navy, 31
"Glacier power," 102–103
Glaser, Peter E., 88
Glass, 117
GM. *See* General Motors
GNP. *See* Gross national product
Gomberg, Henry J., 94
Göttingen University Institute for
    Microbiology (Germany), 204
Graf Zeppelin, 210
Graphite, 91
Great Britain, 56, 91, 98. *See also*
    British Admiralty
Greenborg, J. B., 61, 62

Greenhouse effect, 6–7. *See also*
    "Solar chimney"
Greenland, 102–103
Gregory, Derek, 36, 37, 40, 44, 49,
    175, 185, 187
Grobman, Jack, 150–151
Gross national product (GNP), 61
Grove, William, 22
Grumman (company), 228

Haber process, 58
Haldane, J.B.S., 22, 39, 144
Halides, 72
Hanson, Joe A., 95
Hawaii, 220
Helium, 3, 9, 92, 174, 188, 189,
    190, 191, 211
Heracleitos, 9
Heronemus, William, 24, 98–100
Hess, Rudiger, 197, 198
HEST. *See* Hydrogen Energy
    Systems Technology
High Operating Temperature
    Electrolysis, 68, 70, 72
High-temperature reactors (HTRs),
    6, 60–61, 89, 91–92, 191, 223,
    234
Hildebrandt, Alvin F., 84
Hindenburg, 210–211
Hindenburg syndrome, 127, 188,
    190, 210
HIT. *See* Hydrogen induction
    technique
Hochtemperatur Dampfphase-
    Elektrolyse (HOT ELLY). *See*
    High Operating Temperature
    Electrolysis
Hoechst (company) (Germany), 72
Hohlein, B., 191
Hokkaido University (Japan), 196
Home for Tomorrow, 167, 169
Honda, Kenichi, 76, 79
Honnef, Hermann, 23, 24
Hord, J., 189–190
Hosegood, S. B., 91
Hot air balloons, 13–14

HOT ELLY (Hochtemperatur Dampfphase-Elektrolyse). *See* High Operating Temperature Electrolysis

House Energy Research, Development, and Demonstration Subcommittee, 219

Houseman, John, 135, 136

HST. *See* Hypersonic transport

HTRs. *See* High-temperature reactors

H_2indenburg Society, 40, 42(illus.), 210, 221–222

Humble, Richard, 30

Hybrid cycles, 74–75, 102. *See also* Mark 13 cycle

HYCSOS. *See* Hydrogen Conversion and Storage System

Hydrides, 4, 117, 119–127, 172–173
storage of, 177, 178–182

Hydrobromic acid, 71

Hydrocarbons, 3, 111, 113, 116, 133, 160, 162–163
unburned (CH), 124, 150, 154, 169
See also Fossil fuels

Hydrocrackers, 183, 194

Hydrogen (H_2)
absorption, 186
abundance of, 9
adsorption. *See* Cryo-adsorption
atomic (H), 197–198, 199
atomic weight of, 3
characteristics of, 2–3, 22, 211–212
as chemical fuel, 4, 36, 51, 157, 193
consumption, 194
as conventional fuel, 2, 4, 23, 25, 27–28, 36, 37, 105–106, 181–182, 209–210. *See also* Natural gas, reformed; Transportation, hydrogen-powered
as cryogenic fuel, 3, 4, 37, 117, 118–119, 139, 155, 175, 188
discovery of, 10, 12–17

economy, 4–5, 34, 44, 49, 52, 83, 163, 219–221, 223, 226–229, 237–239
and electricity, 5, 52, 83, 101, 188–190, 204, 228
as energy carrier, 4, 5, 6, 24, 82, 99, 157, 185, 187, 188
flammability of, 188
in food production, 34, 202–207
and helium, 3. *See also* Helium
hyperbaric, 201–202
industrial uses of, 193–197
leakage, 170–172, 174, 186
light. *See* Deuterium
liquid (LH_2), 22, 23, 30, 36, 37, 38, 55–56, 118–119, 120, 127–130, 139, 144–157, 158–159, 161, 162, 163, 165, 175, 176, 189, 190, 195, 199–200, 209, 212, 213, 214, 216, 232
in literature. *See* Iron Pirate, The; Mysterious Island, The
as market commodity, 223–226
medical uses of, 201–202
metallic, 3, 197, 198–201
metering, 221
military uses of, 37–38, 52–53, 106, 159
as nonpollutant, 3, 4, 6–7, 147, 150
as odorless, 187
pipeline for, 170–171, 182–190
production of, 3, 4, 52, 56, 75–79, 162. *See also* Electrolysis; Fossil fuels; Laser fusion; Nuclear power plants, for production of hydrogen; Thermochemical water-splitting process
quasi-perpetual motion machines, 47
research, 44–49
safety studies, 213–218
from seawater, 232
as space rocketry fuel, 3, 37, 56,

144, 162, 176, 188–189,
  216–217
storage of, 3, 4, 24, 83, 99, 109,
  117–130, 136, 173–182
uses of, 3, 36: early, 19–25,
  27–38
volumetric flow rate, 171
water vapor as end product of, 2,
  4, 107, 110, 121, 150, 168
See also Energy Island
Hydrogenase, 78, 205
Hydrogenation, 194, 195
Hydrogen Conversion and Storage
  System (HYCSOS), 180–182
Hydrogen Economy Miami Energy,
  The (THEME) conference
  (1974), 38, 44, 49, 66, 84, 92,
  178. See also World Hydrogen
  Conference
"Hydrogen Economy, The—A
  Preliminary Technology
  Assessment" (SRI), 71–72,
  226–229
"Hydrogen Energy System, A"
  (Gregory), 175
Hydrogen Energy System Society
  (Japan), 46
Hydrogen Energy Systems
  Technology (HEST), 176, 187
Hydrogen Homestead, 172–173
Hydrogen induction technique
  (HIT), 115
"Hydrogen: Make-Sense Fuel for an
  American Supersonic Trans-
  port" (Brewer and Escher), 152
Hydrogenomonas, 36, 203, 204–206
Hydrogen Progress, 120
Hydrogen Tomorrow, 58
Hydrogen Village, 173
"Hydrotreating" process, 193
HYGAS process, 59
Hypersonic transport (HST), 155,
  156(illus.), 157, 161

IBM (company), 231
IEA. See International Energy

Agency
IGT. See Institute of Gas
  Technology
IIASA. See International Institute
  for Applied Systems Analysis
IMC. See International Materials
  Corporation
Inflammable air (hydrogen), 13, 15,
  17
Ingersoll-Rand (company), 186
Institute of Crude Oil Research, 33
Institute of Fuel, 32
Institute of Gas Technology (IGT),
  36, 37, 59, 63, 66, 101, 103,
  154, 158, 159, 167, 168, 169,
  170, 171, 176–177, 184,
  185–186, 195
Institute of High Pressure Physics
  (Moscow), 199
Interatom (company) (Germany), 72
Internal combustion engine, 2, 23,
  25, 27, 107, 111, 114–115, 126.
  See also Transportation,
  hydrogen-powered
International Association for
  Hydrogen Energy, 44, 57
International Automotive Engineer-
  ing Congress (1969), 119
International Auto Show (1975,
  1977), 109, 121
International Energy Agency (IEA),
  45, 55, 81
International hydrogen conferences.
  See Hydrogen Economy Miami
  Energy, The, conference;
  World Hydrogen Conference
International Institute for Applied
  Systems Analysis (IIASA)
  (Austria), 85
International Journal of Hydrogen
  Energy, 44, 79, 130, 147, 152
International Materials Corporation
  (IMC), 115, 116
International Nickel Co., 178
Intersociety Energy Conversion
  Engineering Conference, 40,
  107, 216

Invisible flame. *See* Natural gas,
    reformed
"Invisible Flame, The" (BBC), 7
Iran, 56
Iron, 170, 193, 194, 195–196
Iron Pirate, The (Pemberton),
    21–22, 26
Ishigohka, T., 190–191
Isotope separation, 180
Ispra Research Center (Italy), 35,
    45, 53, 55, 69, 71, 72, 91, 184,
    196, 209
  New Energy Program, 72, 74
Isting, Christian, 217
Italy, 56

Japan, 45–46, 60, 92, 222. *See also*
    Project Sunshine
Jasionowski, W. J., 171
Jet-A fuel, 144, 145, 146, 147, 152,
    153, 154, 157, 161, 211
Jet fuel. *See* Jet-A fuel; JP-4 jet fuel
Jet Propulsion Laboratory (JPL), 58,
    59, 109, 110(illus.), 116, 135,
    187
Johnson, Clarence L. (Kelly), 143
Johnson, D. G., 171
Joint Committee on Atomic Energy,
    94
Joint Research Center. *See* Ispra
    Research Center
Jones, Lawrence, 36, 39–40, 195,
    229
Journal of Metals, 196
Journal of the Institute of Fuel, 22
JP-4 jet fuel, 215
JPL. *See* Jet Propulsion Laboratory
Jülich. *See* Nuclear Research
    Center
Jungk, Robert, 233
Jupiter, 198
Just, J. S., 33
Justi, Eduard, 34
Jute, 170

Katz, Donald L., 195
Kempf, J. F., 33

Kerosene, 140, 144, 146, 152, 153,
    159, 160, 161, 162, 209, 212,
    213, 214
Kilby, Jack S., 68
King, R. O., 23, 34, 39
Klöpffer, Walter, 77
KMS Fusion Inc., 76, 93–95
Knallgas, 77, 205
Knoche, Karl-Friedrich, 74, 75, 222
Konopka, A., 194
Koppers-Totzek process, 58, 59
Kraftwerk-Union (company)
    (Germany), 89
Kweller, Esher R., 168

Landgrebe, Albert, 219
Lanthanium, 178
    -nickel (LaNi$_5$), 180
La Roche, Ulrich, 102–103
Laser fusion, 92, 93, 94, 184
Laskin, J. B., 66
Lavoisier, Laurent, 11, 12, 15–17
Lawaczeck, Franz, 23, 24, 39
Lawaczeck, Franz, Jr., 24
Lawrence Laboratory (company),
    78–79
L/D ratio. *See* Lift-to-drag ratio
Leach, Sam L., 47–48
Leach-and-Mirkin hydrogen caper,
    47–48
Lead, 170
LEAP. *See* Liquid-hydrogen
    Experimental Airline Project
Lemery, Nicolas, 13
Lerner, R. M., 132
Lewis Research Center. *See*
    National Aeronautics and Space
    Administration
Lift-to-drag (L/D) ratio, 153
Lignite, 56, 58
Limits of Growth, The (Meadows),
    230
Linde Division (Union Carbide),
    107–108, 154, 158, 159
Lippert, Jack R., 215
Liquid-hydrogen Experimental
    Airline Project (LEAP),

164(illus.), 165
Liquid natural gas (LNG), 118, 176, 189, 232
Litchfield, John H., 204
LNG. *See* Liquid natural gas
Lockett, G. E., 91
Lockheed Missile and Space Co., 37, 96, 97, 140, 141, 146–148, 151, 152–153, 155, 160, 161, 163, 165, 212, 221, 228
  Tri-Star, 163, 164(illus.)
  See also CL-400 spy plane
Los Alamos Scientific Laboratory (company), 129, 188
Louthran, M. R., Jr., 186
Lurgi process, 58, 64, 67, 70, 179, 192
Lynch, Frank E., 112, 179, 180

McCormack, Mike, 219
McDonald, Patrick, 47
McDonnell Douglas (company), 228
Mach 3 airliner. *See* Hypersonic transport
Mach 6 airliner. *See* Hypersonic transport
Magnesium, 96, 194
Magnesium-nickel hydride, 124–125
MAN (company) (Germany), 28
Mao, David Ho-kwang, 199–200
Marchetti, Cesare, 35, 40, 43–44, 49, 51, 53, 54, 55, 64, 69, 70, 74, 184, 196, 203–204, 206–207, 223, 232–239
Mark 1 cycle. *See* Thermochemical water-splitting process
Mark 13 cycle, 13, 55, 72–74
Martin-Marietta Corporation, 37, 117, 175
Massachusetts Institute of Technology (MIT), 132
Mayerne, Turquet de, 13
Mayow, John, 10
Meadows, Dennis L., 230–232
Medical World News, 201
Meinke, Wayne, 95

Mercury, 53, 69, 71
  oxide (HgO), 11–12, 69, 71
  pollution, 71
"Metal Hydrides as a Source of Fuel for Vehicular Propulsion," 119
Metallurgical embrittlement, 170–171, 186–187, 194
Methanation, 191
Methane, 56, 93, 94, 102, 161, 191, 211, 212
  liquid, 157, 160, 161, 212
Methanol (CH_3OH), 3, 32, 36, 118, 123, 131–136, 138, 194
  -fueled cars, 137(illus.), 223
Method of Chemical Nomenclature, The (Lavoisier), 15
Methyl colanthrene, 202
Methyl ether, 133
M-15, 133, 134
Microbial Energy Conversion, 224
Micro-joules (MJ), 211
Middlesex Polytechnic (Great Britain), 175
Mikolowsky, William, 158, 159
Milesian school of philosophy, 9
Mining equipment, hydrogen-powered, 120
Minnich, Dwight B., 106, 107, 108
Mirkin, Morris J., 47
MIT. *See* Massachusetts Institute of Technology
MJ. *See* Micro-joules
MJM Hydrotech (company), 47
Molybdenum, 194
Montgolfières, 14
MPD Technology Corp. *See* Ergenics Division
Murray, Richard G., 114–115
Musahi Institute of Technology (Japan), 129
Mysterious Island, The (Verne), 20–21

NACA. *See* National Advisory Committee for Aeronautics
Nardecchia, Fredric F., 107, 108

NASA. *See* National Aeronautics and Space Administration
Nashan, Gerd, 183
National Aeronautics and Space Administration (NASA), 36, 44, 88, 116, 145, 147, 150, 154, 155, 158, 160, 161, 163, 186, 187, 197, 204, 215–217, 221
National Bureau of Standards Cryogenics Division, 189
National Cancer Institute, 202
National Gas and Oil Engine Company, 30
National Science Foundation, 101
NATO. *See* North Atlantic Treaty Organization
Natrium, 123
Natural gas, 3, 54, 55–56, 74
  depleted fields of, 173–174
  pipelines, 170–171, 184, 191
  protein from, 203
  reformed, 167–173, 181
  See also Liquid natural gas; Substitute Natural Gas
Natus, Dietrich, 192
Negromycin, 202
Netherlands, 173–174
New Scientist (Great Britain), 76
Newsweek, 47
New York State Energy and Research Development Authority (NYSERDA), 103
New York Times, 47, 48
Niagara Mohawk Power Company, 67
Nicholson, William, 20
Nickel silicate, 177
Niobium, 178
Nissan (company) (Japan), 135
Nitro-aerial corpuscles, 10
Nitrogen, 189, 194
Nitrogen oxides (NOX) emissions, 113, 115, 116, 124, 130, 150–151, 154, 169–170, 173
Nixon, Richard, 151
Noeggerath, J. E., 23, 24

Norsk Hydro, 65
North Atlantic Treaty Organization (NATO), 159
NOX. *See* Nitrogen oxides emissions
Nuclear-Powered Energy Depot, 38, 52
Nuclear power plants, 229
  light-water, 89
  portable, 38
  for production of hydrogen, 4, 5, 6, 35–36, 39, 52, 83, 89–92, 191–192, 222. *See also* High-temperature reactors; Thermochemical water-splitting process
  safety, 88
  second generation, 6, 60, 71
  See also Energy Island
Nuclear Research Center (Jülich, West Germany), 60–61, 89, 191
  Institute for Reactor Development, 91
Nuclear waste disposal, 236
Nuttall, Leonard J., 66
NYSERDA. *See* New York State Energy and Research Development Authority

Oak Ridge National Laboratory, 63, 118
Oberth, Hermann, 24
Oceanic Institute (Hawaii), 95
Ocean mining, 223
Ocean-thermal energy, 95–98
Ocean Thermal Energy Conversion (OTEC) program, 96–98
OECD. *See* Organisation for Economic Co-operation and Development
Office of Technology Assessment, 96, 97
Ohio State University, 37
Ohta, Tokio, 46
Oil. *See* Crude oil; Oil shale; Petroleum
Oil shale, 56, 195

"On the Application of Hydrogen Gas to Produce Moving Power in Machinery" (Cecil), 19
OPEC. *See* Organization of Petroleum Exporting Countries
Ordin, Paul M., 216
Organisation for Economic Co-operation and Development (OECD), 91
Organization of Petroleum Exporting Countries (OPEC), 4, 39, 146
O'Sullivan, John B., 38
OTEC. *See* Ocean Thermal Energy Conversion program
Otto engine, 110, 111
Oxidation, 194, 195
"Oxyburetor," 108
Oxygen, 4, 10–12, 187, 193

Pangborn, Jon B., 169, 170, 171
Paracelsus, Theophrastus, 12–13
Parks, F. B., 116
Pebble-bed reactor, 234. *See also* Nuclear Research Center
Pemberton, Max, 21, 26
"Penstock" pipes, 235
Perris Progress, The, 106
Perris Smogless Automobile Association, 37, 105, 106–108, 113
Peschka, Walter, 127–129, 177–178, 198–199
Petroleum, 56, 162, 196
Phillips Research (company), 178
Phlogiston theory, 10–11, 12
Photon, 78
Photovoltaic collectors, 95
Plasma, 92, 93
Plastic, 170
Platinum, 168
Polaroid (company), 231
Pollution, 29, 34, 39, 62, 71, 105, 109, 149
Polyethylene, 170
Potash, 96
Pratt & Whitney Division (United Technologies Corp.), 140, 143,

167, 178
Presley Companies, 47
"Pressure of the Atmosphere upon a Vacuum Caused by Explosions of Hydrogen Gas and Atmospheric Air" (Cecil), 19
Pressurized water reactor (PWR), 89
Priestley, John, 11–12
Project Sunshine (Japan), 45–46, 161
Protein, 202–207
Proxmire, William, 151
PSE&G. *See* Public Service Electric & Gas Co.
Public Service Electric & Gas Co. (PSE&G), 178
PWR. *See* Pressurized water reactor

Quartz, 194

Radiolytic-thermochemical cycles, 93
Rand Corporation, 158, 159
Readers' Digest, 44
Reed, T. B., 132
Reilly, J. J., 178
Reinstrom, Robert M., 52–53
Renault (company) (France), 35, 117
"Renewable carbon" sources, 76
Renewable wastes, 61–62, 102
Revue de L'Energie (France), 75
Reynolds Metal Co., 97
Rheinbraun (company) (Germany), 72
Ribonucleic acid (RNA), 206
Ricardo, H. R., 23
Rich, Ben R., 140, 141, 142, 143
Richardson, D. M., 63
Rivista Aeronautica (Italy), 23
RNA. *See* Ribonucleic acid
Rockwell International Inc., 88
Rohrmann, C. A., 61, 62
Rolls-Royce (company) (Great Britain), 30
Romania, 49
Roncato, Jean-Pierre, 75
Rosenberg, Robert B., 168
Royal Airship Works, 25

Rubber, 170, 175
Ruhrkohle (company) (Germany), 183
Russell, John L., 74
Ruthenium, 76, 77

Saltpeter, 10
Sandia Laboratories (company), 98, 102, 178
Saudi Arabia, 94
Saüfferer, Helmut, 127, 130
Scheele, Carl Wilhelm, 11, 12
Schlaich, Jörg, 85, 87
Schlegel, Hans Günter, 204–206
Schoeppel, Roger J., 114–115, 127
Schott, G. J., 161–162
Schulten, Rudolf, 91
Science, 39, 40, 201, 221
Science News, 102
Scientific American, 44, 160, 221
Scott, Maurice I., 169, 170, 171
Seawater, 232, 234
Seikei University (Tokyo), 190
Seven Wise Men of Greece, 9
Sharer, John C., 169, 170, 171
Shipbuilding and Shipping Record, 31
Siegel, Keeve M., 93, 94
Siemens (company) (Germany), 116
Sikorski, Igor, 22, 23
Simon, Michael, 85
S.L.X. process, 48
Snape, Ed, 179, 180
SNG. See Substitute Natural Gas
Socialist Industry, 126
Society of Automotive Engineers, 116
Sodium, 123
Solar cells, 68, 82, 190, 195, 204
"Solar chimney," 85–87
"Solar farm" plant, 81–82
Solar furnaces, 69
Solar power, 81, 203
    for electricity, 2, 4, 81, 83, 84–85
    for home heating, 84

and hydrogen, 34, 54, 71, 84–88, 223
    orbiting stations, 87–88, 228
    plant (Barstow, Calif.), 81, 84
"Solar tower," 84
Solid-polymer electrolyte (SPE), 66
Sonic boom, 154, 155
Sorensen, Harold, 115–116, 117
Southern California Edison (company), 81, 84
Southern California Gas Company, 169
Soviet Union, 49, 56, 60, 125–126, 199
Spain, 56, 81, 87
SPE. See Solid-polymer electrolyte
Speer, Albert, 24
Spiegel, Der (Germany), 76
Sprintschnik, Gerhard, 76–77, 78
Sprintschnik, Hertha W., 76, 78
SPTLs. See Superconductive power transmission lines
Squamous-cell carcinoma, 202
SRI. See Stanford Research Institute
SR-71 Blackbird reconnaissance plane, 141, 144
SST. See Supersonic transport
Stahl, Georg Ernst, 10–11, 12
Stanford Research Institute (SRI), 71, 130, 184, 211–212, 213–214, 217, 226
Stanley, William, 158
Steam-Iron process, 59
Steam reforming, 3, 162, 221
Stebar, R. F., 116
Steel, 117, 170, 173, 176, 194
Stern, Der (Germany), 24
Strickland, G., 178
Stuart cells, 65
Submarines, oxy-hydrogen-powered, 31, 38
Substitute Natural Gas (SNG), 56, 58, 93, 189
Sulfides, 196
Sulfur, 55, 75, 193, 195, 235
    dioxide, 72, 74

-iodine cycle, 72, 74
Sunlight. *See* Water, photolysis
Sunsat Energy Council, 228
Superconductive power transmission
    lines (SPTLs), 189–190
Supersonic transport (SST), 151–152,
    153(illus.), 158–159, 221
Swain, Michael R., 115
Swisher, James H., 45
"Synthesis gas," 58
Synthetic Ammonia and Nitrates
    Ltd. (Great Britain), 69

Tanaka, Tokiaki, 196
Tank electrolyzer, 65–66
Tar sands, 195
Teledyne Energy Systems
    (company), 65–66, 178
Tenerife disaster (1977), 209–210
Texas Gas Transmission Corpora-
    tion, 93, 184
Texas Instruments (TI) (company),
    68
Textured vegetable protein (TVP),
    206
Thales, 9
THEME. *See* Hydrogen Economy
    Miami Energy, The, conference
Thermochemical water-splitting
    process, 40, 44, 51, 53–55,
    69–75, 84, 85, 89, 91, 222, 235
Thermonuclear fusion, 76, 93
Thorium, 234
Three Mile Island incident (1979),
    5–6, 89
TI. *See* Texas Instruments
TIME, 44
Timofeev, Y. A., 199
Tison, Raymond, 101
Titanium, 117
    dioxide (TiO₂), 76
    -iron hydride, 109, 119, 120, 122,
        123, 124, 125, 126, 178, 179
    -nickel hydrides, 180
    storage, 132
Torpedo, trackless, 31

Town gas. *See* City gas
Transportation, hydrogen-powered,
    27–29, 34, 35. *See also* Aircraft,
    hydrogen-powered; Buses,
    hydrogen-powered; Cars and
    trucks, hydrogen-powered
Tritium, 93
"Troposkien" wind generators, 98
Tropsch, Hans, 32
TRW Inc., 96
Tsaros, C. L., 59
Tseung, A.C.C., 175
Tungsten, 194
TU-144, 151
TVP. *See* Textured vegetable protein

UCLA. *See* University of California,
    Los Angeles
U-Gas process, 59
Underwood, Patrick Lee, 106, 107,
    108
Union Carbide (company), 136, 158.
    See also Linde Division
United Kingdom Gas Corporation,
    30
United States
    energy crisis, 230–231
    hydrogen production, 56, 194
    hydrogen research, 49, 57,
        219–221, 226–228
    methanol production, 194
    and second generation nuclear
        reactors, 60
    space program, 56. *See also*
        National Aeronautics and Space
        Administration
United States Geological Survey
    (USGS), 101–102
United Technologies Corp. *See*
    Pratt & Whitney Division
University of California, Los Angeles
    (UCLA), 37
University of Denver, Denver
    Research Institute, 179
University of Miami (Coral Gables),
    57

University of Michigan, 40, 175, 195
Uranium, 89, 234
Urban Vehicle Design Competition (1972), 37, 112, 122
U.S. Department of Commerce, Maritime Administration, 96
U.S. Department of Energy (DoE), 45, 57, 67, 68, 74, 81, 88, 96, 97, 103, 163, 219
U.S. Department of the Interior, 174
USGS. *See* United States Geological Survey
U.S. National Advisory Committee for Aeronautics (NACA), 37, 106, 139

Vanadium, 178
Vant-Hull, L. L., 84
Vereshchagin, L. F., 199
Verne, Jules, 20, 21, 23, 24, 39
Veziroglu, T. Nejat, 57
VFW (company) (Germany), 98
Voecks, G. E., 135, 136
Volkswagen (VW) (German company), 32, 118, 131, 132–133, 134, 137, 138
Volta, Alessandro, 20
Von Braun, Wernher, 24
Voth, R. O., 189–190
VW. *See* Volkswagen

Walker circulation, 235–236
Wankel engine, 112
Wasserstoff, 9
Wastes. *See* Nuclear waste disposal; Renewable wastes
Waterfalls, 103
Water Splitter, 54
Water (H_2O) splitting, 5, 52, 99, 181

photolysis, 76, 79
See also Electrolysis, water; Leach-and-Mirkin hydrogen caper; Thermochemical water-splitting process
Weil, Kurt, 23, 27, 29, 111
Weinberg, Steven, 9
West Germany, 45, 46, 59, 60–61, 87, 91, 182–183
Westinghouse (company), 53, 55, 74, 75, 89, 228, 235
Weyss, Norbert, 85
White House Council on Environmental Quality, 228
Whitten, David G., 77, 78
Williams, Larry, 37, 117, 118, 127, 175
Wilson, F. Ray, 201
Wind power, 95, 98–101
Winsel, August, 34
Wiswall, R. H., 178
Witcofski, Bob, 36, 49, 152, 155, 157, 158, 229–230
Wood, 168
World Hydrogen Conference
First (1976), 44, 59, 61, 74, 96, 116, 157
Second (1978), 55, 66, 69
Third (1980), 67, 130, 175, 191
World Power Conference (1930), 27
Worthington (company), 186

Yakovlev, E. N., 199
Yamani, Sheikh Ahmed, 93–94

Zelby, L. W., 100–101
Zeppelin Company (Germany), 25
Zeppelins, 24–25, 190–191, 210